THE IMMIGRANT HERITAGE OF AMERICA SERIES

Cecyle S. Neidle, Editor

Xenophobia and Immigration, 1820–1930

By THOMAS J. CURRAN

TWAYNE PUBLISHERS

A DIVISION OF G. K. HALL & CO., BOSTON

Library of Congress Cataloging in Publication Data

Curran, Thomas J.
  Xenophobia and immigration, 1820–1930.

  (The Immigrant heritage of America series)
  SUMMARY: Examines the fear of and resulting attacks
on foreigners in the United States throughout its history.
  Bibliography: p. 205.
  1. United States—Emigration and immigration—His-
tory. 2. United States—Foreign population—History. 3.
Naturalization—United States—History. 4. Nativism. [1.
United States—Foreign population—History. 2. United
States—Emigration and immigration—History] I. Title.
JV6507.C87   325.73   74-10865
ISBN 0-8057-3294-2

DEDICATED TO
MY FAVORITE IMMIGRANTS:
MY FATHER AND MOTHER

Contents

About the Author

Thomas J. Curran was born to Irish immigrant parents in Brooklyn, New York in 1929, the first of three sons. He was graduated with honors from Manhattan College and then went on to Columbia University for graduate study, where he worked under Professor J. Bart Brebner and Professor David Donald. He completed his doctoral studies under Professor Robert D. Cross. From 1952 to 1954, he served in the United States Army with an overseas tour in Heidelberg, Germany.

From 1955 to 1956 he served as instructor in history at Manhattanville College and has since taught at St. John's University.

In 1973, Dr. Curran appeared on national television as the academic coordinator and host of two television series that dealt with the immigrant and his transformation into the ethnic-American. He and his colleague, Dr. Frank J. Coppa, are jointly serving as co-editors of the *Immigrant in American History,* a book based on the fifty-four part series done for C.B.S. which will be published as part of Twayne's Immigrant Heritage in America Series.

Dr. Curran's articles and reviews have appeared in the *International Migration Review, The Catholic Historical Review,* the *New York Historical Society Quarterly,* and the *Journal of the Behavioral Sciences.*

Acknowledgments

First, I owe a great debt to the staff of Rush Rhees Library at the University of Rochester, and especially to its archivist, now retired, Mrs. Margaret Butterfield Andrews, who not only helped me find my way through the Seward and Weed Papers, but also arranged to make my stay at Rochester a memorable one. Other librarians and archivists have been equally generous. I want to thank publicly all of them for their help and kindness.

Professors Charles McCool Snyder and Luciano Iorrizzo of Oswego College, State University of New York, permitted me to use the Fillmore Collection during their summer vacation. They went out of their way, and I thank them for it.

Others have also helped me. Professor David Herbert Donald of Harvard University and Professor Robert D. Cross of the University of Virginia activated and maintained my interest in immigration history during their years at Columbia University. Other scholars and authors have also been helpful; I mention them in my footnotes.

My colleagues and friends at St. John's University have been more than tolerant about our discussions on xenophobia and immigration. I am particularly grateful to Professors Gaetano L. Vincitorio, James E. Bunce, and Richard Harmond for their penetrating remarks during the course of our talks. Without their comments, this volume might have more shortcomings than it does.

I am indebted to others as well. My editor and friend Cecyle Neidle has been most gracious. She has saved me from many embarrassing errors. My brother, Professor Daniel J. Curran, of Kings College in Wilkes-Barre, Pennsylvania, gave me a great deal of help. He has read various segments of the manuscript with a critical and helpful eye. I am grateful for his

XENOPHOBIA AND IMMIGRATION

help. My wife, Judith, has been my most valuable ally. She has served as researcher, editor, critic, and typist. What would I have done without her!

My greatest debt goes to my parents. I have dedicated this volume to these two Irish immigrants from County Donegal. No man has been more blessed with such understanding parents.

Despite all of the help which I have received, I have still made some errors, I am sure. I, unfortunately, am to blame for them.

CHAPTER I

Introduction

DESPITE THE POLYGLOT POPULATION OF THE BRITISH colonies in North America, English attitudes and institutions dominated the colonies that emerged as the United States of America. And while the cosmopolitan character of its people was reinforced by subsequent waves of immigration, America's dominant heritage continued to be English. Colonial and American naturalization practices emulated the English.

In England, aliens could acquire citizenship either by letters of denization or by naturalization through an act of Parliament.[1] Denization conferred the right of residence plus the right to transfer property to one's heirs. It did not require an oath of loyalty. Neither did it grant full citizenship rights. These could only be obtained through a parliamentary act. Naturalization was required if an alien wanted to qualify for any public office or franchise, to own a British ship, to be a member of the stock exchange, or to enjoy any other right or privilege as a British subject.[2] The English citizenship was a positive privilege which granted power to its holders. While the colonists accepted the idea that naturalization was a privilege, they were faced with the need to attract aliens to their colonies. Thus colonial promoters and land speculators were constantly scheming to entice foreigners to come to the British colonies. One method of encouraging immigration was to make not only land but also citizenship available. In 1699, the crown denied to the colonies the right of issuing letters of denization.

In their immigration and naturalization policies, the colonies reflected their ambivalence toward the newcomers. This tension between welcome and rejection can be found throughout America's history. On the one hand, there was the encouragement of immigration; on the other, the xenophobic effort to limit naturalization so as to maintain political, religious, and ethnic control.[3]

Xenophobia, that is, the distrust of strangers because of the fear that they pose a threat to the culture of the natives, is endemic to most societies.[4] In the case of the colonists, they established the xenophobic pattern that would be followed throughout the history of the United States. The pattern would eventually culminate in the exclusion acts of the 1880s and the quota acts of the 1920s.

What was the colonial pattern? It was a combination of official action by colonial authorities coupled with the private actions of the colonists themselves. Official policy is easiest to follow in the various legislative enactments passed by the colonial assemblies and the British Parliament to regulate immigration and provide for the naturalization of the non-English. The legislation usually aimed at restricting the admission and naturalization of those who were considered a threat to the security and well-being of the colonies. These would include religious nonconformists, usually Catholics and Jews, convicts, and paupers.

Despite the admission of certain Protestant groups who were acceptable to the authorities, there were xenophobic outbursts directed against three major ethnic groups: the French Huguenots, the Scotch-Irish, and the Germans. These became so intense at times that the authorities themselves responded by passing restrictive legislation directed at these groups.

As early as 1637, Massachusetts prohibited strangers from settling in the colony without permission. This act was meant to discourage non-Puritans from entering the area. It was as much a religious measure as a xenophobic act, since it was directed against native-born citizens of the other colonies and aliens alike. The English code of laws made divergence from the established creed a crime, so that the Massachusetts General Court in its rule of 1637 attempted to keep out non-Puritans. It was a practice followed by all of the other New England colonies except Rhode Island. Even Rhode Island, however, denied citizenship to Roman Catholics, as did the other New England colonies.[5]

Roman Catholicism was anathema to the Protestant English. All the colonies, even Maryland after 1654, consistently tried to thwart the immigration of Catholics. In 1654, Maryland refused to admit Roman Catholics to the colony. In 1704, no Roman Catholic priests were to be admitted, and in 1715, a fine of twenty shillings was levied on Irish servants in the province as well as an additional tax of twenty shillings on Catholic property. The same practices were followed in the other Southern colonies. Thus, Maryland which passed the first naturalization act in the colonies in 1666, limited the privilege of becoming citizens to foreign-born Protestants.[6] So, too, did Virginia in 1671 and South Carolina in 1696.[7]

These naturalization acts, it was hoped, would encourage the emigration of Protestants and would prevent Catholics and Jews from gaining citizenship. Jews did not receive a cordial reception in the colonies. For example, a group of New Yorkers claimed the election of 1736 was fraudulent, since Jews had been permitted to vote.[8]

All of the colonies had laws against voting and office-holding for Catholics and Jews, and all of the colonies agreed to a policy of restricting the importation of criminals. For example, Virginia's naturalization act stipulated that jailbirds could not become citizens. So, too, the act in South Carolina restricted the rights of felons. In 1676, Maryland prohibited the importation of felons and levied a fine of 2,000 pounds of tobacco on anyone convicted of violating the act. Pennsylvania passed an act in 1683 that no felons would be permitted in the colony. Even after Parliament declared in 1717 that felons would be transported to the colonies, the Pennsylvania legislature in 1722 and again in 1730 reiterated its opposition to convicts. These acts could not prohibit what Parliament had decreed, but they did levy a fine of five pounds on each convict carried into the colony, and the shipmasters were required to post a one-year bond for the good behavior of the felons. The fear of a crime wave made the colonists as "law and order" conscious as any of our current citizens.

Colonists were also alarmed over the prospect of immigrants becoming public charges. All of the colonies, at one time or another, made strenuous efforts to restrict strangers who might become public burdens on the community. Rhode Island in 1700 demanded a bond of fifty pounds from each vessel master carrying foreigners, to insure that aliens likely to become dependent on public help would not be brought into the colony. In many ways, the eighteenth-century Massachusetts statutes served as models for the other colonies. In 1709, an immigration law required the masters of all vessels to provide a complete list of their passengers, and the financial status of each. It also decreed that no lame, improvident, or infirm immigrants would be permitted to land. The law was amended in 1722 and again in 1724, and in 1756 a new immigration act emphasized the prohibition against the sick and the infirm, although they would be allowed to land if they received permission from the authorities.

While colonial immigration and naturalization were generally left to the colonial legislatures, the British Parliament, at times, directly intervened both to encourage and discourage immigration. In 1709, the Protestant Protector, the British Parliament, passed an act providing for the naturalization of those German Palatinates who fled from Germany to England. Many were then sent to New York. And in 1740, Parliament passed a general naturalization act which granted citizenship to any subject who had been a resident of the colonies for seven years, without an absence longer than two months, and who swore loyalty to the crown. In 1747, Parliament extended the naturalization privilege of 1740 to the Moravian Brethren, many of whom came to the colonies, and in yet another act passed in 1747 granted naturalization to all foreign Protestants, even those who refused to take an oath of loyalty because of their religious convictions.[9] These acts encouraged foreigners to come to the colonies. On the other hand, England tried to disrupt the immigration of foreigners to the colonies by the heavy stamp duty called for by the Stamp Act of 1765. All naturalization was abruptly halted by an Order in Council in 1773. And finally, in 1774, a parliamentary act ended immigration to the colonies, since it was thought that the influx of newcomers would strengthen the call for independence.

These interferences were condemned by the colonists. In the Declaration of Independence, one of the charges levied against the King was his attempt to keep the colonies depopulated.[10]

In addition to the colonial and parliamentary restrictions, there were also reactions by the common people in the colonies against the Huguenots, the Scotch-Irish, and the Germans. Colonial authorities from Massachusetts to South Carolina welcomed the Huguenots because of their special skills. But with the outbreak of the Anglo-French wars in 1689, the French Huguenots' loyalty was suspected. Only in South Carolina did they go unmolested.[11] In New York and Pennsylvania, their loyalty was questioned, and in Pennsylvania some were even imprisoned. Virginia petitioned the British government to stop sending Huguenots to the colony. And in 1691, a Rhode Island mob attacked and dispersed the Huguenots in Frenchtown.[12] The French Acadians were similarly treated in 1755.

The Scotch-Irish faced the same hostile reaction as the French immigrants, but here the motivation was not the suspicion of their loyalty, so much as the fear of their large number and their poverty. This enmity was particularly noticeable in New England and Pennsylvania. In 1718, when 600 to 800 arrived, the Bostonians blamed the Scotch-Irish for the scarcity of food and the concomitant inflation. Numbers of them were warned to leave, or to post bonds for their support. This antagonism intensified when the increase in the price of wheat from six to ten shillings a bushel was blamed on the increased numbers of Scotch-Irish. It caused a fear of famine. In 1729, a Boston mob refused to permit the landing of a number of immigrant ships with passengers from Belfast and Londonderry. And a Worcester mob in 1734 destroyed a new Presbyterian church built by the Scotch-Irish.[13]

Similarly, the Pennsylvanians were alarmed at the numbers of Scotch-Irish who flooded the colony in the eighteenth century. Coming as they did from Ulster, these people were already citizens of Great Britain. Nevertheless, their numbers and their turbulent relations with the Indians and the Germans led the Pennsylvania proprietors to seek an act of Parliament that would halt the Ulster invasion. The Pennsylvania legislature also passed an act in 1729 which placed a head tax on alien passengers who might become burdensome to the colony.[14]

Pennsylvania's reaction to the Germans was much harsher. From 1720 to 1750, approximately 2,000 Germans a year settled in the province. By 1750, there were about 100,000 Germans in Pennsylvania.[15] Benjamin Franklin reflected the Anglo-American's view of the Germans. He delighted in pointing out their "political immaturity and social incivility." He was also suspicious of German business honesty and political loyalty.[16]

The question of German loyalty was particularly intense during the French and Indian Wars. In 1750, in a letter to one of his correspondents, Franklin pointed out that "because of the disagreeableness of the dissonant manners of the Germans their English speaking neighbors would have preferred to move away."[17] Again, in 1753, Franklin presented the American stereotype of the German: "Those [Germans] who come hither are generally the most stupid of their own nation... not being used to liberty they know not how to make a modest use of it. And as Holbein says of the Hottentots, they are not esteemed men until they have shown their manhood by beating their mothers, so these seem not to think themselves free, till they can feel their liberty in abusing and insulting their teachers."[18]

But, by far, Franklin's most xenophobic outburst directed against the Germans can be found in his *Observations Concerning the Increase of Mankind* (1751). There he asked, "Why should the Palatine Boors be suffered to swarm into our settlements and, by herding together, establish their language and manners to the exclusion of ours? Why should Pennsylvania founded by the English, become a colony of aliens who will shortly be so numerous as to Germanize us instead of our Anglifying them?"[19]

The Pennsylvania legislature reacted to this alarm by the passage of an act in 1729 directed against the foreign-born as well as against Irish servants. This act, as noted above, laid a duty of five shillings on each foreigner coming into the colony. In 1755, however, the assembly passed a bill that would prevent the importation of Germans and other passengers in too great numbers in any ship. The Governor refused to sign the bill. Nevertheless, the assembly bill reflected the xenophobic fears of the English residents. Delaware and New Jersey followed the lead of Pennsylvania in setting their policies toward the immigrants.[20]

In this brief summary of colonial attitudes toward new-comers, a number of points should be emphasized. First, the English colonists discriminated against non-English immigrants on both ethnic and nonethnic grounds. They did oppose the French Huguenots because they appeared more French than Protestant during the Anglo-French wars. This nationalistic feeling could also be found in the reactions of the Pennsylvanians toward the Germans in their midst during the course of the French and Indian Wars. But the opposition to the Germans can also be traced to their large numbers; a fear existed that they would take control of the colony. The same situation applied to the Scotch-Irish in Massachusetts. Here, not only their numbers, but also their poverty and their Presbyterianism, were considered a threat to the colony.

But if every non-English group was treated with suspicion, if not with outright hostility, by the English, it is also true that their laws were not based on ethnic factors alone, but rather also on religious affiliation, economic status, and moral condition.[21] These religious and social factors had little to do with the ethnic composition of the immigrants. The English colonists' antipathy towards the Catholics and Jews, convicts, and paupers was reflected early and often in their statutes. This opposition persisted even when the colonies became states and then a nation.

Two other factors which served as a basis for opposition emerge clearly: one, a color bias, and the second, an opposition to the immigrants' ideas. We will not deal in this study with the English bias against Blacks and Indians, since these groups were not voluntary immigrants, except to note that this bias does indicate a color consciousness.[22] That color bias has existed became most obvious in the Oriental Exclusion Act, 1882, directed against the "yellow peril."

The need for conformity was noted by Tocqueville in the 1830s.[23] The desire for agreement in thought as well as practice was inherent in the opposition to the beliefs of Catholics and Jews. This bias was apparent in the attitude of the Federalist party towards the immigrants and would again be the basis for the antialien feeling in the closing decades of the nineteenth century.

It is evident that the English attacks on Catholics, Jews, the poor, and the morally suspect were not restricted to the foreign-born. Attacks were made on English Catholics, Jews, and convicts as well. This study will focus on the xenophobic attacks on the foreign-born and will not deal with the attacks on the native-born because of their ideas, organizations, or religious practices. The focus will be on the organized response of the natives to the immigrant. At times, that opposition would be based wholly or in part on the foreigners' religion, economic situation, race, and radicalism.

The ambivalence which characterized the colonial policies toward immigrants continued in the new government established by the United States Constitution. It has even been pointed out that the Founding Fathers were ethnocentric since they limited the office of President to native-born citizens. Still immigration was encouraged by the liberal Naturalization Act of 1790 which required only a two-year waiting period for aliens before they were eligible for citizenship. But the influx of aliens which followed the outbreak of the French revolutionary wars in 1792 alarmed many members of Congress, especially the Federalists, who then pushed through the Naturalization Act, 1795, which extended the waiting period to five years. When immigration continued, and especially when many of the naturalized foreigners voted with the Jeffersonians, there was a movement in the Federalist party to destroy the foreign vote.

The Federalist effort led to the passage of the Naturalization Act, 1798, which extended the waiting period to fourteen years, and the infamous Alien and Sedition Act.[24] In the discussion of this problem of the aliens in the war crisis of 1797–98, two broad approaches were debated: one, for some form of control, and the other, for immigrant restriction. That is, many individuals—Harrison Gray Otis of Massachusetts was one—wanted to find some way to limit the political power of the immigrant. Thus, Otis, in a letter to his wife, warned, "If some means are not adopted to prevent the indiscriminate admission of wild Irishmen and others to the right of suffrage, there will soon be an end to liberty and property."[25] Therefore Otis supported a measure that would have placed a prohibitive twenty-dollar tax on all certificates of naturalization. Otis not only wanted to limit the impact of the foreign-born vote, but he also insisted that "no alien born, who is not at present a citizen of the United States, shall hereafter be capable of holding any office of honor, trust, or profit, under the United States."[26] These proposals were aimed at the political power of the immigrants.

But if Otis and his Federal allies, John Allen of Connecticut and Robert Goodloe Harper of South Carolina, wanted to limit the political power of the naturalized citizens, they made no serious effort to forbid immigration. Yet, even this early in our national history, there were voices that pushed the xenophobic argument to its limit. President John Adams's nephew and private secretary, William Smith Shaw, declared that since foreigners were prone to be difficult, "Let us no longer pray that America may become an asylum to all nations."[27] This meant that Shaw favored a closing of the gates. This element would dominate the thinking of the post-Civil War nativists, though arguments for control and restriction coexisted throughout America's xenophobic outbursts.

The Federalists' antipathy toward the immigrant did not abate with the election of Thomas Jefferson in 1800. The Jeffersonians returned to the naturalization procedure of 1795 and permitted the Alien and Sedition Acts to lapse in 1801. The optimistic Jeffersonians generally found little to fear in the immigrant—he was a source of political power and an indication of America's growth and development. But the more pessimistic among the Federalists continued to view with alarm the influx of immigrants in the first years of the nineteenth century. This hostility was clearly evidenced at the Hartford Convention. The Hartford Convention Report, undoubtedly written by Harrison Gray Otis, clearly indicated that the nativism of the Adams administration had not died.

As the Federalist party went into decline, two divergent tendencies emerged among the party's members. On the one hand, there was a growing belief that the Federalist failures were the fault of foreigners who by their corrupting, revolutionary doctrines and conspiracies, their unaccustomed manners, rejected the best political party available—the Federalists.[28] On the other hand, there was a movement to entice the immigrants. It was first initiated in 1802 by Alexander Hamilton with his call for the formation of the Christian Constitutional Society, which would aid the immigrants.[29] Although Hamilton's idea was not acceptable, nonetheless, certain Federalists did make some efforts to win the support of the immigrants. The Philadelphia Federalists even established a committee to aid in the naturalization of foreigners.[30] But the Hartford Convention's demands on the Madison administration in regard to the problem of immigration was a clear indication that the Federalists were still waging their xenophobic crusade. The convention called for a constitutional amendment that would bar all naturalized citizens from holding public office. The Federalists' faith in America as a sanctuary had declined so far that it was no longer visible. What did appear was a xenophobic tradition that would reappear time and time again in the century of immigration, 1820–1930.

CHAPTER II

Early Xenophobic Movements

THE FEDERALISTS' FAILURE TO WIN POPULAR FAVOR after the Hartford Convention was an indication that the majority of the American people accepted the tradition of America as a sanctuary and as a place for strangers to make a new start. "It was here then," wrote Crèvecoeur in 1782, "that the idle may be employed, the useless become useful, and the poor become rich; but by riches I do not mean gold and silver, we have but little of those metals; I mean a better sort of wealth, cleared lands, cattle, good houses, good clothes, and an increase of people to enjoy them."[1]

This idea has dominated the American immigrant experience.[2] Yet the demise of the Federalists did not kill the xenophobic spirit in America. Many Americans shared the Federalists' distrust of foreigners, but only one out of every three Americans joined nativist groups.

The root cause of xenophobia was the fear that the stranger threatened the culture of the native-born. At times this fear became so intense that it impelled nativists to search for a measure of security in organizations that promised to perpetuate those traditions they called their own.[3]

This nativist belief, like that of the Federalists, expressed opposition to a liberal, universalistic view of citizenship. The American xenophobes thought that they belonged to a national community and were intent on preserving the character and integrity of the community by retaining control of it. As a result, they favored a more restrictive view of citizenship which they preferred not to confer on the foreign-born or, at least, not to confer readily. In this sense we may certify them as conservatives.[4]

Although xenophobia can occur whenever different

ethnocultural groups come in contact with each other, organized nativism in the century of immigration, 1820–1930, was more episodic. It trod an uneven path. The distrust of foreigners usually appeared after a series of bewildering changes. Then the nativists sought an explanation for these changes, and the xenophobes found their answer in a foreign menace. Professor David Brion Davis has shown that certain common themes persist in nineteenth-century American nativist literature. He found that the white, insecure Protestant Americans reacted to confusing social changes by uniting against a common enemy who threatened their existence through some form of internal subversion. Thus nativistic writers emphasized the frauds of the enemy; and, in the words of Professor Davis, "sought to establish the legitimacy and just authority of American institutions."[5] Nativist writers prejudged the foreign-born, and even native religions—the Mormons, for example—and such native organizations as the Masonic Order were subjected to attack. But even here, Freemasonry and Mormonism were associated with the anti-Catholic motif.[6]

The immigrant influx of close to thirty-eight million in the years 1820–1930 produced periodic tensions that often found release in the organization of xenophobic movements.[7] Basically, American xenophobia can be divided into two major movements. The first groups tried to control the power of the immigrants admitted to the United States, as outlined by Harrison Gray Otis. The second type tried to restrict the numbers, or even eliminate, the immigration of foreigners. The effort at control motivated the formation of the xenophobic Native American party of the 1830s, the American Republican party of the 1840s, and the Know-Nothings of the 1850s. Again there were efforts mainly aimed at limiting the aliens' right to be naturalized and to hold public office. While xenophobic groups did organize in places such as Washington, D.C., (1837) and Saint Louis, Missouri, where a future Know-Nothing, Vespasian Ellis, the Virginia-born editor of the *Saint Louis Democrat* (1841–44), founded a nativist group, the successful movements of the 1830s and 1840s were confined to the urban centers of the Atlantic seaboard, New York, Philadelphia, and Boston.[8] The Know-Nothings in the 1850s, however, were national in scope.

The second movement aimed at restricting the numbers and kinds of immigrants who would be admitted to the United States. Thus, in the 1870s and 1880s, the first successful efforts at national restriction took place and culminated in the Oriental restriction acts, which excluded Asians. This success led the xenophobes to a renewed attack on immigration in general, especially to prevent admission of the illiterate poor. Finally the Immigration Restriction League, joined by other interested groups, was able to push through Congress a variety of federal quota laws which were meant to preserve the status quo. In the 1920s, these laws brought one hundred years of open immigration to a close.

Two differing types of xenophobic organizations appeared in the organized nativist groups: the first directed at the religious beliefs of the immigrants and the second at their political power. Both religious and political nativism were basically conservative and reformist, in the sense that they hoped to maintain the status quo or, at least, to mold society in the image of the nativists' idea of the past.

For the most part, these nativists were sincere Americans, alarmed and confused at the changes taking place around them. And while there was an irrational element in the stereotypes and scapegoats created by them, it is also true that it was not unreasonable for them to attempt to protect themselves against the groups that were damaging their community and destroying their sense of status.[9] Generally they were in the minority, but occasionally they would be reinforced by other Americans who were angered at specific grievances generated by the two major political parties. And almost inevitably, demagogues appeared who used the nativist creed to advance their own careers.

In the period 1830–60, immigration had profound political and social implications for the nation, though the Eastern cities were the first to feel the impact of these newcomers. As immigration increased from approximately one half million in the decade 1831–40 to almost one and three quarter million in the succeeding decade and to two and a half million in the years 1851–60, a feeling of alarm spread among some of the native-born because the bulk of these foreigners, mostly Roman Catholics, were Irish and German peasants.[10]

Among the native-born urban dwellers, reaction to the Irish immigrant was generally much harsher than to other foreigners; the nativists saw the Irish immigrant as a positive menace.[11] Many of these xenophobic nativists were inclined to believe that all the Irish in the United States were immigrants, and all the immigrants were Irish—thus the immigrant became the symbol of change.[12]

Simultaneously with this influx of immigrants, substantial political changes marked the end of one era and the opening of a second. In the 1820s and the 1830s, revisions of state constitutions permitted universal white male adult suffrage, which meant the end of the rule of the patrician families and the introduction of the era of the practical politician.[13] Suffrage extension also marked the end of important appointive offices: for example, in New York by 1826 sheriffs and justices of the peace were elected; in 1834 city governments were permitted to vote for their own mayors. By the year 1835, those who wanted a voice in municipal affairs had to secure popular approval.[14] By 1835, throughout the nation the convention system had replaced the legislative caucus. Again this change meant that candidates would be selected by professional politicians interested in gaining party victories through the selection of candidates who could win.[15]

Xenophobes believed the immigrants were taking unfair advantage of these changes. This was particularly true in New York City, where the newly-created Whig party and some native-born Democrats found their role in local affairs diminished. The easiest explanation was to blame the newcomers. In addition, many nativists were members of the various reform societies which, as early as 1830, warned their members of the serious threat posed by the flood of Catholic immigrants. These warnings, emphasizing the efforts of Catholics to subvert America, were part of the creed of the national reform societies, such as the American Bible Society, the American Tract Society, the American Home Missionary

Society, the American Education Society, and the American Sunday School Union.[16] By failing to play a significant role in the social reforms of the day, particularly the temperance movement, the Catholic church stood condemned in the eyes of the Protestant reformers.[17] It did not take very long for conservative New Yorkers, already upset at their declining political power, to ask whether the Catholic church did not encourage the political power of immigrants as part of its conspiracy to subvert the American Republic. These xenophobic nativists were encouraged by some professional politicians who were anxious to exploit nativism as their vehicle to political power.

Philip Hone, former mayor of New York City (1825), and a wealthy Whig merchant, echoed the sentiments of many others when he described the political power of the Irish: "These Irishmen, strangers among us, without a feeling of patriotism or affection in common with American citizens, decide the elections in the City of New York. They make Presidents and Governors, and they send men to represent us in the councils of the nation. . . ."[18] Other nativists also wondered why these ignorant foreigners should be allowed to participate in the governing of the nation. For example, in 1844 one nativist asked: "Will the chances of a wise and honest administration of affairs be increased by extending to foreigners the privilege of voting?"[19] And that same year, Lewis Charles Levin, the well-traveled South Carolinian and editor of the xenophobic *Philadelphia Sun* insisted that "the Irish Catholic vote is to be organized to overthrow American Liberty."[20]

Of course, not all foreigners were a detriment; William L. Prall of the *New York Courier and Enquirer* pointed out that "A comparatively small portion . . . are men of intelligence, of learning, and of virtue. Some are worthy of our firm confidence and friendship."[21] These immigrants were usually Protestant in religion.[22] The special objects of vilification by the xenophobic nativists of the 1830s and 1840s were the Catholic Irish.[23]

This resurgent anti-Catholicism received additional support in 1832, from the artist Samuel Finley Breese Morse. The son of the militant Reverend Jedediah Morse, he returned to his home in New York City after a tour of Europe. He had discovered the Leopoldine Foundation, which financially supported the American Catholic missions.[24] Condemning this organization for its alleged plot to subvert America, Morse believed that he should now expose the Papist conspiracy which his father and the American reform societies had denounced in the past.

Morse's series of letters to the *New York Observer*, then edited by his brother Sidney, accused the Austrian government of using the Leopoldine Foundation and the Holy Alliance as means of gaining control of the United States by subsidizing the emigration of Catholics to America.[25] Anxious to do more, Morse in 1834 helped to organize the New York Protestant Association to combat this threat. Influenced by his action, the weekly *American Protestant Vindicator and Defender of Civil and Religious Liberty against the Inroads of Papacy* made its appearance in New York City with the expressed purpose of halting the further extension of Catholic influence.[26] The paper was edited by Parson William Craig Brownlee, the former editor of the bitterly anti-Catholic newspaper the *Protestant*.[27] This vigorous divine was noted for his heavy Scottish burr and his single-mindedness in preaching against what he termed, "papery."[28]

By catering to the prejudices of its readers, the *Protestant Vindicator* increased their anti-Catholic feelings. It gave wide publicity to Rebecca Theresa Reed, whose wild fabrications about life in an Ursuline Convent in Charlestown, Massachusetts, led to the burning of the convent in 1834. When Miss Reed published her accusations in a best-selling monograph, *Six Months in a Convent*, the *Vindicator* carried numerous advertisements for the book.[29] It also published the sensational distortions of Maria Monk, whose articles were printed in book form in 1836 as Maria Monk's *Awful Disclosures of the Hotel Dieu Nunnery of Montreal*.

Maria, an alleged nun, claimed to have escaped from the Montreal convent where innocent girls were forced to submit to priests who gained entrance to the convent via secret tunnels. Those nuns who resisted were killed. The children born of those meetings were baptized, then strangled and thrown into a lime pit. The baptized infants, free of all sin, would go directly to heaven where they would intercede for those who had baptized them.[30] Maria's readers were given a heady mixture of sex and religion. Other anti-Catholic tracts were also circulated in the country at this time.[31]

Support for Parson Brownlee's campaign against Catholicism came from three other religious-oriented organizations which were established to fight the Catholic menace. In May, 1841, Samuel Morse, frustrated in his scientific endeavors to perfect the invention of the telegraph, turned again to nativism, organizing the American Protestant Union to help fight the subjugation of the United States by the Pope at Rome.[32] Three years later, James W. Beekman, wealthy New York landholder and a fierce anti-Catholic, helped establish the American Protestant Society, which hoped to convert Roman Catholics to Protestantism, but which spent most of its time and energies attacking rather than converting them.[33] The American and Foreign Christian Union was organized in 1849. It was a fusion of several societies interested in preventing the spread of Catholicism as well as overcoming its "worst" practices in Europe. In the 1850s it was spending upwards of $80,000 a year on its tasks.[34]

Interestingly enough, the outbreak of war against Catholic Mexico in 1846 added little stimulus to religious nativism. Even when President James K. Polk asked Bishop John Hughes of New York to help in improving the anti-Catholic image of the United States in Mexico, there was little open reaction from the xenophobic nativists.[35] American Protestants simply did not correlate the defeat of Mexico with the elimination of the Roman Catholic religion. Furthermore, American Protestant opinion, particularly in the North, for the most part opposed involvement in the war.[36]

If the Mexican War did not exacerbate relations between Catholics and Protestants, events in Italy did tend to elicit sympathetic support from American Protestants for the Pope. The ascension of the liberal Pope Pius IX in 1846 was followed by a number of liberal reforms in the States of the Church and brought about a temporary abatement of anti-Catholicism.

The former nativist mayor of New York City, James Harper, served on a committee which called a public demonstration of support for the liberal Pope Pius IX.[37] Even Philip Hone, the xenophobic diarist, marveled at the change in attitude toward the Catholics. He attended a dinner sponsored by the New England Society of New York in December, 1847, at which Bishop Hughes presided and Pope Pius IX was praised.[38] He did not believe that he would see the day when a body of conservative Protestants would dine with a Catholic bishop and toast the Pope of Rome, whom they had recently called the "red harlot," and the "whore of Babylon."

Religious nativism—that is, Protestant opposition to Roman Catholicism—was organized in the 1830s and 1840s. As already noted, it lost some of its fervor in 1847. When we examine the political scene, we shall see the same trend among the political xenophobes. In the 1830s, the first formal organization took place in New York City. Political nativism increased its activities in the 1840s, but by 1847 open opposition to foreign-born voters had all but disappeared.

The early manifestations of political nativism showed a mixture of religionationalistic feeling: a combination of anti-Catholicism and antiforeignism. The Whig defeat in the first New York mayoralty election in 1834 caused the Whigs some misgivings.[39] The Democrats had been able to control the naturalized voters.[40] Though Tammany Democrats had at first (1782) excluded foreigners, their record of support for immigrants had become well-known by 1817.[41] Nativist Whigs were upset at the loss of this hard-fought election.

Then on March 13, 1835, the Irish Catholics disrupted a meeting of the New York Protestant Association, which met to discuss the question "Is Popery compatible with Civil Liberty?" Parson Brownlee, chairman of the meeting, explained that "a great number of persons, chiefly if not exclusively Roman Catholics," invaded the hall and assaulted the ministers on the speaker's platform.[42] But the police made no arrests among the two hundred or so attackers. This incident sparked the beginning of an organized political nativist movement.

Almost immediately afterwards, Uriah C. Watson, a New York mechanic, began publication of the *Spirit of '76,* which called for the limitation of the political power of the foreign-born; simultaneously, a few nativists in several wards tried unsuccessfully to organize for the spring elections of 1835.[43] Unfortunately for their hopes, the Democrats carried not only the mayor's office but they also won control of the Board of Aldermen, thus giving them complete access to the city patronage.[44]

This exhibition of power, coupled with the organization of an Irish-American regiment, the O'Connell Guards, as part of the state militia system, raised the nativists' fears to awesome heights, and in July they organized on a citywide basis. The Native American Democratic Association had two objectives: to halt the growing political power of the foreign-born by making only native Americans eligible for public office, and to end the efforts of the Roman Catholic hierarchy to control the United States.[45] These two aims became the common threads which united all of the xenophobic nativists in pre-Civil War America.

By the end of the year, the "Native Americans" and the Whigs cooperated in presenting a single ticket for the state legislature and the congressional seat vacated by the resignation of the incumbent.[46] The ticket was unsuccessful.[47] It did not engender any great enthusiasm among the native-born Democrats, perhaps because it did appear to be but another name for the Whig coalition. Then, again, the nativists were racked by factional disputes that did not foster harmony.

The Association, or Native American Party, as it was called, existed for three years. It had two splits—one in 1835 over the wording of its platform and the second in 1836 as a result of the nomination of the Democrat, Samuel F. B. Morse. These struggles indicated that, for the most part, the nativists were predominantly Whigs.

The first break occurred at the party convention in September, 1835, when the organization divided over the platform: one group, led by the combative Origen Bacheler, the Boston-born, nativist Whig editor and temperance supporter, wanted to declare its hostility to all Catholics, native- as well as foreign-born. Another, more tolerant segment, headed by Uriah C. Watson, the former Whig turned Democrat, was hostile only to the foreign-born.[48] The Bacheler faction prevailed, though they moderated their opposition to native-born Catholics as voters. Still they were loud in their opposition to President Jackson's elevation of the native-born Catholic, Roger B. Taney, to the United States Supreme Court.[49]

In April, 1836, the second split occurred. When two Whigs declined the Native American nomination for mayor, Samuel Morse accepted, but in this presidential year, the Whigs refused to endorse him.[50] Morse was an ardent Jacksonian and a supporter of Martin Van Buren, the Democratic nominee for the presidency. When Morse refused to repudiate the Democratic leaders, the Whigs turned on him. James Watson Webb, the fiery editor of the conservative nativist-Whig journal the *Courier and Enquirer* accused Morse of cunningly foisting himself upon the honest men of the American party.[51] Without the Whig endorsement, however, he received fewer than fifteen hundred votes.[52]

This election was the only one in which the Native Americans failed to cooperate with the Whigs of the city. Most native-born Democrats accused the xenophobic nativists of being Whigs in disguise; and most Whigs agreed.[53]

The Native Americans and the Whigs renewed their alliance in 1837. At that time, the Native Americans merged officially with the Whigs and endorsed for mayor the Whig Aaron Clark, the former clerk and parliamentarian of the New York State Assembly. He became subsequently a successful landowner and businessman.[54] Elected in 1837 and reelected in 1838, he was narrowly defeated in 1839.[55]

Who supported the Native American Party? The party appealed mainly to the Whigs and to some native-born Democrats who opposed the policies of Tammany Hall toward the immigrants. Some foreign-born Protestants, especially the Irish Presbyterians (or Orangemen), also favored the party.

With the amalgamation of the Native Americans and the Whigs in 1837, most of the nativists returned to the Whig party. Democrats continued their appeal to the foreign-born, and nativist Whigs, especially in the cities, pointed to the growing power of the naturalized Irish in politics as an important factor in the decline of Whig political fortunes. In 1838, Philip Hone still labeled the naturalized Irish as "unprincipled foreigners."[56]

The merger of the Native Americans with the Whigs of New York City did not end either the political or religious xenophobia of the 1830s. The Whig party in other states—Illinois is a prime example—also took a xenophobic stance, as much for political considerations as for fear of the foreigners. The Illinois Constitution of 1818 permitted any adult male alien to vote so long as he had resided in the state for at least six months. This measure was intended to encourage immigrants to come into the area. But by 1839, some ten thousand foreigners were voting and, according to most authorities, nine out of every ten were voting Democratic.[57] The Whig party made several efforts to expunge the alien-vote provision from the constitution.[58] Even the Irish-born James Shields of Belleville, a Democrat, found himself, as a state legislator in 1836, introducing a petition from his constituents asking first that all aliens be removed from public office, and second that the constitution be amended to deny aliens the right to vote.[59] By 1839 these resolutions were aimed at supporting the Whig circuit court judge Daniel Stone's 1839 decision against the aliens' right to vote. To protect themselves against the Whigs on the court, the Democrats reorganized the judiciary: they legislated the circuit court of appeals out of existence and added five new members to the supreme court.[60] But while similar attitudes on the part of the Whigs were to be found in other states as well, by and large, they did not call forth any new xenophobic political organizations.

New nativist groups did organize, however. The Catholic demand for public aid to parochial education coupled with the controversy over the Bible in the public schools aided the nativists in the formation of the American Republican party in the 1840s. This issue was a perennial one. It has continued to exacerbate relations between Catholics and Protestants right up to the present day.

CHAPTER III

The Bible Controversy:
the American Republicans

WHAT REALLY AROUSED THE IRE OF BOTH POLITICAL and religious xenophobes of the 1840s, often one and the same, was the school question: that is, the Catholic practice of establishing their own parochial schools, and their efforts, particularly in the 1840s, to obtain public funds to support these schools. Growing numbers of immigrants created a problem for the Catholic hierarchy of most of the urban centers of the nation: where was the church to get the money to pay for these schools?

Other factors were involved in the willingness of many native Americans to become part of the nativist movement. The years, 1842–43, if not a period of depression, were certainly a time of economic stagnation. Money was scarce, prices were low, people were in debt, and many banks had suspended specie payments.[1] These occurrences caused unrest and a sense of unease among many artisans and small businessmen. And, as the Irish Catholic editor of the *Boston Pilot* noted, many native workingmen were also restless because they "have been brought into competition with, and frequently undersold by, emigrant workmen."[2] Both groups came to feel that the cause of their difficulty was the immigrant, especially the Catholic immigrant. Added to these groups were other sincere Americans who were alarmed at the growth of political corruption as a result of the increased participation of naturalized immigrants.[3]

The first outburst of this nativist reaction took place in New York. Other areas also felt the tensions, but only in New York, Philadelphia, and Boston did the nativists successfully organize and carry some of their candidates to political victory.

In New York, Governor William Henry Seward, in his annual

32

address to the legislature in 1840, made a bold bid for the political support of the foreign-born by advocating a policy of providing the immigrants' children with schools and teachers who spoke the language of the children and professed the same faith.[4] Among nativist Whigs, a suspicion grew that the Whig governor had succumbed to the influence of the Roman Catholic Bishop of New York, John Hughes; and within the Democracy, certain influential elements believed the governor was trying to lure the naturalized citizens away from their party.[5] The plan was ignored by both the Whigs and the Democrats in the legislature, but when the governor again called for aid to the immigrant children, many Whigs protested vigorously.[6] This opposition encouraged Samuel Morse and several others to form in March, 1841, a new nativist organization, the Democratic American Association.[7] They hoped for Whig support.

But when the Democratic Americans insisted on nominating Morse for mayor of New York City, the Whigs balked. Notices appeared on the day of the election declaring that Morse had withdrawn from the race. He had not. The ruse worked, however, and he received but 77 votes.[8] The Democratic Association was crushed, and it was clear that, at this time, the nativists required the organizing and financial talents of political professionals plus the active support of the Whigs if they were to be successful.

The Irish-born Bishop Hughes now entered the fray. Cooperating with the Seward Whigs of the city, he decided to endorse candidates favorable to Seward's school plan.[9] The so-called Carroll Hall ticket of Bishop Hughes was accepted by the Seward Whigs as a method of splitting the Democrats in the city, but many of the nativist Whigs condemned what they termed Bishop Hughes's "unblushing attempts to mix up religion with politics—an unpalatable dish in this country...."[10] It was, to say the least, an error in judgment on the part of the Bishop, and a clear violation of the American doctrine of the separation of church and state.

After the appearance of Bishop Hughes's Carroll Hall ticket, Seward was warned by a rural-county Whig, "I have heard Presbyterians say 'we must cut loose from Seward and [Gulian

C.] Verplanck [a Seward Whig at this time] or the Whig party must go down.' This class of man must be reconciled and all is well.... The word Roman Catholic sounds frightfully in this country."[11] The Carroll Hall ticket provided the margin of victory for those Whigs who were elected in New York City.[12]

Despite these Whig admonitions, Seward again, in 1842, called for changes in the state's educational system. But the bill that finally emerged from the legislature, the so-called Maclay bill, was a far cry from the plan initially offered by the governor. Both the governor and the bishop, however, endorsed the bill which became law in 1842. The act replaced the centralized Public School Society—dominated by the Protestant clergy of New York City—with decentralized boards of education elected in each district in New York City each year. The boards had the right to tax and dispense funds as they saw fit; they could not, however, provide any public money to church schools.[13]

Many citizens in New York City were upset: they excitedly condemned the Maclay Act as a victory for the Catholic bishop. Riots broke out, and a mob even attacked the home and church of Bishop Hughes.[14]

Even those Whigs who wanted to continue the alliance with the Catholic Bishop of New York believed that he controlled the Irish Catholic voters of New York City. These Whig politicians declared that once the Catholics openly supported the Whig party, Whig opposition to the naturalized Catholics would decline.[15] But Bishop Hughes refused to continue his political activities; while he had made a point, the nativist rioters also had made theirs.[16]

Catholic tactics shifted somewhat. Since it was impossible to acquire public funds, Bishop Hughes now tried to replace the King James Version of the Bible with the Catholic version, for Catholic students in the public schools.[17] This decision transformed the local school board elections into religious disputes. The appearance of Protestant ministers in these contests was, if not defensible, then certainly understandable. This decision by Bishop Hughes was emulated elsewhere. For example, Bishop Francis Kenrick of Philadelphia initiated similar actions to replace the King James Version of the Bible.[18] The results were somewhat similar; an increase in activity of Protestant ministers to save the Bible for the public schools.[19]

In Boston, Bishop Benedict J. Fenwick faced similar difficulties.[20] The heritage of the Charlestown convent burning of 1834 intensified religious friction, and, of course, Boston had been the home of the Reverend Lyman Beecher, who was one of the most bitter opponents of Catholicism.[21] Beecher, as part of a fund-raising tour, was in Boston in 1843 on behalf of the Lane Theological Seminary of Ohio. He still believed that the Catholic Church wanted to subvert America. "No human means can so certainly meet and repel this invasion of Catholic Europe," he declared, "as a competent evangelical ministry and revivals of religion. . . ."[22] And, of course, he insisted on the use of the Bible in public schools. The Catholic effort to establish parochial schools and eliminate the King James Version of the Bible from the public schools exacerbated relations between the Catholics and their Protestant neighbors.

Bishop John Baptist Purcell of Cincinnati, Ohio, faced the same problems. The parochial school system precipitated anti-Catholic feelings. Then when he, too, entered the Bible controversy, a number of Protestant ministers became involved in nativist attacks upon the Catholics, predominantly German immigrants.[23]

But while other sections of the country took part in the Bible controversy, the nativists and their newspapers gave particular attention to the situation in New York. The American Bible Society, under the leadership of the New York merchant, Hiram Ketcham, for example, emphasized the conflict in New York. Almost all Protestant religious denominations, except the Unitarians and the Episcopalians, took part in this defense of the Bible, and a concomitant attack on Catholicism.[24]

This religious battle became political in 1843. When the American Republican party was formed, it was a religio-nationalistic group aimed at both Catholic and immigrant power. It enjoyed success in New York and Philadelphia in 1844 and Boston in 1845.

The American Republican movement was obviously not an

exclusively anti-Catholic group. Many areas with a strong anti-Catholic bias did not become involved in the movement.[25] Only where the political and economic control of the native-born was threatened did the nativists find political support.[26]

When the Democratic party in New York City, with the aid of the naturalized voters, won the mayoralty election in 1843, Hiram Ketcham and several other members of national reform societies denounced the fraud and corruption of the Tammany Democrats.[27] These reformers joined with certain dissident Democrats in June, 1843, to form the nativistic American Republican party.[28] These Democrats were out of favor with Tammany because of their role in the unsuccessful anti–Van Buren and pro-Calhoun movement of the previous year.[29]

The party had three major objectives: only native Americans should hold public office; the Bible should be retained in the public schools; and the naturalization process must be extended from five to twenty-one years.[30] These aims were the same in other places, particularly in Philadelphia, Pennsylvania, and Boston, Massachusetts.

In defending their platform, the American Republicans used the nativist stereotype for the naturalized American—wicked, ignorant, and priest-ridden.[31] The xenophobic fears of the period were reflected in the words of a Boston nativist written in 1844: "Too long, fellow citizens, too long, has this nation suffered its sympathies for oppressed humanity in Europe to predominate over its perception of its own true interest.... It has forgotten to exercise that charity which begins at home, and dictates its self-preservation."[32] Other nativists watching the number of immigrants arriving in New York declared: "we state but a simple truth when we say that so filthy and ignorant a mass of humanity we have never seen on the face of the earth as is congregated in the cargoes of from two to ten or eleven hundred men, women and children."[33] The same source went on to ask, "And is it of no account to be an 'American born'?"[34]

Bible reading for all, they believed, would end the domination of the priests. "Ignorance is the means employed by the Catholic priest to perpetuate his influence and power over the devotees of his faith," one Philadelphia nativist insisted.

"Give a people intelligence and they are no longer Catholics. Ireland is an oppressed country, but made so by the Catholic religion."[35]

The need for alterations of the naturalization laws was a major plank for the American Republicans. The nativist press insisted that the changing character plus the tremendous increase in immigration required an extension of the waiting period to at least twenty-one years.[36]

But there were no serious efforts to restrict immigration. Most Americans accepted the idea that the increase in a state's population was evidence of its prosperity.[37] There was also a belief that the nation suffered from a scarcity of labor, though as we have indicated, there was a strong element of economic nativism among the American Republicans. The newer states, nevertheless, sought to encourage immigration.[38]

Catholicism was attacked because of "the prevailing Romish system of luxurious profligacy, opulent vice and bloated sensuality."[39] Reform and an emotional anti-Catholicism were closely intertwined.[40]

But while the American Republicans were reform-minded they were decidedly xenophobic as well. For example, in the early months of 1844, the General Executive Committee of the party both in New York and Philadelphia purged themselves of their foreign-born members.[41]

The American Republicans of New York City, though unsuccessful, were encouraged by their vote-pulling power in the election of 1843.[42] They now prepared for the spring mayoralty campaign. James Harper, the book publisher, a devout Methodist and strong supporter of the temperance crusade and a Whig in politics, accepted the nomination to run for mayor. While the Whigs did not endorse Harper, because they wanted to maintain the party organization in the city for the November gubernatorial and presidential contests, they did assure him that he would have their quiet support.[43]

The preparations made by the American Republicans reflected their professional talent. They checked the various courts to get additional naturalization lists, and they canvassed their wards.[44] They warned their supporters to be on guard against the Irish Democrats' efforts to colonize special wards through the use of the Alms and Pauper House residents.[45] They even offered a hundred-dollar reward for the detection and conviction of illegal voters, and at least one American collected.[46]

These efforts were successful. On April 10, the Whig diarist and prominent attorney, George Templeton Strong, reported enthusiastically, "Hurrah for the Natives! They've elected Harper by a majority of 4,000 and stand two to one in the Common Council...."[47] Harper's main support was in the Whig wards.[48]

Harper's success encouraged the American Republicans not only in New York, but in Philadelphia.[49] The efforts of the American Republicans to generate support for their movement helped precipitate a series of riots in the Philadelphia area in May and July, 1844. The May riots took place in Kensington, an Irish ghetto in Philadelphia. The July riots took place in Southwark, a middle-class, and blue-collar area which had not undergone the population changes of Kensington, which had evolved from a fashionable residential area into a commercial and business section and finally into an immigrant slum.[50]

In May, the American Republicans called for a meeting in Kensington, right in the stronghold of the Catholic Irish. The meeting was disrupted. Shots were fired; men were killed; houses were burned. The nativists, led by Lewis C. Levin, blamed the "foreign rabble" for the riot. One New York nativist reported that "the Minions of a Despotic Priesthood *shot down with* Musket *Balls* in the Streets of the Second Greatest City in the Union, *native American* citizens because those descendants of Revolutionary Heroes met peaceably publicly to discuss questions relative to the Good of the Country."[51] The riot lasted four days, from Monday to Thursday, May 7 to 11. The most active participants were youngsters, sixteen to twenty-one years old, and some older adults under the influence of strong drink.[52] The nativist rioters were anti-Irish as well as anti-Catholic.[53]

Numerous injuries were inflicted on both sides, and, in addition, the nativist rioters managed to burn Saint Nicholas and Saint Augustine's Roman Catholic churches. These acts won the American Republicans the name of "Churchburners." In order to defend themselves against these charges, the American Republicans issued an address defending their acts. They insisted that these acts were the results of the "unprovoked" slaughter of Americans, though the address did condemn, defensively, the acts of arson.[54]

The New York nativist, Philip Hone, condemned the church attacks; they were the results, he believed, of "incendiary newspapers and fed by political demagogues."[55]

The second series of riotous activities took place in Southwark in July, 1844. On July 4, the American Republicans held a big parade; many of those wounded in May were at the parade as guests of honor. There were scuffles between the Irish and the paraders, but cooler heads prevailed; there was no riot. On July 5, however, the nativists noticed that arms were being taken into Saint Philip Neri Roman Catholic Church.[56] Great excitement ensued. On Saturday, July 6, crowds threatened the church. The sheriff removed a number of firearms, and though the state militia attempted to disperse the crowd, it continued to swell. Finally the troops fired on the crowd, and the mob retaliated. The result was the death of two state militiamen and fifteen civilians plus many wounded among both groups.[57]

Despite the adverse reactions to the Kensington riots, in Philadelphia the American Republicans managed to elect Lewis C. Levin and John H. Campbell to Congress in the October 1844 elections.[58] During his campaign speeches, Levin had insisted that the American Republicans were composed of the useful classes: mechanics, farmers, manufacturers, and workingmen. It had no aristocrats.[59] But the Whig Sidney Fisher summed up the major ideological ingredients in the Philadelphia party after the October election victory in these words:

The movement of the "native" party is decidedly conservative, because by excluding foreigners so much democracy is excluded, so much of the rabble, so much ignorance and brutality from political power. The natural ally of this party are the Whigs. Their object harmonizes with the instincts and secret wishes and opinions of the Whigs. The consequence is they have combined forces so far in this election, and I hope to see the one merged with the other, and the principles of this party announced with authority in Congress. I think they are destined to spread, possibly to triumph.[60]

In Boston, the Bible controversy had excited the enmity of the Protestant Bostonians as well as of the immigrant Catholics. These fears had been increased as a result of the Philadelphia riots.[61] The American Republican party was formed and ran Thomas Aspinwall Davis, former jeweler and Whig, as their candidate for mayor in 1844. Not only was the protection of the Bible an issue, but the American Republicans promised, if elected, to improve the water-supply system for the municipality.[62] The election in Boston was a three-way affair; both the Whigs and the Democrats were in the field. In the first voting—an absolute majority of the votes cast was required for victory—no candidate pulled a majority. Not until February 21, 1845, after eight ballots, did Davis obtain that bare majority. It was apparent that as Davis's totals went up, the Whig candidate's vote came down.[63]

In his inauguration address, Davis touched defensively on a point that always proved embarrassing to the nativists, and especially so to the American Republicans because of their riots in Philadelphia—their violation of the American tradition of tolerance. "It is not the object of the American party," he insisted, "by word or act, to engender unkind feelings between native-born and foreign-born citizens. Its object is, by the establishing of general and salutary naturalization and registry laws, by education and moral means, to place our free institutions upon such a basis that those who come after us, the descendants both of the foreign and the American citizens may be free and independent."[64]

Soon after his election, Davis fell ill and tried to resign, but his resignation was not accepted. He did not succeed in his efforts to improve the water system.

The success of American Republicans in New York and Philadelphia encouraged both groups to outline an ambitious political program: they would attempt to organize first on a statewide basis, then throughout the nation.[65] In Boston, however, after the election of Davis, interest in nativism declined as the Whigs assumed the rhetoric of the nativists. Then, too, it did not appear that the relatively small number of Irish voters in Boston posed any great threat to the political hegemony of the native-born.[66]

Whig leaders frowned upon the nativists' efforts to widen the scope of the movement. They did, however, cooperate with them in New York and Pennsylvania in the November gubernatorial and presidential elections. The Whigs of Pennsylvania agreed to support the national legislative candidates, while the nativists accepted Henry Clay, the Whig presidential candidate.[67] In New York City, the Whigs and the American Republicans endorsed a fusion ticket in the local New York City election, and both pledged to aid Henry Clay.

In Pennsylvania, the American Republicans denied what they considered a Democratic charge: that there was a coalition between the Whigs and the Native Americans.[68] Still the fusion went forward. The agreement was kept in Pennsylvania.

In New York, however, though the Whigs supported the nativist candidates, the Democratic nativists, numbering no more than 1,500 voters, refused to support Henry Clay.[69] The result was success for the nativists in the local election and defeat for the Whigs in the national election.

The New York Whigs decided to abandon their formal coalition with the American Republicans for two reasons: they blamed Clay's defeat on the treachery of the nativists, and secondly, the decision of the Native Americans to set up a state and national party jeopardized their own existence.[70] The nativists in New York insisted that Clay's defeat was brought about by foreign voters naturalized for the purpose.[71]

When Mayor Harper came up for reelection in 1845, the Whigs refused to endorse him and Harper was defeated.[72] His administration had not lowered taxes, and this disappointment coupled with Whig party defections brought about his defeat. As one Whig wrote, "I shall never change my name to any other party, nor be called by any other name but Whig." The same writer went on to explain that the nativists "were almost made up from Whigs."[73]

While some of the Whigs were alarmed, many former supporters believed the American Republicans to be "politically dead" in 1845.[74] Even Bishop Hughes felt that the nativists were in decline in 1845.[75]

But the Native Americans did hold a national convention. It met on July 4, 1845, in Philadelphia. Thirteen states were represented, but over 80 percent of the delegates came from Pennsylvania, New York, and Massachusetts. Henry A. S. Dearborn of Roxbury, Massachusetts, was selected President of the convention. He was the most prestigious member present. His father, a Revolutionary War hero, had been Secretary of War during the Jefferson administrations and subsequently a member of Congress and a diplomat. His son had succeeded him to the post of Collector of the Port of Boston, a position he held from 1812 to 1829, when he was removed by the Jacksonians. Elected to Congress in 1832, he had been defeated in 1834 by his Democratic opponent.[76] The convention warned of the growing power of the foreign-born voters and endorsed the use of the Bible in the schools as the "divine authority for rights of man." They also called for a national convention to meet in May, 1847, to nominate candidates for President and Vice President of the United States.

As a result of the efforts to expand the xenophobic doctrine of the American Republicans into a national movement called the Native American party—the two names were used interchangeably—the Whig professionals formally dissolved the arrangements with the nativists.

The result of the Whig party opposition was a significant drop in the nativist vote totals.[77] In Pennsylvania, only Levin survived as a successful nativist candidate after 1846, though it is true that many Whig party candidates assumed the rhetoric of nativism.

The Native American party did meet in Pittsburgh in September, 1847, to nominate candidates for the presidency and vice presidency of the United States. They chose General Zachary Taylor and Henry A. S. Dearborn for the two offices respectively, but the nativists ran no campaign. The nominations were its last formal act.

Generally, the party appealed to the middle classes: the small businessmen, artisans, and craftsmen, plus the native workers. The bulk of these people were Whigs, but they also enjoyed the support of an important element of the Democratic party, those who were alarmed at the changes and the methods employed by their political party.

The Native Americans failed because leading Whigs began to make serious efforts to discourage the Whig-Nativist alliance. They came to believe that the nativists posed a threat to the national aspirations of the Whig party. Then, too, the nativists flew in the face of the national tradition for toleration and the belief that immigrants were beneficial to the American society. The Philadelphia riots also cast the nativists in a bad light with their more moderate supporters among the Whigs.[78]

And, of course, Levin, the lone avowed nativist in public office after 1846 was ineffectual as a symbol for many reasons, not the least of which was his extremism and his self-delusion. Indeed, his vehemence made him appear juvenile.[79]

But the decline of the nativist movement in 1844–45 became obvious with the formation of a number of secret fraternal nativist organizations, particularly the establishment of the nationally famous Order of the United Americans. The nativists could no longer afford publicly to be known as supporters of the party of proscription, especially if they were businessmen or had political ambitions which they hoped to gratify among the Whigs or the Democrats.

CHAPTER IV

The Shift to Secrecy

THE SECRET NATIVIST FRATERNAL SOCIETIES THAT HELPED foster the major xenophobic movement of the 1850s, the Know-Nothings, began simply as organizations where the American-born wished to maintain their sense of an exclusive community. Of course, it was to be a community devoid of foreigners. Members joined because they felt the need for an association in which the threat of the un-American immigrants could be discussed without fear or reprisal from the growing influx of the foreign-born.[1] The societies wanted to maintain America as they thought it had been before the arrival of the immigrant, that symbol of many unwanted changes.

The first secret fraternal society with nativistic aims, the American Brotherhood, made its appearance in New York City at the end of 1844. Simeon Baldwin, prosperous real estate and insurance broker, disagreed with the Seward analysis of the Whig defeat in 1844. Baldwin believed that the foreign vote was the cause. He thought changes were needed in the naturalization laws, or "it will soon be too late to prevent an entire foreign control of our government."[2] On December 16, 1844, with James and John Harper and a number of others, he helped organize the first of the nativist chapters at the home of Russell C. Root, owner of a printing and stationery shop. The following week, December 21, a constitution was approved and officers chosen.[3] In January, 1845, the name of the order was changed to the Order of United Americans, usually abbreviated OUA. The first chapter, headed by John Harper, a successful book publisher and brother of Mayor James Harper, was called the Alpha Chapter. It served as the arch-chancery or governing body of the OUA. Within eight months, four other chapters were founded.

Most of the organizers of the Alpha Chapter were business and professional men. John Harper and his brother owned the Harper Brothers Publishing Company; Simeon Baldwin was an insurance broker; Daniel Talmadge and Lancaster Burling were merchants; Charles Whitney was a wealthy banker; George E. Belcher was a physician.[4] These men feared the growing power of the immigrants and thus believed in the need for secrecy. Both Baldwin and James Harper were well-known in nativist circles, Baldwin was elected to the board of education of the common schools by the nativists in June, 1844, and Harper was elected mayor by the American Republicans.[5]

The aims of the OUA were fraternal and patriotic. They hoped to inculcate "right notions of liberty" and "a true love of country" among themselves and others, as well as to aid any member who might possibly fall upon hard times.[6] The members took an oath not to "disclose any of the transactions or secrets of this Order to any being in the known world."[7]

As more and more men took the oath, a state chancery was organized in 1846, and national organization soon followed.[8] Local chapters were governed by a sachem; the state organization was controlled by a chancery made up of three chancellors from each chapter and presided over for one year by a grand sachem; and national control was vested in the arch-chancery formed by three arch-chancellors chosen from each state chancery and headed for a year by an arch-grand sachem.[9]

While the OUA proceedings and ritual were secret, the organization operated openly. Meetings were advertised in the press. The organization made its first massive appearance in October, 1847, at the Washington Monument celebration. When John Quincy Adams died February 23, 1848, the OUA held a public memorial service.

Other nativist fraternal organizations were established at the same time. The Order of United Americans had its women's auxiliary, the United Daughters of America.[10] The United American Mechanics, a fraternal and benevolent nativist association hostile to immigrant labor competition, began operation at Philadelphia in July, 1845.[11] It helped its members obtain employment and also helped defray funeral costs. Three councils were organized quickly and in November, 1845, a state council for Pennsylvania was established.[12] Two years later, Jacob Broom of Philadelphia, son of former Delaware congressman James Madison Broom, formed the United Sons of America.[13]

While other organizations developed, the OUA remained the most important of the secret nativist groups. As the OUA grew throughout the nation—it had fifty-three chapters by 1851, and four years later was established in sixteen states—its interest in politics developed.[14] In 1848, when the New York state legislature was preparing to choose a candidate for the office of United States Senator, the *order's* organ, the *OUA*, hoped William H. Seward would not be chosen.[15] The nativists still remembered the Maclay Act, which eliminated the Protestant-dominated Public School Society's control of education in New York City, as a betrayal of Americanism. But Seward became a senator nonetheless.

The following year, 1849, the order in New York pointed with pride to the election of two of its members on the Whig ticket.[16] Though the order insisted it was above partisan politics,[17] its members were often told that one political organization, the Democratic party, was catering to the foreigners who demanded the right to sit in the legislative halls of the government.[18]

The earliest manifestation of the use of the OUA for nativist political purposes came during the New York City election of 1849. George H. Purser of the Fourth Ward, nominated by the Democrats for comptroller of New York City, had the temerity to ridicule the nativists. The OUA issued a circular urging his defeat. "George H. Purser," it declared, "is ... bitterly opposed to our Order.... Let us show this man of foreign birth and foreign prejudice that he cannot hold and control the funds of our city."[19] It was a Whig year, and Purser, the Democratic candidate, was defeated by his Whig opponent. Still he ran behind his ticket by a thousand votes, indicating that there may have been at least a thousand Democrats in the New York City OUA.[20]

The OUA continued its involvement in politics and, in 1850, helped the Union Safety Committee, a group of one hundred New York City businessmen, in its support of the Compromise of 1850.[21] In May, 1850, the chancery set up a nine-man Grand Executive Convention for this purpose. The convention also successfully organized the OUA membership to vote in the same year against the repeal of the Free School Amendment, which Bishop Hughes had hoped could be changed to permit public funds to go to parochial schools.[22] By 1851 Thomas R. Whitney, editor of the nativist magazine, the *Republic*, asserted that the OUA was developing its political strength quietly but effectively.[23]

While religious nativism persisted throughout the 1840s, by 1850, the character of organized political nativism had changed throughout the nation. Secret societies had replaced the earlier political parties interested in maintaining "America for Americans." Basically these new groups were organized by middle-class elements, particularly in New York and Pennsylvania. They appealed to the artisans, craftsmen, mechanics, and the native workers in the cities and towns, where the immigrants' presence was obvious. They disclaimed any interest in partisan politics, though it was apparent that the members were basically Whig in composition with, however, an important element of Democrats. But by 1850, a new element began to appear among the nativists: not only did anti-Catholicism and antiforeignism remain a potent issue in the nativist creed, but the nativists also began to stress their nationalistic, pro-Union outlook.[24] This factor made these nativist societies attractive to many individuals, particularly in the South, who were growing alarmed at the increased slavery agitation that split the two major political parties.

Even some prominent Whigs became concerned. Henry Clay, in a speech before the Kentucky state legislature in November, 1850, saw the need for a National Union Party. Most Southern Whigs, at that time, rejected the idea.[25] When Winfield S. Scott received the Whig presidential nomination, the Union Safety Committee of New York viewed him as the candidate of the Seward wing of the party and, thus, as tainted with the charge of abolitionism. They denied him their support. Instead the committee set up a National Union ticket with Daniel Webster as the candidate. But he refused to take the nomination seriously.[26]

The inability of the committee to generate enthusiasm for

Webster's candidacy in effect ended the political activities of the Union Safety Committee. Many of the conservative members of the committee were attracted to the nativist movement because of the help provided by the OUA.[27] The committee detested what they termed the abolitionism of Senator William H. Seward; the nativists were angered by Seward's catering to the foreign-born. The increased political power of the "Foreign Desperadoes and Irish Politicians," as one nativist editor later (1856) put it, was a cause for deep concern.[28] In New York, both the nationalists in the Union Safety Committee and the nativists in the OUA came to agree that the nation's most pressing problem was the question of how to thwart the twin menaces of abolitionism and political Catholicism.

Thomas R. Whitney had an answer: political organization of the OUA. In a series of rules drawn up by the executive convention of the order in New York State in December, 1851, to guide its political activity, the order's executive committee was permitted to endorse political candidates, and the membership was enjoined "to sustain" these nominees.[29] They opposed all candidates who catered to the foreign-born, but they were most condemnatory of any Whigs who might seek political support from the foreign-born by granting concessions to them. For example, they helped defeat a Whig alderman in Brooklyn because he favored an appropriation for that city's Catholic Orphan Asylum.[30] Whitney hoped to extend this power by a union of the conservatives and nativists. "Thus we see a conservative party *taking its cue from the doctrines set forth* by the Order of United Americans...." he wrote. "This party must and will become the party of the nation—the great American party...."[31] In order for such a party to become effective on a national scale, Whitney in 1851 and again in 1852 called for the nativist societies—the United Mechanics, the United Sons of America, and the Sons of Liberty—to affiliate with OUA, as the first of the nativist societies.[32]

His initial appeal was ignored, but he persisted, believing there was a genuine need for a new party which would embrace all parts of the union. "The party will embrace the entire conservative Whig strength in the North, in contradistinction to the Abolitionists of that party; the entire Whig and a good portion of the Democratic parties of the South; the American influence of New York, Pennsylvania, New Jersey, and the West, and the friends of the Union everywhere."[33]

In the summer of 1852, Whitney's appeal bore results. On July 5 and 6, a new party, the American Union party, convened at Trenton, New Jersey, for the first time. Thirty-one delegates from Pennsylvania, New Jersey, New York, Massachusetts, Illinois, Ohio, Maryland, Virginia, and Georgia met and nominated Daniel Webster for President and George C. Washington of Maryland for Vice President on a nativist ticket.[34] Washington, grandnephew of the first president of the United States, declined the nomination and was replaced by Dr. Reynell Coates of Camden.[35] Friction soon developed among the delegates on the issues of naturalization. It was the same difficulty which had faced the nativists in 1835: many wished to proscribe all Catholics; others simply wanted to maintain opposition to the foreign-born as the sole criterion. The decision of the party to eliminate the demand for a twenty-one-year waiting period for naturalization in favor of a call for general reform of the naturalization laws antagonized the more militant nativists.[36]

Essentially, the new party had no influence. In New York, the OUA, which was thought to control between ten and fifteen thousand votes, ignored the nominations,[37] as Whigs in the order attempted to keep this bloc in the Whig party, or at least prevent it from being controlled by anyone else.[38] When Webster, who ignored the nomination entirely, died in October, the National Executive Committee of the American party on October 28 chose as his replacement Jacob Broom of Philadelphia, the chairman of the Trenton convention.[39] Lacking any substantial support, the party did not conduct a campaign and after the election quickly disintegrated.[40]

Although the effort to organize the American Union party failed, some concerned conservatives were still alarmed at the trend in American political life; they feared the political power of the foreign-born and were equally frightened by the danger of disunion. Many of them found their way into a new secret nativist organization which came to be known as the Know-Nothings. It emphasized the importance of continuing the unity of the American nation and the superiority of the native-born over the foreign-born.

The unwillingness of the OUA leadership to become politically involved, except in special cases, plus the failure of the American Union party, caused the political nativists to seek some other organization that might help them overcome the growing power of immigrants and save the nation. They found their nativist vehicle in the Order of the Star Spangled Banner. Established in New York City in the spring of 1850 by Charles B. Allen, a thirty-four-year-old agent[41] and former Whig who had been born and educated in Boston, Massachusetts, the society emphasized the need for secrecy.[42]

This emphasis was an acknowledgment of the power of Jacksonian political ideology which stressed the democratic principles of equality, for the charge of proscription forced the nativists to conceal their purposes. The anxious guarding of their order and the attempt to make it invisible reflected a need for protection. The emphasis on secrecy was not permanent, of course, for as the order grew and became powerful, it would no longer require such protection.[43]

There were many attacks on these secret societies. The Democrats regularly attacked the secrecy of the nativist societies as un-American, and the nativists reacted to these barbs. Thomas Whitney felt it necessary to defend the use of secrecy, explaining: "So strongly have foreign prejudices become fixed among us, that few Americans dare to be American in their external habits, and especially in their political opinions, lest perchance they should suffer in their business or their prospects of advancement."[44] In other words, men with political ambitions could not afford to avow nativist principles openly; the party leadership might thwart them. Other native-born citizens, particularly the merchants, were well aware of the growing economic power of the immigrants.

Religious groups also attacked the idea of secrecy, though the bulk of their attacks were on the Masons and the Sons of Temperance. For example, the Baptists made serious efforts to purge the Masons in their midst.[45] These religious opponents emphasized that no laudable object required secrecy; only the Jesuits, the Papacy, and tyrants needed secrecy to accomplish their ends.[46]

Still, even among the Protestant ministers there was some support for specific secret societies. Their arguments rested on the premise that secret societies, for example, the Sons of Temperance, did a good deal of Christian work.[47] In general, while there was support for the Sons of Temperance, most of the Protestant clergy were firm in their opposition to the Masons because of the liberal religious ideas of Freemasonry, while they remained ambivalent about the various secret nativist groups.[48]

The opposition to secrecy did not hamper the organization of the Order of the Star Spangled Banner. Members of the order referred to themselves as the "Sires of '76" so as to conceal their true identity. When questioned by outsiders about their secrecy, they answered, "I know nothing," for which Horace Greeley, editor of the *New York Tribune*, in 1853, labeled them the Know-Nothings.[49] The purpose of the order was to influence and control the nomination of candidates of the major political parties and to prevent the selection of naturalized Americans for public office.[50] To preserve harmony it also determined to avoid completely the divisive issues of slavery and temperance.[51]

For the first two years of its existence the new organization grew slowly. But by the summer of 1852 this situation changed. The members of the OUA from New York City, who played an active role in the creation of the weak American party "investigated" the Know-Nothings and found an organization of only forty-three members.[52] Moving into a dormant society, the members of the OUA quickly took control and installed their own leadership. So completely did the OUA capture this organization that Thomas Whitney actually viewed the Know-Nothings as an auxiliary of the OUA.[53] Installation of new leadership had an immediate effect; membership expanded to over a thousand in 1852, primarily in New York City. The bulk of these Know-Nothings were sincere, middle-class Americans who were convinced that all the political, economic, and social changes taking place meant that something was wrong, and that somehow the Irish Catholics were responsible.

Almost simultaneously with the penetration of the Order of the Star Spangled Banner by the membership of the OUA, the conservatives formed a City Reform League to eliminate municipal corruption and reduce the growing rate of taxation.[54] Nativists were anxious to reform the city government, but they used the City Reform League to cloak another of their objectives—punishment of all politicians who seemed to side with the foreign-born. Such prominent nativists as the Harper brothers played significant roles in this reform movement, and even Horace Greeley became a member of the league. The existence of the nativist groups became public knowledge as a result of the City Reform League's refusal to endorse the Whig district attorney, Nathaniel D. Blunt, who successfully ran for reelection. Greeley reported in the *Tribune* that some of the reformers claimed Blunt had failed to prosecute an Irishman, who had injured an omnibus driver in a July 4 riot, because the District Attorney was soliciting Irish votes in the election of 1853.[55] In place of Blunt, the league supported the antislavery Democrat and Temperance candidate, Chauncey Shaffer, who also was a member of the Know-Nothings.

Two factors helped the Know-Nothings: first, an outburst of anti-Catholicism; and secondly, the continued disruption of the major political parties, particularly the Whigs, over the slavery issue. In the 1850s, after the lull of 1847, there was a rampage of anti-Catholicism in the nation which led many of the native-born to believe that the Catholics were attempting to control the United States. Discoveries and confessions of orators and former priests, Louis Kossuth's activities in 1851–52; the trustee controversy, and the visits of Allessandro Gavazzi and Monsignor Gaetano Bedini, which will be explained below, all exacerbated relations between Protestants and Catholics. Then, too, it appeared as if there was an increase in the political power of the foreigners within the Whig and Democratic parties. These events helped the Know-Nothings to gain a hearing.

In the 1850s throughout the nation, speakers catered to the anti-Catholicism prevalent among their audiences. Apostate priests were especially popular speakers if they presented startling revelations about the plots of the Catholic hierarchy and the debauchery of the priests and nuns.[56]

From 1851 to 1852 the most compelling orator in the country

was Louis Kossuth.[57] The former premier of Hungary had fled from Austrian authorities to Turkey after the movement for Hungarian independence had been crushed by Russian, Croatian, and Austrian troops. The United States had helped win his release from the jails of Turkey,[58] and Kossuth arrived in New York City on December 4, 1851, hailed as "the great representative of freedom, of liberty, and the rights of man...."[59] In speeches throughout America, he condemned Catholic Austria and Catholicism in general and brought down upon himself the wrath of the Catholic press which attacked his "Protestant appeal to bigotry."[60]

But there was opposition to Kossuth among the more xenophobic Whigs. They were upset at the prospect of this foreigner involving the United States in the affairs of Europe and possibly pushing the United States into war.[61] Thomas R. Whitney was adamant in his opposition to Kossuth to whom Whitney referred as "the meddler."[62]

The result of the Kossuth movement, however, was an increase in violent and abusive language directed against the Catholic Church, its doctrine, and its government.[63] This abuse mounted in intensity during 1852–53, when the trustee problem arose again to plague the Church. Bishop John Timon of Buffalo was having difficulty controlling the German trustees of the Saint Louis Catholic Church.[64] Archbishop Hughes had the answer: instead of having trustees control the church property, have the state legislature pass a bill providing that all church property in a diocese be held by the bishop of that diocese. Such an act had been passed by the Pennsylvania legislature in February, 1844, on behalf of the bishops of Philadelphia and Pittsburgh. The original idea had come from Archbishop Hughes.[65]

The plan was condemned by the Catholics of Buffalo and Rochester,[66] and conservative Protestants became almost hysterical because they thought that this plan "would virtually establish popery in the state."[67] Others thought the proposal would increase Catholic power to such an extent that the Pope would be able to nominate the President of the United States.[68]

No sooner had this "threat" to the security of Protestant America become law than Monsignor Gaetano Bedini,

Archbishop of Thebes and Apostolic Nuncio to the United States, arrived in New York City. He came to settle the trustee controversy in Buffalo as well as to visit the various episcopal sees. Three months earlier, on March 20, 1853, his fellow Bolognese Allessandro Gavazzi, a defrocked priest, had arrived in America under the auspices of the American and Foreign Christian Union.[69]

In clear English, Gavazzi had given a series of lectures, warning both of the Jesuit conspiracy and of the identification of Romanism and Paganism, and describing the present situation as a war of European Roman Catholicism against American Protestantism.[70] He insisted to his audiences that "Irish emigration is intended to overthrow your American freedom."[71] In an address before the American Protestant Association in New York, Gavazzi warned Americans to guard against the secret organizations of the Catholic Church and advised Protestants to work for the extension of the naturalization period for foreigners.[72]

Other fanatics and demagogues emulated the successful Gavazzi, and disturbances between the protectors of these anti-Catholic street preachers and the Irish and German defenders of Catholicism became common, especially where Bedini and Gavazzi were active.[73]

In New York City, the Know-Nothings became the defenders of one of these street preachers. In an effort to prevent riot and bloodshed, Mayor Jacob Westervelt, himself a Whig, refused to license a fiery street preacher, Daniel Parsons. When Parsons tried to speak anyway he was arrested on December 11, 1853. Know-Nothings secretly and speedily generated a protest rally on behalf of free speech at City Hall on December 14. Chauncey Shaffer presided, and James W. Barker, wealthy Whig merchant, was present on the platform. Know-Nothings blamed the Catholics for the tumult. According to George Strong, they depicted Parsons as a "Protestant martyr."[74]

Paradoxically, Archbishop Hughes had a nativist explanation for the trouble: he placed the blame for the reaction evoked by Bedini and the concomitant riots on "renegade Italians and the infidel Germans. . . ."[75] The culmination of the affair saw the unfortunate Papal Nuncio Bedini smuggled aboard the ship that returned him to Italy in January, 1854.

Bedini's visit to the United States had helped the nativists raise the threat of papal subversion of America, but according to the political nativists, the major threat to the welfare of America was the increased political power of the Catholic hierarchy and their blind followers, especially the Irish.[76] Both Whigs and Democrats made overtures to the foreign-born, whose votes, they thought, Archbishop Hughes largely controlled.

Although Hughes denied time and again any political influence, he ruefully admitted that "among public men, from the President down, there are very few who are not under the impression that a spoken word of mine, or even a hint is sufficient to vibrate, especially among the Catholics, from one extremity of the United States to the other."[77] Politicians seemed bent on proving him right: in 1852, Elihu B. Washburne of Illinois, Whig candidate for the United States House of Representatives, wrote to Seward requesting him to obtain from Bishop Hughes a letter of endorsement which would carry weight with the Irish Catholics in Illinois.[78] Two days later, Truman Smith, United States senator from Connecticut, and Schuyler Colfax, Indiana congressman, agreed that Thurlow Weed should devote all his efforts in 1852 to influencing Hughes and the Catholics to vote for the Whigs.[79]

Democrats also catered to the foreign-born. President Pierce indicated his intention to appoint naturalized citizens to represent the United States abroad[80] and named the Irish-American James Campbell of Pennsylvania, postmaster general.[81] Such developments did little to diminish the nativists' fear of the political power of the naturalized citizens.[82]

Then, too, both of the major national political parties were beset with difficulties caused by the territorial expansion of the 1840s and its concomitant, the explosive slavery question.

James K. Polk, elected president of the United States in 1844 on an expansionist platform, created serious political quarrels for both great parties when he realized territorial expansion through a war with Mexico. Introduction of the Wilmot Proviso, which would prevent the extension of slavery into any territory acquired from Mexico, aggravated the antagonism between the two factions within the Whig party: the Conscience and the Cotton Whigs. Conscience Whigs were antislavery; Cotton Whigs were not necessarily proslavery, but they were willing to live with the institution as the price of Union. Within the Democratic party there was a similar cleavage: radical Democrats who opposed slavery were known as Barnburners; conservative Democrats willing to support a proslavery position were known as Hunkers, because of their "hunkering" after political office.[83]

The controversy continued into 1850 over the problem of admitting California into the Union. President Zachary Taylor encouraged the Californians to draw up a constitution and to petition Congress for admission as a state, hoping thereby to avoid a protracted debate which would embitter relations between the sections.[84] Senator Seward and most of the northern Whigs in the Senate eventually supported the President's plan; in effect, it meant California's admission as a free state. The Southern Whigs in the Senate joined by Senator Henry Clay of Kentucky and Daniel Webster of Massachusetts urged a conciliatory policy that would not exclude slavery from the state, because they were aware that the climate was not suitable for raising cotton. They expected few slaveholders to carry their slaves there. The Democratic Senators were split along similar lines.[85]

In February, Clay offered a set of soothing resolutions calling for concessions and forbearance on both sides.[86] Essentially the resolutions provided the admission of California as a free state in exchange for which the South would receive a strong fugitive slave law. Webster, and Sam Houston of Texas, won the applause of the moderates for their support of Clay's resolutions;[87] but Clay's compromise was defeated by President Taylor and the Northern Whigs. Taylor's death in July, 1850, turned the tide. Millard Fillmore, leader of the Cotton Whigs, became the President. He pushed vigorously for the compromise measures which were enacted into law by September.[88]

The result of this struggle was a widening of the Whig party split. This factor was especially true in New York. President Millard Fillmore, who had endorsed the Compromise of 1850, and Senator William H. Seward, who had opposed the Compromise, struggled for control of the Whig party. In the September, 1850, convention of the Whig party in New York State, Seward's control of the state party was obvious: resolutions supporting his stand were passed. As a result the Fillmorites walked out.[89] The contest then continued in the Whig national nominating convention in 1852. Sewardites resolved to prevent the nomination of Fillmore. Again, Fillmore and his followers failed. As already noted, General Scott received the nomination, though the antislavery Whigs did have to endorse the Compromise of 1850. The election of 1852 resulted in a thorough defeat for the Whigs, and to some it seemed the "end of the Whig party."[90]

The Fillmorites found themselves in a frustrating position. They were being merely tolerated in the Whig party. In New York, they began to move into the Know-Nothing movement, since it appeared to be one means of maintaining some sense of power.[91] In the New York election of 1853, the Know-Nothings endorsed six Whigs and four Democrats. No Sewardites received their support. The ticket of the Know-Nothings was recognized by one Whig organ as the work of a "few individuals who have been prominent in former troubles, and who make no secret of their bitter hostility to the party they have abandoned. . . . Some of those who have been drawn into the movement may be sincere, but will eventually find it to be the 'last card' of a few ex-office holders, who have forfeited the confidence of the party from which they have received so many favors, we entertain no doubt."[92] The Know-Nothings nevertheless displayed some strength. They had roughly two thousand votes, most of them centered in New York and Kings counties.[93]

By the end of 1853, the Know-Nothings were not numerous, but they were growing. Still largely urban, the movement would spread to the rural areas where the anti-Catholic orators, the Kossuth activities, and the "threat" posed by Monsignor Bedini would win a hearing for any movement that promised to curtail Catholic power. And now, as a result of the Seward-Fillmore feud in New York, a large bloc of professional politicians were available to provide their organizational expertise to the movement. The movement would spread nationwide in 1854.

CHAPTER V

Nativism and Nationalism

THE KNOW-NOTHINGS WERE ORGANIZED NATIONALLY. BY late 1853, Daniel Ullman and the former President of the OUA James W. Barker (1851), both New York Fillmorites and OUA members, were affiliated with the Know-Nothings. Their presence indicated that organizational discipline would soon come to the order. These men realized that consolidation on a nationwide basis was essential if the order was to serve as a springboard to political power. Already it had branches in New York, New Jersey, Maryland, Connecticut, Massachusetts, and Ohio, though in some of these states it existed only in a few councils.

In New York, a serious division had to be healed before planning on a national scale could be begun. There, the influx of OUA members into the order had caused Charles B. Allen and his supporters to secede and form a rival wigwam in May, 1853,[1] and the order thus consisted of two factions: the Allen group of original Know-Nothings, and the Barker group, whose membership came from the OUA. After lengthy negotiations between the two factions, the wigwams and the councils in New York were again united on May 11, 1854, with the formation of the Grand Council of New York State.[2] James W. Barker, the New York City dry goods merchant whose interest in the Union Safety committee led him to see the desirability of forming a new party, became president of the New York State Grand Council as a reward for his efforts in conciliating the rival factions.

With state party harmony restored, the Know-Nothings made plans for national organization. Taking the initiative in this endeavor, Barker sent letters to all other state councils, asking them to send delegates to a Grand Council of the Order, scheduled to meet in New York City. The meeting took place but was adjourned until June 14 because there were insufficient delegates present to constitute a working body.[3] When the convention reassembled with the required number of delegates on June 14, Barker was chosen president of the National Council; three days later the group drew up a constitution and new ritual.[4]

Under the new constitution, the Know-Nothings had a hierarchical chain of command moving downward from national council to state council to district or territorial councils to local councils. The National Council of the United States of North America had the power to determine all matters concerning national politics. It met annually, though special meetings could be called by the president at the request of five state councils. Sixty-days notice had to be given to the state councils before such a meeting could be held.

State councils had the power to establish local councils whose constitutions and bylaws had to be approved by the state councils or by the district or territorial councils, if such had granted the enabling charter.

In New York, Barker appointed district deputies to facilitate the formation of local lodges. Nine men could form a local council. In North Carolina, thirteen men were necessary. The number fluctuated from state to state. Meetings were held weekly. In most lodges, chaplains attended the weekly meetings.

The four stated aims of the order were:

1) to protect every American citizen in the legal and proper exercise of all his civil and religious rights and privileges;
2) to resist the insidious policy of the Church of Rome, and all other foreign influence against our republican institutions;
3) to place in all offices of honor, trust or profit... none but native-born Protestant citizens; and
4) to protect, preserve and uphold the union of these states and the constitution of the same.

Membership in the order was restricted to Protestant native-born citizens who were at least twenty-one years of age. The state council could extend or refuse, as it saw fit, membership to native-born Protestants married to Catholics. In New York, the Grand Council at first permitted these men to join as members.

To become a member, a man had to be introduced by a council member. A three-week interval had to elapse between the conferring of the first and second degrees, but a dispensation could be granted by the president of the local council so that a prospective member could be received privately into the order and invested in the first and second degrees on the same day. The dispensation was granted for the induction of Millard Fillmore in 1855.

Each of the three degrees had secret grips and passwords, and meetings were called by secret postings of different cut shapes and colors of paper. All proceedings of the national, state, and local councils were kept secret, and anyone divulging the secrets of the order would be expelled. The ritual, with its grips, passwords and meeting arrangements, was confirmed by a Know-Nothing convention, which met in Cincinnati on November 15, 1854. Here former Whig congressman Kenneth Rayner of North Carolina added a so-called Third, or Union, Degree.[5] The Union Degree swore members to do all in their power to maintain and preserve the Union, making the necessary political compromises required.

This Union Degree was a direct response to the slavery question which again exacerbated relations between North and South. It was also an indication that the Know-Nothings were moving from a purely xenophobic stance to one that emphasized the American Union.

The renewal of the slavery extension issue in 1854 tended to push the problems of "Liquor and Catholics" somewhat aside. It was both a help and a hindrance to the nationally organized Know-Nothings. The slavery debate intensified the factionalism within and among both the Democrats and the Whigs. For example, the New York Democrats split in 1853 and again in 1854: both years they ran a Softshell and a Hardshell ticket. Some members of both factions, upset at the direction that their particular party was taking, sought shelter among the Know-Nothings.

Nationally, Democratic Senator Stephen A. Douglas of Illinois had pushed through Congress the Kansas-Nebraska

Act (1854), which called for the organization of these territories on the basis of popular sovereignty—the people of the territory to decide the question of slavery themselves. The act also implied the repeal of the Missouri Compromise (1820), which had prohibited slavery in the territory north of 36° 30'.[6] Once again the slavery issue flared into prominence. Many members of both major political parties were free-soilers, thus anti-Nebraska Democrats joined with anti-Nebraska Whigs in condemning the act and formed the basis for a new antislavery extension party, the Republican party.[7] Others, unwilling to join with old rivals or to participate in a sectional party, looked for help to the Know-Nothings.

Temperance was also a prominent issue in the 1850s. Though it had been an element of some political significance in the 1840s, the success of Neal Dow in passing a restrictive act in Maine (1851) gave new vigor to the nation's Sons of Temperance. The American Temperance Society sponsored a World Temperance Convention which met in New York City in September, 1853. One of the resolutions passed by this group insisted: "That while we do not design to disturb political parties, we do intend to have, and enforce, a law prohibiting the liquor manufacture and traffic as a beverage, whatever may be the consequences to political parties, and will note accordingly."[8]

Although not all temperance men were Whigs, nevertheless, the movement found its chief support among them.[9] And though not all temperance men were xenophobes, a large majority of the nativists favored a prohibitory law.[10] The connection between the influx of immigrants and the use of alcoholic consumption was not lost on the temperance and nativist advocates, often one and the same. Consumption in the United States increased over 50 percent in two decades: from 4.17 gallons per person in 1840 to 6.43 gallons in 1860.[11]

Any organization that promised help against rum and Romanism was bound to win a sympathetic hearing from many Americans. If, in the process, the issue of slavery agitation could be submerged and replaced by appeals to the Americanism of the nation, such a group would find an audience, especially among Southern Whigs and some Democrats.[12]

But the Know-Nothings themselves splintered on the rock

of slavery. The first intimation of the party's failure to substitute antiforeignism for antislavery came early in February, 1855, when despite the official opposition of the Know-Nothing order, United States Senator William Henry Seward was reelected by the New York state legislature to a second term with the help of some Know-Nothings.[13] What was particularly embarrassing to the Know-Nothings of New York was the recognition that they could not afford to attack Seward's radical antislavery record. To do so would have alienated many former Whigs and Softshell Democrats, turned Know-Nothings, who opposed the expansion of slavery and the Kansas-Nebraska Act. The Know-Nothing leadership rather emphasized the Senator's pro-Catholic past. But Seward as the chief New York antislavery politician was able to overcome his past pro-Catholic association. This fact was a portent of the future; the slavery question would wreck the Know-Nothings as a national party.

Despite Kenneth Rayner's Union Degree, the Know-Nothings did express themselves on the slavery question. Know-Nothing members of Congress from New England expressed antislavery feelings on occasion.[14] The New England members of the order were staunchly antislavery.[15] They denounced the political cooperation of Catholic Democrats of the North with Southern Democrats.[16] In the West, the Know-Nothings were considered predominantly antislavery.[17] In the Southern states, however, the movement was regarded by some as a possible "avenue of escape" from the explosive slavery issue.[18]

Any discussion of slavery was bound to have an adverse effect upon the Know-Nothings. Know-Nothings in the South were disturbed by the actions of their Massachusetts brothers, who rejected the Union Degree and condemned the institution of slavery. Kenneth Rayner pleaded with the Northern Know-Nothings: "We do not ask you," he wrote, "to say one word in favor of slavery.... All we ask you to say, is that if this order is to be *National*, it must, *as an order*, ignore questions that are sectional."[19]

But the Know-Nothings' discussion of slavery was renewed when the National Council met at Philadelphia on June 5,

1855, to draw up a national platform for the party. Fireworks were expected. One astute political observer noted, that "the K. N. of the Free States will *Bolt*, the Convention, at Philadelphia if [they] undertake to make a National Platform."[20] This is what actually happened.

On June 12, the platform committee brought forth a majority report of eighteen states. Section 12 of the majority report stated that "Congress ought not to legislate upon the subject of Slavery within the Territories...."[21] While the platform was accepted by a majority of the states and their delegations, Henry Wilson of Massachusetts, who called for a return to the Missouri Compromise, led a bolt of the delegates of Massachusetts, Ohio, Indiana, Michigan, Illinois, New Hampshire, Vermont, Maine, Iowa, Connecticut, Rhode Island, and Wisconsin.[22]

Some of these antislavery nativists organized their own brotherhood, the Know-Somethings. They opposed three things: the extension of slavery, immigrant political power, and the rum-sellers.[23]

While concern over the slavery issue divided the party, the Know-Nothings were in complete agreement in emphasizing the Catholic menace. For many hysterical New Yorkers, the Catholic peril became a reality in 1855. One New York woman, when asked in April, 1855, why she carried a pistol, retorted, "Why for the same reason that my husband does—to protect himself against the Catholics."[24] This outburst of anti-Catholicism was probably the result of the murder of the leader of the Ninth Ward's Bowery Boys' gang, the notorious "Butcher Boy" Poole. Poole and John Morrisey, a Democratic gang leader, had been feuding for years, and in a brawl with Morrisey and his gang the "Butcher Boy" was shot by Lew Baker, a Morrisey supporter; he died on March 8, 1855, and Baker fled to a Caribbean island.[25] George Law, former Democrat and wealthy shipowner with strong political aspirations, sent one of his vessels to the Caribbean to capture and return Baker for trial. It was a grand and expensive gesture on the part of Law, who had joined the Know-Nothings to advance his political career, and it brought him to the attention of the nativists in New York and throughout the nation. Baker was tried and acquitted, and as a result, the *Express* and the nativist press, in general, transformed Poole into a true American patriot.[26]

The Know-Nothings, despite their division over the slavery plank in their platform, did exceptionally well in the 1855 state elections. They controlled New York and Massachusetts and enjoyed great success in other states as well. After their 1855 showing, the nativists' attention centered on the presidential election of 1856. George Law, Millard Fillmore, and Sam Houston aspired to be the party's presidential choice. Houston's chances really depended on a deadlock between Law and Fillmore. Barker and Rayner became Law men; Ullman and Fillmore's former law partner, Congressman Solomon G. Haven, became the dominant spokesmen for Fillmore.[27]

Section 12 became an important ingredient in the struggle between Law and Fillmore. To enlist Southern support, the Law men declared their willingness to endorse section 12.[28] Vespasian Ellis, editor of the chief Know-Nothing publication, the Washington *American Organ* was anti–section 12; he joined the Fillmore supporters.[29] He insisted that the party would be destroyed if it continued to support that portion of the platform.[30]

Using the alteration of section 12 as a pivotal weapon, the Fillmore men succeeded in destroying the influence of Barker in the order and in weakening Law's prospects for the presidential nomination. Charles B. Allen agreed to have the so-called Allen Know-Nothings support Ullman in his efforts to thwart Barker and Law and to alter section 12;[31] and at a secret national meeting of the two groups held in New York on December 2, the Allenites and the anti-Barkerites discussed alterations in the Know-Nothing platform, particularly section 12.[32]

The meeting, one of the best-kept secrets of the order, led to the calling of a special meeting of the National Council on February 18, 1856.[33] The meeting would discuss the issue of secrecy, the admission of Catholic members, and—most important—the alteration of section 12. Fillmorite success in calling the special meeting indicated Barker's loss of control.

In December, 1855, Barker declined to be a candidate for reelection as state president of the Grand Council, claiming that he was "weary." The New York *Times* queried, "Can it be that his vote in favor of the Philadelphia Platform has anything to do with the matter?"[34] With the loss of Barker's influence, Law's presidential hopes dimmed.

In addition to the difficulty caused by the Law-Fillmore conflict and section 12, those antislavery Know-Nothings who had bolted the platform meeting continued to agitate for an antislavery extension plan. Foes of slavery under Henry Wilson called a convention to meet in Cincinnati in November, 1855.[35] This antislavery element of the American party, the so-called North Americans, declared that the Missouri Compromise should be restored, and if it was not, then Congress should refuse to admit any slave states from the territory formerly controlled by that compromise.[36] Though still part of the national order, the North Americans were giving fair warning that they intended to transform the American party into an antislavery extension organization.

The slavery issue also plagued the party in Congress, where, in December, 1855, party members failed to maintain party unity in organizing the Thirty-fourth Congress. In caucus, Know-Nothings decided to support Henry M. Fuller of Pennsylvania for Speaker of the House. There were approximately ninety members of the order in the House, and, though they could not organize it, they did hold the balance of power between the Republicans and the Democrats.[37] In the floor vote, all but one of the Southern Know-Nothings supported William Aiken of South Carolina, a Democrat; they refused to support the Northerner, Fuller.[38]

This vote indicated the caliber of the Know-Nothing congressional delegation, many of whom were not sincere believers in the nativist character of Americanism. "These men," Valk charged, "knew that in the fall of 1854, the American party would sweep everything before it; and that their only hope of success was to seem to be what they were not. . . . The struggle for the Speakership disclosed the naked truth."[39] The charge was well founded, and the Know-Nothings found it impossible to accomplish anything in Washington. Their efforts to alter the naturalization laws failed, as all such attempts were tabled by a combination of Republican and

Democratic votes. The "K. N. Party, it is evident, cannot hold together," an opponent stated. "The rock on which they have and must split is the 12th section. *With* it, the party at the North is powerless. *Without* it, the K. N.ism is annihilated [sic] at the South. . . ."[40] These words summarized the essence of the slavery problem for the Know-Nothings.

At a special meeting of the National Council called to order by the new president, E. B. Bartlett of Kentucky, on February 18, 1856—four days before the American Know-Nothing Convention was to meet for the purpose of discussing the slavery issue, the admission of Catholics, and the ending of secrecy —the section-12 question dominated the proceedings. Northerners, led by Massachusetts and Connecticut, demanded its elimination; Southerners or South Americans, as they were called, insisted on its retention.[41]

Debate at this special meeting grew bitter. At one point, the excitement became so intense that President Bartlett threatened to leave the chair.[42] Finally, a delegate from the District of Columbia proposed a motion to have the National Council accept the platform used by the district. Its second plank called for the perpetuation of the Union; its sixth for the "unqualified recognition and maintenance of the reserved rights of the several states . . . [and the] non-interference by Congress with questions appertaining solely to the individual states;" and its seventh supported the doctrine of popular sovereignty.[43] Nowhere in the platform was slavery mentioned.

Two other questions were also settled at the special Council meeting: whether to admit Catholics and whether to end secrecy. These issues, though not as burdensome to the order as the slavery question, still posed difficulties and had a history of their own.

Basically the Know-Nothings appealed to Protestants. Know-Nothingism differentiated between the Protestant and the Catholic immigrant. As one nativist tract writer declared in 1856, *"We do not wish one word in these pages to be considered as referring to our PROTESTANT FOREIGN-BORN CITIZENS unless they are particularly mentioned. We have tens of thousands of such, who were an honor to the country that gave them birth and are equally an honor to the country they have made their home.*"[44] Other nativist writers of the 1850s also accepted this distinction between Protestant and Catholic foreigners, especially in regarding the Irish Catholic foreigners as the real danger.[45] Bayard Clarke, Know-Nothing congressman, gave two reasons for being a Know-Nothing: "[1] I am an American. . . . [2] I am a Protestant."[46] The Know-Nothings maintained this distinction, and many of them continued their appeal to the Protestant foreign-born.[47] Charles G. Irish, Jr., a Buffalo Know-Nothing, hoping to capture the foreign-born Protestant vote, organized in March, 1855, the American Protestant Assembly, whose object was to free the United States from "that monster," Catholicism.[48]

Know-Nothings, in an effort to avoid the label of bigotry, tried to maintain a distinction between political Romanism and religious Romanism. Insisting that the two were different, they declared their indifference to Catholicism as a religious creed. In February, 1855, one of the Know-Nothing (New York) Councils declared: "We disavow any inference, therefore, which may be drawn from this free expression of our opinion against political Romanism, that the American party is intolerant toward the Catholic religion. With the principles and doctrine of that faith we have no concern."[49]

In some parts of the country, there were nativists who were not anti-Catholic. In Louisiana, Know-Nothing candidates sometimes were members of the Catholic Church,[50] but these Know-Nothing Catholic Creoles were not practicing Catholics and were considered to be anticlerical.[51] Along with the wealthy American elite, they formed the upper stratum of New Orleans society, and the tide of incoming immigration was repugnant to them. Yet the overriding majority of the Louisiana Catholics were anti–Know-Nothing.[52]

Nationally, the existence of these Louisiana Catholic Know-Nothings, in the face of the controversy over the admission of Catholic members, caused difficulties. At the Cincinnati convention in 1854, the order refused to seat or solicit Catholic members,[53] though there had been an attempt to seat the Catholic members from Louisiana at the Philadelphia convention. Kenneth Rayner had blocked this move, asserting that

Northern politicians wanted to admit the foreign-born voters, while Southern politicians were interested in gaining the admittance of the Catholic native-born voters. In a letter to Ullman in the summer of 1855, Rayner asked, "What inducements have the true and devoted friends of the Order—those who have maintained and fought for it *on principle*—to continue the struggle, if this organization is to be used as the mere stalking horse of politicians...."[54]

Know-Nothing politicians were, however, looking to the native-born Catholic and foreign-born Protestant for help. On May 8, 1855, after the order had failed to defeat Governor Henry A. Wise of Virginia, some Virginians added their voices to those from Louisiana and called for a strengthening of the order by permitting native-born Catholics to join.[55] The issue of Catholic membership was finally resolved at the special National Council meeting of 1856 which, after a spirited and caustic debate, agreed to admit Catholics as members by a vote of 66 to 50.[56]

The same principles which moved nativists to admit Catholics and foreign-born Protestants also led them to question the need for secrecy. Benoni Thompson proclaimed that there were many conservative voters in the state who refused to support the Know-Nothings because these voters were opposed "to secret political societies."[57] S. H. Hammond of the Albany *State Register* and Erastus Brooks of the New York *Express* also believed the time had come to end secrecy.[58] Before joining the order, Millard Fillmore had noted, "My chief objection to the Know Nothings is its secrecy...."[59] Senator John Clayton of Delaware and others also demanded that the order throw off its secrecy.[60] Those opposed to the order, who condemned not only its objectives but its secret methods, strengthened the rhetoric of their attacks. America, they insisted, was a land for all the people; there was no need for secret, clandestine groups who undermined the foundation of good democratic government.[61]

Very often, as a result of their secrecy, the Know-Nothings found themselves the object of ridicule and scorn. The new Order of the Knights of the Star Spangled Banner was labeled by one opponent as the "Guardians of the Tail Feathers of the American Eagle," and its purpose as "devotion to the bottle and hostility to everybody else."[62] Greeley, of course, dubbed the order the "Know Nothings" who ought to say and do nothing since they know nothing. One antinativist facetiously set the qualifications for the order: toenail scalloped and hair cropped.[63]

By 1856, however, the special meeting provided a solution to the secrecy issue. The right of local option was approved, and the National Council agreed to end secrecy in its own deliberations. Reporters were invited to attend all of its sessions.[64] State Grand Councils had the option of following the path of the National Council or of retaining secrecy.

The American party's 1856 presidential nominating convention opened on February 22.[65] The Catholic delegation from Louisiana was seated, and an anti-Catholic delegate from Louisiana was ejected for protesting vociferously.[66] Southern delegates as well as New Englanders condemned with equal vehemence the compromise platform arranged by the National Council, and members on both sides temporarily withdrew from the convention.[67]

Southerners were upset because the convention would not accept section 12; and Northerners declared the National Council had no power under the order's constitution to draw up a platform.[68] Antislavery Know-Nothings then went ahead with the plan arranged at the Merchants' Hotel meeting. They introduced a motion on February 25, declaring that no one should be chosen as the candidate for president or vice president "who is not in favor of interdicting the introduction of slavery north of 36° 30'."[69] When it was tabled by a vote of 141 to 60, Connecticut left the convention, followed by Massachusetts, Rhode Island, Ohio, and portions of the delegations of Indiana, New Hampshire, Iowa, and Pennsylvania.[70] Of the 227 delegates, 42 bolted, and others would join shortly.

After acceptance of the special council platform, the convention then turned to selection of a national ticket. The three major candidates for the nomination were Law, Fillmore, and Sam Houston of Texas. To generate additional support for the

Texan, Charles Edwards Lester had prepared a campaign biography in 1855.[71] Houston was a Southerner who had supported the Clay Compromise of 1850 and had opposed the Kansas-Nebraska Act in 1854. His candidacy had been endorsed by the New Hampshire Democrats, and he himself hoped for the American party nomination.[72] But his past personal excesses, and his visit to Boston's Tremont Temple to speak before the Antislavery Society at the very time that the convention opened, snuffed out any hopes Houston had, especially when the antislavery nativists bolted the convention.[73]

At the convention the delegates showed their preference very quickly, choosing Fillmore on the second ballot. After selecting Fillmore, the convention then picked Andrew Jackson Donelson of Tennessee for second place on the ticket.[74]

When their candidate failed to secure the presidential nomination, some supporters of Law and Houston left the hall and joined the antislavery bolters at their rival convention. The bolters accepted the New Yorkers, despite the knowledge that Law men had been supporters of section 12. Together they censured the work of the Fillmore convention and issued an address condemning the repeal of the Missouri Compromise.[75]

The Know-Nothings were preparing for their first national campaign. In doing so, they had tried to broaden their appeal by admitting foreign-born Protestants and native-born Catholics. They also altered their national platform, much to the chagrin of Northern and Southern extremists. As a result, the Know-Nothings split into North Americans and South Americans, and some of those who joined the North Americans were disappointed in the selection of the party's presidential candidate. Despite their earlier acceptance of section 12, they now became bitter opponents of the party because of its pro-Southern bias. Antiforeignism could not camouflage the real breach caused by the issue of slavery and the frustration of Law's supporters at the selection of Fillmore.

During the campaign of 1856, more and more Know-Nothings left the American party because they believed that it could not win. These desertions embittered relations between the Northern and Southern groups in the party and posed the question as to whether the two groups could function as a national organization. The failure to defeat Seward, the antislavery Cincinnati convention of 1855, the failure of Northern and Southern Know-Nothings to cooperate in Congress, and the bolt of the Northern faction from the Know-Nothing convention all provided an answer: the Know-Nothings could not ignore the slavery issue, and once its attention was directed to the problem, some elements in the order were antagonized. The three-cornered race for the presidency was emotionally charged. In 1856 the Democrats nominated James Buchanan of Pennsylvania, and the Republicans selected John C. Fremont.[76] "Bleeding Kansas" was the major topic of the campaign, for whoever exercised authority in Kansas determined the survival of slavery and the validity of land sales. Fillmore supporters took no stand on slavery extension, but denounced the sectionalism of both the Republicans and the Democrats. The Democrats favored the principle of popular sovereignty: the residents themselves should solve the problems in Kansas. The Republicans adamantly opposed the extension of slavery into Kansas.

The lack of complete Know-Nothing support for Fillmore posed problems. In the South, where the prospect of a Fremont victory was being employed by the Democrats to win support for Buchanan, the defections by the Northern Know-Nothings caused confusion. The "Americans of the South scarcely know how to act," reported one Know-Nothing from Virginia.[77] They wanted to elect Fillmore, but they did not want to support him if it would give the victory to Fremont.[78] Kenneth Rayner reported that Fillmore was strong in the South and could be elected if all the Know-Nothings, North and South, supported him; but by June, 1856, even Rayner was discouraged.[79] The Northern Know-Nothings' preference for Fremont ruined the party in the South.[80]

During the summer, the effort to remain united was further exacerbated when the news became known of the May attack of Congressman Preston Brooks of South Carolina on the antislavery leader, Senator Charles Sumner of Massachusetts. Southern firebrands talked of imitating Brooks; Northerners were outraged at the assault.[81] By September, 1856, astute observers of the Southern Know-Nothings agreed they would withdraw and vote for Buchanan as the only way to defeat Fremont.[82]

Anti-Catholicism was employed by the Know-Nothings in a desperate effort to break Fremont's hold on the Northern Know-Nothings. The Know-Nothings circulated the story that Fremont, an Episcopalian, was a Catholic. Nathan Sargent, Philadelphia newspaperman and a Fillmorite, informed Ullman that Colonel William Russell of Mississippi, who was with Fremont in California, testified that Fremont was a Catholic and attended Catholic Church services.[83] Others supported the story.[84] Thurlow Weed reported: "The Catholic story is doing much damage. . . .[85]

Fremont ignored the charge, but delegates who visited him made categorical statements denying the allegation. This charge was at once a reflex of prejudice and an appeal to this emotion. Why it was believed is difficult to explain.[86] Both the Democrats and the Know-Nothings also attempted to discredit Fremont by utilizing the information that his mother had eloped, and inferring thereby that he was illegitimate.[87]

Still, Fillmore's chances, not good to begin with, declined as the campaign progressed.[88] He tried to bolster his supporters. In July, 1856, he wrote, "Our political prospects are brightening daily . . . my friends are sanguine of success."[89] The Know-Nothings tried to capture portions of the foreign vote. They knew they had no chance to capture the naturalized–Irish Catholic vote, but they believed the German Protestant, Irish Protestant, and the Louisiana French Catholic vote might support their ticket.[90] The Irish Protestants of New York State did give strong financial support to the Fillmore campaign.[91] But in August the Fillmorites were continuing to lose ground, especially in North Carolina and Kentucky.[92] Southern Know-Nothings of Virginia had switched to Buchanan by mid-September.[93]

When the results came in they showed the Democrats had won the national election. Fillmore and the Know-Nothings carried but one state, Maryland.[94] Now the major concern of the Republicans was to effect a fusion with the nativists. Buchanan was a minority president: the combined votes of the Know-Nothings and Republicans composed a majority of the Northern voters.[95] Many others called for a union of the Republicans and the nativists to defeat the two strongest elements of the Democratic party—the foreign vote and the slavery supporters.[96]

The election of 1856 was disastrous to the national aspirations of the Know-Nothings, for it made it obvious that they were unable to surmount the slavery issue. Just as the Whig party had failed to keep both the Conscience Whigs and the Cotton Whigs united under one banner, so too the American party was unable to keep both Northerners and Southerners united under a single party label. The result was the inability of the party to pose a serious threat to the other major national parties.

After the Fillmore defeat and the permanent division of the party into Northern and Southern Americans, the national organization so painstakingly established by Barker and Ullman disintegrated. In 1857, the National Council held its last meeting in Louisville, Kentucky, then adjourned sine die. Many of the state Grand Councils followed its lead. The OUA divorced itself from the Know-Nothings. Simeon Baldwin, who had helped organize the OUA, and was serving as its arch-grand sachem, declared in his annual report that his group was now retiring from active political participation in the Know-Nothing movement, reaffirming the principles of political neutrality which had characterized the order at its inception.[97] Many of the former members—Ulysses S. Grant and others had moved into the Republican party—would carve out significant political careers for themselves. Others would try to form the pro-Union, Constitutional Union party for the election of 1860. But this party was no longer xenophobic. Jonathan Pierce of the OUA insisted that the nation needed an independent, conservative party, "making the Constitution . . . its platform, the preservation and perpetuity of the Union . . . its brightest aim." He added that the party must respect all foreigners and religions, a radical departure from past OUA policy.[98] Thus when the Constitutional Union party came into being, it was not a nativist movement, but rather a nationalist one.[99]

The Know-Nothings were destroyed because of the slavery

extension issue. Most Americans remained antiabolitionist, almost violently so.[100] But many Americans were equally opposed to the extension of slavery because they feared the prospect of competing with cheap slave labor. Thus, the newly created Republican party was able to overcome the fear of Catholics and foreigners by substituting a different fear: the loss of free lands for free men.[101] Thus Negrophobes and abolitionists could find a home among the Republicans and draw this strength away from the Know-Nothings. But as we shall see, the end of the Know-Nothings did not mean the end of xenophobia. Jews, Chinese, and Catholics, as well as the immigrants from Southern and Eastern Europe, would become the focus of renewed attacks.

CHAPTER VI

Beginnings of Exclusion

ORGANIZED NATIVISM DID NOT CONTINUE INTO THE 1860s. Both major groups, the Know-Nothings and the Order of United Americans did not survive nationally, though a few OUA councils did remain in existence. But xenophobic sentiments, though muted, could be heard, especially against the Jews and, of course, the Catholics. Yet the loudest, and most successful, clamor was made against the Chinese.

While the California-based Workingmen's party did not become a national nativist group, its racial opposition to the Chinese was so successful that for the first time the gates of immigration were closed to the Chinese and, as we shall see, to other Orientals as well.

The Civil War apparently helped to improve the status of the foreign-born in the eyes of most native-born Americans.[1] One of the more positive assertions of this new stance was presented in the *New York Times* in 1863: "One of the grand results of this war is to be the assimilation of all American blood ... their [immigrants'] fighting side by side with the descendants of those who laid the foundation of the Republic will do more to Americanize them and their children than could be effected in a whole generation of peaceful living.... The blood that mixes in the battlefield, in one common sacrifice, will be a cement of American Nationality nothing else could supply."[2]

This view of the foreign-born, especially the Irish, was submerged temporarily by the outburst of the draft riots in July, 1863. The introduction of the draft, with its exemption clauses available to the rich and the rising fear of black job competition, precipitated one of the most violent racial outbursts in New York City.[3] The New York draft riots, and the Irish participation in this racial holocaust, brought scathing denunciations from all sides. Perhaps George Templeton Strong reflected the initial reaction to the Irish as a result of their violent actions:

I am sorry to find [he wrote] that England is right about the lower class of Irish. They are brutal, base, cruel, cowards, and as insolent as base. . . .
No wonder St. Patrick drove all the venomous vermin out of Ireland! Its biped mamalis supply that island its full average share of creatures that crawl and eat dirt and poison every community they infest. Vipers were superfluous. But my own theory is that St. Patrick's campaign against the snakes is a Popish delusion. They perished by biting the Irish people.[4]

But within a month, the press shifted emphasis. Archbishop John Hughes's efforts to restore order among his fellow-Irishmen caused some newspapers to place the blame on the Democratic press and the propeace Copperheads.[5] By and large, the performance of the Irish, as well as of other foreign-born troops, helped improve the native-born's view of America's naturalized citizens.

If the war temporarily allayed the nativist suspicion of the foreign-born, especially the Irish Catholics, the 1860s saw the rise of a formerly dormant anti-Semitism. As already noted, some colonial Americans had a tendency to be anti-Semitic.[6] But even the Know-Nothings, while centering most of their ire on Irish Catholics and, in some areas, on the Germans, also reflected the earlier anti-Semitic tendencies. The national organ of the Know-Nothings referred to the Jews as "this peculiar race of people," and projected them as avaricious Shylocks.[7] August Belmont, the Democratic national chairman, found the greatest epithet that the Know-Nothings could label him with was "the Austrian Jew, and agent of the Rothschilds."[8]

During the Civil War, this anti-Semitic impulse again reappeared. Not very numerous at this time, the Jews, nevertheless, were singled out for censure. They were accused of being disloyal smugglers. One naval officer, for example, declared, "There is entirely too much smuggling done . . . and as usual chiefly by Jews."[9] As a result of these unwarranted charges the former Know-Nothing General Ulysses S. Grant issued

General Order Number 11, which expelled all civilian Jews from his military jurisdiction because he thought they were engaged in cotton speculation and smuggling.[10] Lincoln revoked the order on January 4, 1863. Even George Templeton Strong manifested his antipathy towards Jews by suggesting that August Belmont was "a mere successful cosmopolite adventurer and alien, who ... has no real affinity with our country or people."[11]

This antipathy towards the Jews, in the 1860s persisted in the 1870s, though no specific xenophobic organizations were established. One reason was the lack of Jewish immigrants. Most Christians viewed the Jews as different, and Americans were no exception, but since the Jews—native and foreign-born—even in 1880 numbered approximately 250,000, less than one half of one percent of the total population, they could not be viewed as a serious threat to the nation. While this was a fact, still the depression years, 1873–77, saw an intensification of hostility to the Jews. Social discrimination against the Jews was practiced consistently. The outstanding example was the barring in 1877 of the famous New York banker Joseph Seligman from a Saratoga Springs hotel.[12] It was not, however, until the 1890s that a more virulent anti-Semitism manifested itself as part of a larger and broader movement against the "new immigration" of Southern and Eastern Europe. We shall take this movement up subsequently.

The Catholic issue also reemerged in the 1870s, but without too much vigor. Once again, the major issue was the parochial schools and the demands of the Catholics for public money to support and sustain these schools. This issue, as already noted, had done more than anything else to cause friction between the Catholics and their non-Catholic neighbors.

During the Reconstruction period, both North and South came to accept the idea of public-financed secular education. Thus private schools and church schools were replaced by these public institutions as the major source of education for America's youth.[13] Catholics not only insisted upon public funding for their own schools, but they also opposed the idea of secular, nonreligious education.

Non-Catholics tended to emphasize the fact that the ignorance and superstition of Catholic children would not survive the education which they received in public schools. One Boston magazine reported in 1870: The free school system has long been understood by Protestants to be not only a direct attack upon ignorance, but incidentally, a flank movement upon Romanism, sure, in the process of time, to turn its position and put it to rout.[14] Other Protestant periodicals concurred.[15]

This education issue, that is, the demands of the Catholics for tax money to support their schools, threatened to foster a new wave of anti-Catholic organizations. Even President Grant, in his seventh annual message to Congress (1875), made a plea for the public education of every child in which no sectarian tenets could or would be taught.[16] Catholics were incensed. They wanted not only money for their own schools, but they also opposed the idea of secular or nonreligious education on the grounds that it was a form of "indifferentism," that is, a willingness to accept the nonimportance of religious training.[17]

But because Catholics received no funds and because the fact of Republican opposition to public aid for religious schools was implicit in President Grant's message, there was no immediate need for a separate nativist organization. Of course, New York City residents were upset that the Irish seemed to be running their town. But despite the brilliant cartoons of Thomas Nast, whose apelike Irishmen appeared in *Harper's Weekly*, there were no serious xenophobic reactions.[18]

There were those, however, who hoped to return to Know-Nothingism. Daniel Ullman, for example, received a letter in 1876 which called for the formation of a secret organization which would organize and distribute an antipapal newspaper.[19] This short-lived group, the American Alliance, called for all citizens to vote for the native-born for all public offices and to oppose political Romanism in all its forms.[20] By far the most xenophobic clamor was directed not against the Jews or the Catholics, but rather against the "heathen Chinese."

The Chinese were never really accepted in nineteenth-century America.[21] Particular groups and individuals—certain busi-

nessmen and missionaries active in China in the middle of
the nineteenth century—did defend the Chinese, but the overwhelming majority of the American people agreed with their
more xenophobic neighbors and the prevalent stereotype of
"John Chinaman."[22]

The Chinese, most of whom landed at Pacific ports, came
for the same reason as many other immigrant groups: they
hoped to improve their economic conditions. Unlike other
immigrants to America, however, the Chinese always planned
to return to their homeland. Often they came as indentured
servants, in Chinese, *k'u-li* ("coolie").[23] Despite their cool
reception in America, they continued to come. The T'ai Ping
rebellion of the 1850s in Kwantung province exacerbated their
life in the homeland, and the promise of riches induced them
to emigrate.

The nativism of the 1850s did not bypass the Chinese, especially in California where the nativist tradition was already
well entrenched.[24] As early as 1852, groups of American
miners, upset at their own precarious financial condition and
the growing competition from the Chinese miners, attacked
the "Capitalists, ship-owners and merchants" who encouraged
the immigration of these Chinese competitors. Thus they
resolved: "That no Asiatic or South Sea Islander be permitted
to mine in this district [Columbia mining district, Tuolumne
County] either for himself or for others, and that these resolutions shall be part and parcel of our mining laws."[25] The State's
Democratic governor, John Bigler, supported their stand,
although the California legislature did not.

But even in the eastern half of the country, there was opposition to the Chinese among nativists and nonnativists alike.

The Know-Nothings also sounded the alarm against the
Chinese. The leader in this movement was a Kentucky congressman, Humphrey Marshall, who had been our Commissioner to China in 1853–54. Marshall, for example, warned
in 1854:

> To be overrun by the diverse races of Europe is doubtless evil
> enough, but whether Celtic, Teutonic or Anglo-Saxon, confraternity,
> if impossible, is at least approachable. But even the Dutchman and

the Irishman would join in the national horror at the curse with which the prospective inundation of oriental barbarism threatens our country.... Assimilation is not possible.... Nature has erected an eternal barrier... can Americans think of such an amalgamation without indignant disgust?.... [They are] devoted to the most absolute of despotisms, without conceptions of human rights, underdeveloped in intellect, with the plainest truths of Christian virtue and morality extinguished in the most hideous and monstrous idolatry, they must forever be a distinct race! ... [If] charity begins in China, it will end in America—in national suicide.[26]

Even Horace Greeley, editor of the New York *Tribune,* supported the policy of excluding the Chinese; he found little cause to recommend them.[27]

Initially the Oriental threat was only the Chinese. There were no Japanese recorded in the United States as late as 1860. Only forty-six Chinese immigrants came to the United States between 1820 and 1850, but in 1854 some 13,100 were admitted.[28]

By the last years of the 1850s, 35,000 Chinese were estimated to be in California, with some two-thirds of them working as miners, much to the consternation of the white miners, native and foreign-born alike.[29] Over 70,000 more Chinese entered the United States in the period 1860–70, and again almost all came through the Pacific ports, particularly San Francisco. This influx almost doubled the number of Chinese in California. It also made one out of every five residents of San Francisco a Chinese, and since there were fifteen males for every one female (recall the Chinese were not settlers, but sojourners), almost all of the Chinese population were employables. During the next decade the number of Chinese more than doubled.

With their admittance there came a threatening feeling on both the East and West coasts, though the major thrust against the Chinese would center on the West Coast. The major opponents of the Chinese could be found in the emerging labor unions and in the press.

Labor saw coolie workers as a threat to its standard of living.[30] Yet inconsistently they also claimed that John Chinaman was good only for women's work in laundries. The Chinese were considered racially inferior, a group which kept to themselves and would make no effort to assimilate. Then, too, they had their opium dens, their female slave traffic, and their gangster element, Chinese hatchet men called the Highbinders.[31] Ethnic slurs were applied: "moon-eyed leper", "yellow leper", "yellow-belly", and "slant-eyes" were among the more colorful descriptions of the Chinese.[32]

This stereotype of the Chinese had a highly emotional basis in the notion that the coolie labor was fraught with danger. Even the American Federation of Labor made the exclusion of Chinese labor a major issue throughout the pre–World War I years.[33]

But even before the organization of the AFL (1881) Eastern labor was opposed to the entry of the Chinese. The fear grew among native-American workers that the Chinese willingness to work long hours for low wages would cause a widespread depression of wages and a concomitant reduction in America's living standards. Widespread opposition to the Chinese thus developed even in the East.[34] By 1870, there was a growing demand for some action by the government of the United States to halt this threat to America.[35] Mass meetings of workers were called in several cities, including Boston, Massachusetts, and New York City. The powerful shoemakers' union, the Knights of Saint Crispin, was also vehement in its denunciation of the Chinese, because Chinese workers had been used to break a strike of the shoemakers in Northampton, Massachusetts.[36]

Major opposition to the Chinese, as already noted, came from the West Coast, where the bulk of the Chinese lived. In 1862, Governor Leland Stanford, in his inaugural message to thé legislature, declared:

To my mind, it is clear that the settlement among us of an inferior race is to be discouraged by every legitimate means. Asia, with her numberless millions, sends to our shores the dregs of her populations.... There can be no doubt but that the presence of numbers among us of a degraded and distinct people must exercise a deleterious influence upon the superior race, and to a certain extent repel desirable immigration.[37]

Stanford's racial argument against the Chinese grew in strength with the continued influx of Chinese immigrants.

At first, local ordinances were employed somewhat similar to the miners' resolutions already noted. There was also harassment and intimidation of the Chinese, as well as anti-Chinese riots in 1871 and 1878. To have a "Chinaman's chance" became synonymous with no chance at all. There were also attempts to have the California state legislature do something to alleviate the distress.

Finally, in an attempt to halt the Chinese influx, the Burlingame treaty between China and the United States took up the problem of Chinese immigration. It was negotiated and ratified in 1868. The treaty was specifically aimed at what was called involuntary immigration of Chinese, supposedly controlled by the Six Companies, Chinese groups who signed Chinese workers to "a term of service." The treaty did not interfere with voluntary immigration. It explicitly asserted the right of people to emigrate to the United States. But as we have indicated, the decade after the treaty saw a larger influx of immigrants than the period that preceded it. The treaty had no impact.

Congress, however, reacted to the growing demands that something be done about "coolie" labor. In 1875, therefore, Congress tried to reinforce the Burlingame treaty injunction against involuntary immigration by passing the Immigration Act of 1875. The law provided in part:

That in determining whether the immigration of any subject of China, Japan or any Oriental country, to the United States, is free and voluntary . . . it shall be the duty of the consul-general or consul of the United States residing at the port from which it is proposed to convey such subjects . . . to ascertain whether such immigrant has entered into a contract or agreement for a term of service within the United States, for lewd and immoral purposes, and if there be such a contract or agreement, the said consul shall not deliver the required permit or certificate.[38]

This act also outlawed the immigration of prostitutes and convicts, but not political prisoners.[39] It also restricted citizenship to whites and those of African ancestry. This first effort at selectivity did not have the desired result; Chinese immigration was not slowed.

And the Chinese remained a highly visible group. As Mary Roberts Coolidge pointed out, the American view of the Chinese was not influenced by the increased knowledge that was become available. Americans still saw a Chinese as a "left-handed, cunning, industrious, cruel and inhuman creature. . . ."[40] But the real problem was not so much the Chinese who were here, but the threat posed by "Asia, with her numberless millions," as Governor Stanford phrased it. According to Coolidge, the Chinese never exceeded 132,000 at any one time, and their average number ran about 110,000.[41]

Yet if the xenophobic hostility to the Chinese was constant, based on both racial and economic factors, what caused the final, successful push for exclusion? After all, the California state legislature had tried unsuccessfully in 1855 to pass a law that would exclude the Chinese.

The desire for the China trade was one important reason for that failure. If the threat of inundation by some four hundred million Chinese posed a problem, the prospect of trade with that same mass of humanity presented the possibility of profit. For this reason, the legislature avoided antagonizing the government of China by a direct affront, but continued a policy of licensing the Chinese miners at rather high fees.[42]

Essentially, the furor over the Chinese led in 1862 to the formation of the first anticoolie clubs in San Francisco. Yet the organizations did not develop any effective solution to the problem. Many businessmen and Protestant religious groups did not support the anticoolie movement. Then, too, both major political parties in California continued their anti-Chinese rhetoric, though there is some suspicion that Republican leaders in reality opposed any legislation that would restrict Chinese immigration, since many of their major supporters benefited from the cheap wages paid to these laborers.

Other anti-Chinese groups in California had proven no more effective than the anticoolie clubs, though they did make life miserable for the Chinese. In 1870, there was an anti-Chinese convention in California dedicated to opposing all political candidates who either employed Chinese laborers or favored their admission to the United States. Several other such groups were organized. These were the precursors of the anti-Chinese movement of the late 1870s.

The period from 1873–77 was a strained economic time throughout the country. The great railroad strikes of 1877 and the violence that accompanied them were but one manifestation of these economic difficulties. California was particularly hard hit, especially by the drought of 1877. Wages fell precipitously: for example, shoemakers, who had previously earned twenty-five dollars a week, now worked, if they could find a job, for nine dollars a week. These skilled artisans found the Chinese to be the cause of their decline in wages and status.[43] Similar situations could be found in other crafts. Then, too, almost half the factory employees in California were Chinese. To the American- and foreign-born whites, the answer to their problem was simple: get rid of the Chinese.

Thus in 1877 many idle workers, craftsmen and unskilled alike, often heard from the sandlot speakers (they had no funds to hire meeting halls) that the white worker would not be safe so long as he competed with low-paid coolies. On a number of occasions, particularly in San Francisco, attacks on the Chinese sections followed these fiery speeches. These riots were indications that the social fabric was disintegrating, but they afforded no real relief to the San Francisco workers.[44]

On July 23, 1877, the Workingman's party of the United States, a national Marxist organization with a local in San Francisco, held a meeting to sympathize with their fellow workers in the East who were then participating in the great railroad strikes of 1877. This meeting also was followed by an attack on Chinatown.

During the month of August, a new organization came into being to handle the Chinese threat: on August 22, 1877, the Workingman's Trade and Labor Union of San Francisco was established. John Day, Denis Kearney, and J. J. Hickey, all Irish-Americans, were its first board of officers. Then, in September, preliminary meetings were called for the purpose of establishing the Workingman's party of California. Day and Kearney claimed that the major political parties were both corrupt and that they neglected the needs of the workers. In these preliminary meetings, one aim dominated the group: the elimination of the Chinese in California.[45]

Finally, on October 5, 1877, a meeting was held to establish a permanent organization. Denis Kearney was elected president. The plaform had four major planks: (1) expel the Chinese workers, (2) take control of the government from the rich, (3) destroy the California land monopoly, and (4) elect none but competent workingmen to office. These purposes, it was insisted, would be achieved peaceably.

Who was Kearney? Denis Kearney was born in County Cork, Ireland, in 1847. In 1868, as the first officer, he had sailed into California. He bought a drayage business (teamster), married, and settled in San Francisco in 1872. He was ambitious and self-taught. He had become a naturalized citizen and a union member. In August and September, 1877, he was the outstanding sandlot Sinophobe. His appeal was always the same: "the Chinese must go!"[46]

Under Kearney, sandlot meetings continued in an effort to recruit more members to the party. The rhetoric of the movement was both anti-Chinese and anticapitalist. Kearney even held meetings on Nob Hill, where many wealthy San Franciscans lived.

In November, Kearney was arrested for the first time. But instead of hampering the party, his arrest helped by arousing the sympathies of the California workers. Kearney was acquitted of the charge of inciting to riot, though the rhetoric of the Irish-born leader was certainly reminiscent of the demagogic.

Kearney now expanded the movement. He toured the cities of California and established branches of the party in Gilroy, Santa Barbara, and even Los Angeles. His speeches became more violent. In December, 1877, he cried out, "There isn't an honest man in office today.... The only way to get laws passed in our favor is to surround the Capitol with bayonets and shoot those who vote against us."[47] As a follow-up to this speech, military clubs were established in a few of San Francisco's wards. Then, on January 3, Kearney led a parade of a thousand unemployed workers to the San Francisco City Hall and demanded work, food, or a cell in jail.

This increased potential for violence brought about Kearney's arrest again. Freed on bail, he was rearrested almost daily from January 9 to 16, when bail became so prohibitive that he remained in jail. On January 22, however, he was acquitted.

On January 21, 1878, the party's first state convention met in San Francisco; Kearney served as chairman of the proceedings. The party platform which was adopted called for: (1) restrictions on the Chinese, (2) an eight-hour day, (3) state regulation of the railroads and other corporations, (4) tax reform, (5) compulsory education for all in public schools, and (6) the popular election of United States senators. Most of these measures were progressive.

But the Workingman's party's big chance came, not in its successes in many of the local elections, but in the decision of the legislature to try to alleviate the distress by setting up a new constitution for California and choosing the delegates by an election to be held in June, 1878.

Yet the party did not capitalize on this opportunity to control the convention. It had always been troubled with defections and revolts. For example John Day, the vice president, had resigned in a dispute with Kearney over the latter's bombastic rhetoric.[48] Others, too, had unsuccessfully tried to wrest control of the party from Kearney.[49] And now that it had a chance for real success—it had clubs scattered throughout the state—Kearney hobbled it further by proposing in May, 1878, to the state central committee that all officials of the Workingman's party be made ineligible for nomination to public office. This deprived the party of capable candidates. A majority of the central committee thought such a move would weaken the party, but Kearney ignored them. He appealed to the workers. Thus the party split into two factions: both selected delegates for the coming delegate election in June.

The election did not appear to hold much interest for the electorate. Only a small vote was cast. The split in the Workingman's party, however, reduced its strength in the convention. Only 51 of the 152 delegates were members of the Workingman's party' and because of Kearney's insistence on the exclusion from the delegation of the party's officers, they were not the most able men in the movement.

Still the Workingmen were able to place some of their xenophobic ideas in article 19 of the new constitution, though the fear of unconstitutionality did limit the anti-Chinese sections.[50] The article declared that the state should provide all the necessary regulations to protect citizens from "dangerous aliens." It also forbade private corporations from employing the Chinese in any capacity and insisted that no Chinese be employed on public works. It called for curbs on coolie labor entering the state.[51] But these provisions would not stand up in federal courts because they conflicted with both the Burlingame treaty and the Fourteenth Amendment.[52]

This constitution was presented to the people of California. It passed by a narrow margin. But, most important, it showed that the split in the Workingman's party continued. Kearney toured the state on its behalf, while other members of the party, men like John Day, campaigned for its defeat because it did not go far enough.[53]

At the state convention of the party in June, 1879, called to select candidates for the September gubernatorial race, the party platform explicitly repudiated both Communism and agrarianism, and endorsed the new state constitution. Otherwise, it was similar to the 1878 platform.

The party nominated a full slate of candidates for state office, led by William F. White of Santa Cruz and W. R. Andrus for governor and lieutenant governor, respectively. Many of the Workingmen's candidates, especially for judicial offices, were endorsed by the Democrats, as well as by a new party, the Constitution party, which was based on support for the new constitution. Kearney, in fact, was asked to drop the name Workingman's party and replace it with the more appealing name, Constitution party. Kearney refused and became involved in a name-calling conflict with the Constitution party.[54]

Although the Workingman's party enjoyed some success in the state election, its gubernatorial candidates failed. While it did elect eleven state senators and sixteen assemblymen, they were unable to accomplish anything in the state legislature. The major parties stymied their efforts. In 1880, Kearney tried to preside over a merger of the Workingmen with the Greenback party, but most of the Workingmen were former

Democrats and preferred to return to that party, especially since the Democrats had made overtures by endorsing many of the Workingmen's candidates in 1879.[55] The party was in effect destroyed by this quarrel between the pro-Greenback and pro-Democratic factions. By 1881 the party was dead.

What had the party accomplished? We have mentioned article 19 in the new constitution. Perhaps its most important contribution was to transform the anti-Chinese agitation into a national issue.

Most of the support for the Workingman's party came from both skilled craftsmen and unskilled workers frightened by both the capitalists and the Chinese. They were alarmed at the spread of the large corporations and their own declining status. They were appalled at the wage competition provided by the Chinese workers. Kearney's unwillingness to broaden the appeal of the party by a name change indicated that the party would have a short life. As soon as economic conditions improved, as they did in 1880, the workers would return to their jobs. They would have neither the time nor the energy for any additional politicking. The Chinese agitation now centered on the Congress of the United States, where both major political parties emphasized their opposition to the Chinese immigrants.

As early as 1876, Congress had sent a congressional investigative team to look into the issue of Chinese immigration.[56] During the course of this investigation, it emerged that those who supported the Chinese were not averse to implanting the idea that the real menace lay not in the Chinese, but in the Irish Catholics who had shown their true character in the draft riots of 1863.[57] But the Irish, rather than being the object of xenophobic ridicule, were, in California, the xenophobes who directed their attacks on the Chinese. The committee, however, did recommend to the Congress that the Chinese scourge be terminated in order to protect the Pacific area.

Congress, after prolonged consideration, finally acted in February, 1879. The bill, which passed both houses of Congress, unilaterally denounced the Burlingame treaty, especially those sections that were in favor of free and voluntary immigration between the two countries, China and the United

States. It also, to all intents and purposes, excluded the Chinese from entering the United States. President Rutherford B. Hayes, who believed that the Chinese were invaders not immigrants, nevertheless, vetoed the bill.[58] He based his actions on two points: treaties could not be abrogated unilaterally, and, secondly, he felt that such a bill placed in peril our traders and missionaries in China.

But Hayes did begin negotiations with the Chinese to alter the Burlingame treaty. On November 17, 1880, the treaty was modified. It now stated that the United States could "regulate, limit, or suspend the immigration [of the Chinese], but may not absolutely prohibit it."[59] The Senate ratified the treaty in 1881. The following year, Congress tried to suspend all Chinese immigrations for twenty years. President Chester A. Arthur, however, vetoed the bill. His grounds were the same as Hayes's: the bill violated the treaty.[60] On May 6, 1882, however, Arthur did sign into law the Chinese Exclusion Act, which suspended for ten years the immigration of Chinese laborers, but did not interfere with Chinese merchants or students. The act also required all Chinese laborers who left for China and wanted to return to the United States to have a certificate of eligibility before they left. And the act denied the right of naturalization to the Chinese and other Orientals. Although it, too, appeared to violate the Treaty of 1880, nevertheless, it did become law.

Although the Chinese Exclusion Act was successful in that the number of immigrants was reduced by half in the ten-year period after it became law, the agitation against the Chinese continued, especially in California, where the local ordinances were again used to harass the Chinese. In 1885, for example, some two hundred Chinese laundrymen in San Francisco were arrested.[61] That same year, some fifteen Chinese were killed in anti-Chinese riots in Wyoming.

Congress, therefore, reacted to the pressure of the Western states as well as the AFL and other labor groups and tried to close the loopholes in the Exclusion Act of 1882. On July 5, 1884, Congress restricted the rights of Chinese merchants to emigrate to the United States. They would have to receive visas. Many people thought that laborers were coming in under the guise of merchants. Congress also extended the exclusion period an additional ten years.

Again Congress acted, in 1888, when the Chinese were slow to ratify a treaty negotiated in the years 1886–88. Introduced by the Pennsylvania Democrat, William Lawrence Scott, the act forbade the readmission of Chinese laborers who left the country, even though they had certificates of eligibility.[62] Furthermore, in 1892, the Geary Law extended the Scott Law for another 10 years. In addition Chinese laborers in the United States had to obtain within one year a certificate of residence; otherwise, they would be deported.[63]

The primary object of the Geary Law was to halt the illegal entry of the Chinese across the Canadian and Mexican borders. The California Democrat, Representative Thomas J. Geary, defended the act in much the same terms as the early anti-Chinese xenophobes. He insisted:

> The Chinese laborer brings no wife and no children and his wants are limited to the immediate necessities of the individual while the American is compelled to earn income sufficient to maintain his wife and babies. . . . If this immigration is permitted to continue, American labor must surely be reduced to the level of his Chinese competitor. . . . The protection of the American laborer is an essential duty of the American Government. . . .[64]

Additional legislation to restrict the Chinese was passed by Congress in 1893, 1894, 1898, 1902, and finally the act of 1904 extended the exclusion provisions without limitation.[65]

The anti-Chinese movement was crowned with success. For the first time, the federal government had prohibited the immigration of a distinct group, the Chinese. The reason given for these legislative acts was protection of American labor. Certainly that was a good reason. It was obvious that with the industrialization of America, some limits would have to be put on the influx of immigrants, but the anti-Chinese rhetoric displayed a racial bias that is hard to ignore.[66] Those who defended the Chinese in 1892 pointed to specific instances where European immigrants, particularly the Poles and the Italians, were paid lower wages than the Chinese for comparable work.[67] But the fear of the yellow race was too great.

This racial argument would reemerge in 1900 when the anti-Japanese movement struck America, with the most important anti-Japanese spokesmen again coming from California and the labor movement.[68]

At the very time that the "Chinese must go" slogan had reached the pinnacle of success by the enactment of a national exclusion act plus the local harassment by way of municipal ordinances, the Japanese began to arrive in noticeable numbers. Between 1890 and 1900, over 25,000 Japanese came to America.[69] The following decade more than 125,000 arrived.[70] With their arrival, there came again the specter of the yellow peril. This time the menace was the Japanese. And again the center of this fear was in California, where the bulk of the Japanese lived.[71]

The same basic stereotype was applied to the Japanese: there was the rejection based on his race, nationality, and religion. Organized labor and the press were again the leaders in this xenophobic movement.[72]

And as with the Chinese, large agricultural interests, businessmen in need of cheap labor, and some missionaries remained opposed to the exclusion of the Japanese immigrants. But, by the opening of the twentieth century, the overwhelming majority of Americans again had developed a degree of race consciousness and willingly agreed to the need to exclude the Japanese.

Japan, a bustling, aggressive, and ambitious nation, which had shown its modern capacity in the Sino-Japanese War, 1894–95 and in the Russo-Japanese War, 1904–1905, agreed to the voluntary "Gentlemen's Agreement of 1908," which restricted the numbers of Japanese coming to the United States. It did cut back on the numbers; Japanese immigration was reduced by a third. But this fact did not diminish the myth of the yellow peril held by the more xenophobic racists, especially in California where the Asiatic Exclusion League, organized in 1905, continued to operate.[73] These racists would presist until the Immigration Act of 1924 excluded all Asiatic peoples.

The most important element in the anti-Oriental immigration movement was the use of the racial argument in defense of exclusion. As one San Francisco editor, in 1909, put it, "The opposition to Oriental immigration is justified upon the single ground of race.... It is not a matter of tongue, of color, or of anatomy, although in each of these respects the difference is very clearly marked, but of morality and intellect."[74] Similar thoughts can be found in much of the American writing on this question in this period.[75] But this concept of racial purity could not be restricted to the Asiatics. As we shall see, the beginnings of the restriction policy which manifested itself in the Exclusion Act, 1882, would also bring a clamor for the suppression of the far more numerous European immigration, which now began to come from Southern and Eastern Europe. Now some businessmen would join hands with organized labor in an effort to limit the numbers of immigrants coming to the United States. Again the targets would be Catholics and Jews from Southern and Eastern Europe.

CHAPTER VII

Renewed Assault on the Papacy in America: The American Protective Association

FROM THE 1880S TO THE POST–WORLD WAR I ERA, AMERICA was a nation in flux. Even before the assertion (1893) of the American historian Frederick Jackson Turner that the year 1890 had witnessed the closing of the frontier, and with it the end of the optimistic view of America's future, many Americans had become alarmed over the changes in American society.[1] Its values had shifted. The rural, agrarian ideas of the 1880s were being transformed into the bureaucratic middle-class values of the 1920s.[2] This process generated a good deal of unrest: increased labor strikes symbolized by the Haymarket riot (1886) and the Pullman strike (1894), the depression years 1893–96, the burgeoning of the urban slums, and the difficulties of the farmers reflected in the Granger and Populist movements.

But the frustrations of the 1880s and the 1890s were not due solely to social and economic problems. The Protestant churches also began to react to these changes.[3] They began to see the full significance of these alterations, which helped create what the late Professor Richard Hofstadter has called "the psychic crisis of the 1890's."[4] They were especially concerned about the increased power of Catholicism.

The increased immigration of the period did nothing to alleviate this growing feeling of uncertainty. Beginning in the 1880s almost a half million immigrants arrived each year, the largest portion of whom flocked to cities of the urbanized East and the increasingly urbanized Midwest. Of course, it was not until 1896 that the "new immigrants from Southern and Eastern Europe surpassed in number those coming from Northern and Western Europe. Still the differences between the older immigrant groups and the newer ones became a publicized factor in the xenophobic outbursts of the period. As early as the 1880s there was a growing sense of unease.

Many Americans found an outlet for their discomfort by joining associations based on background and heredity as well as the more xenophobic movements. These organizations emphasized the ancestral lineage of their members. As one contemporary commentator noted, "more and more we [native-born Americans] are developing a faith in the heroism and worth of those who first settled in this country."[5] Thus there appeared the Sons of the Revolution (1883), the Colonial Dames (1890), the Daughters of the American Revolution (1890), and many others.[6] Between 1880 and 1900 the bulk of the recognized patriotic and hereditary associations were organized.[7] These groups reflected the uneasiness of some Americans about the events taking place in the United States.

Generally, the members of the hereditary societies, the SAR, DAR et al. belonged to the well-to-do and more educated classes.[8] They saw in the immigrant the source of much of the corruption and radicalism which they believed were undermining American values.

The membership of the patriotic societies, on the other hand, belonged to the lower middle class. These groups stressed patriotic and national ideals, as their names indicated; for example, the Order of Native Americans, the Patriotic League of the Revolution, the American Patriotic League, and the Loyal Men of American Liberty. The largest and the most powerful of these groups was the Grand Army of the Republic, the organization of the Civil War veterans. By 1886, the GAR membership was being warned about the dangers of the "immigrant scum."[9] There was a large number of other such groups operative during this time. They, too, agreed that the immigrant was one of the major problems that faced Americans.

Was the American Protective Association the only exclusively xenophobic group of the period? Why and how did it come to dominate the other nativist orders? What was its program? Who joined the group? What geographic areas provided the bulk of its membership? Why did it fail? To answer these questions we must look more closely at the anti-Catholic and anti-immigrant rhetoric and organizations of the 1880s and 1890s.

The APA was essentially anti-Catholic and anti-immigrant. It was one of a number of groups that emerged in the 1880s and the 1890s to combat the menace of Catholicism and immigration and their alleged concomitants—ignorance, conspiracy, corruption. A number of actions by the Catholics created a storm of protest in the 1880s.

In 1884, the Catholic hierarchy brought the parochial-school issue once more before the American people and provided another excuse for some vehement anti-Catholic propaganda. The Third Plenary Council of Bishops, meeting in Baltimore, made attendance at parochial schools, where they existed, mandatory for Catholic children. Pastors of churches where such schools did not exist were enjoined to establish them as soon as possible.[10] Protestants, who, as we have seen earlier, believed that Romish superstition would not survive public education, were alarmed.

The Catholic position in education was a highly debated issue. This increased role of the parochial school (there were over four thousand in existence by 1900) brought demands for state aid.[11] Then, too, the Catholic Indian Bureau became the most successful Indian-school contract bidder during the 1880s and 1890s.[12] Protestants began to insist that the Indians be taught in nondenominational schools.

State efforts at regulating parochial schools caused considerable controversy. Massachusetts was rocked by such efforts in the years 1887–89. In the Midwest (Ohio, Illinois, and Wisconsin) there were efforts to compel attendance in all schools and to require that all teaching in schools be done in English. Some German Catholics and Lutherans used the German language.[13]

A wave of anti-Catholic propaganda and organization followed in the wake of these events. These protests did not restrict themselves to attacks on the parochial schools.

The assault began when the Reverend Josiah Strong published *Our Country.* The book, which went through a number of editions, accused the immigrants of crime and immorality, of corrupting municipal government, of debasing the Anglo-

Saxon bloodstream, and of swelling the ranks of Catholicism and socialism.[14] Strong's book emphasized the three nativist themes which dominated the xenophobic outbursts of the 1880s and 1890s: anti-Catholicism, Anglo-Saxonism and anti-radicalism. These themes, along with anti-Semitism, were the core complaints of the xenophobes.

Strong, himself, became the secretary of the Evangelical Alliance of the United States in 1886. While the organization was not primarily dedicated to nativism, it participated, nevertheless, in combating the "menace of Rome," especially on the school question.[15]

Charles P. T. Chiniquy's *Fifty Years in the Church of Rome* was another major anti-Catholic work published in 1885. It pointed to Rome as the major threat to America's freedom and also alleged that Abraham Lincoln was aware of the "Catholic menace." Chiniquy, a former priest, insisted that on a visit to the White House during the Civil War, Lincoln had told him of the growing menace of Rome to the future security of the United States.[16]

Other books added to the anti-Catholic chorus. The former Know-Nothing the Reverend Justin H. Fulton published *Rome in America* (1887), which condemned the parochial-school system as a threat to America's liberty.[17] This book was followed by his *Washington in the Lap of Rome,* which insisted that the office of the president of the United States was controlled by Rome *via* the office of Cardinal Gibbons in Baltimore.[18] In the same year Fulton published yet another attack on Catholicism. In his *Why Priests Should Wed,* he emphasized the moral shortcomings of the Roman Catholic church.[19]

American Protestants of the 1880s and 1890s also had their own Maria Monk. Mrs. Margaret Lisle Sheperd published her autobiography in 1887. She claimed to have been an escaped nun, and her story was widely believed.[20] Actually she was the daughter of an Irish-Catholic father serving in the British Army. She appears to have been no better than she had to be: a swindler who had spent some time in prison for theft and had deserted her husband.[21]

Other works stressed this anti-Catholic theme. The Reverend Isaac J. Lansing of Worcester, Massachusetts, picked up on the Lincoln theme of Chiniquy. Lansing accused a Catholic conspiracy of the assassination of Abraham Lincoln. He also condemned the Catholic church for its efforts at thought control.[22] The Reverend Robert P. Sample was another clergymen who stressed the idea that Catholicism was inimical to freedom of thought and expression. Only the Protestant religions, he declared, provided and guaranteed human freedom.[23] This notion was also emphasized by the Reverend James M. King of New York City in his book, *Facing the Twentieth Century* (1899). It categorically condemned Catholic efforts to secure public funds for parochial education. It declared that only public education that was nondenominational could safeguard American freedom.[24] King served as the secretary of the National League for the Protection of American Institutions, a group organized in 1889 to safeguard the American common school. The group had an anti-Catholic bias.

There were countless other works that dealt with the Catholic problem, but the ones noted above all had large sales and sounded the clarion call for Protestant action in the 1880s and the 1890s.[26] As Professor David Brion Davis has noted about the nativist literature of the pre-Civil War period, the anti-Catholic literature of the 1880s and 1890s emphasized the conspiratorial nature of Catholicism.

Immigration was seen as part of that conspiracy. The Reverend Daniel C. Eddy, a former Know-Nothing legislator in Massachusetts and later a Brooklyn pastor, pointed out in 1889 that the church was in fact trying to gain control of the United States through immigration. Eddy declared:

The hope of the Catholic Church to overthrow our common-school system and substitute the parochial system, is based on immigration. . . . The determination of the Church of Rome to capture our great cities, those centres of life and power, rests on immigration! . . . Our dangers as a free people, dangers against which the wisest men of the world have warned us, spring from immigration.[27]

Eddy retained the Know-Nothing idea of immigration control; he opposed immigration restriction, though he did accept the immigration law of 1875 which excluded paupers and criminals. He endorsed the old Know-Nothing idea that public office be held only by native-born Americans. However, he believed immigration restriction to be un-American. Others, of course, did move toward the idea of exclusion as already practiced in the case of the Chinese.

But this oratory and propaganda went hand in hand with organizations that were predominantly nativist in their purpose. A number of secret anti-Catholic societies were established in the 1880s but they remained minor nativist organs.[28] These groups generally were composed of self-styled patriots who assumed a negative and positive stance: they were anti-Catholic and anti-immigration; but they were also pro–public school.

Groups of foreign-born Protestants joined these native anti-Catholic groups. The anti-Catholic American Protestant Association organized in the 1850s by Charles Irish continued its existence in the post–Civil War period. It was made up of Protestant militants. The Loyal Orange Institution went international: it came to the United States in 1870.[29] These groups were reenforced by the British-American Association in 1887.

These nativist groups, whether they consisted of native-born or foreign-born, were decidedly anti-Catholic. They were alarmed at the growing political power of Catholics in the cities of the United States.[30] There was even an effort in 1886 to set up a nativist political party to combat this menace.

In 1886, an anti-immigration political movement began in California, as a result of the Haymarket riot of 1886. Peter D. Wigginton, a railroad attorney, coupled immigration with revolutionary radicalism. The party enjoyed some success in the San Francisco area.[31] It failed to excite much national enthusiasm.

The party, however, did offer New York City's Mayor Abram Hewitt its support in his reelection bid. Hewitt had attacked the role of Irish-Catholics in the affairs of the city. He accused them of being overrepresented on both the city's payroll and its charity rolls.[32]

The election did cause a wave of anti-Catholicism, however. Henry George, the California Sinophobe and a proponent of the single tax on landholders, was also a candidate in the mayoralty contest. He was supported by the outspoken Catholic priest Father Edward McGlynn and opposed by the conservative New York cleric Archbishop John Corrigan. For his refusal to submit to the control of his bishop, Father McGlynn was excommunicated, a condition imposed on him for five years. Anti-Catholics used him as proof that freedom of thought and political action was forbidden to church members.[33]

Hewitt refused to accept their endorsement. It was apparent that a separate nativist party had little hope of success. Thus, the more xenophobic Americans continued to join and organize patriotic societies which operated as distinct pressure groups within the major political parties.[34]

By far the most successful anti-Catholic group of the period was the American Protective Association. It was founded March 13, 1887, in Clinton, Iowa, by Henry F. Bowers and six other men.[35] Clinton was a growing city with a population approaching 15,000. Two out of every five of its inhabitants were foreign-born, mostly Irish and German.

In addition to the widespread feelings of unease already alluded to above, the spark that set off the organization of APA was the mayoralty election of 1887 in Clinton. Arnold Walliker, the incumbent, was defeated for reelection. There were several reasons for his defeat, but the one which Walliker, his campaign advisor Bowers, and their friends preferred to accept was the opposition to him by the Irish-Catholic–dominated Knights of Labor. Thus these seven men came together to battle the Catholic menace.[36]

Obviously, these men had real grievances. It is understandable that people in positions of authority should feel their loss of status, especially when they believed they had been removed by alleged Catholic conspiracies. However, in retrospect these do not appear to have been real.[37] Certainly, it is safe to say that many Protestant Americans were alarmed over the "un-American" aspects of Catholicism, particularly the papacy and the church's emphasis on authority. Many Protestants obviously were upset—some were almost hysterical—at the appearance of the Italian-speaking Apostolic

Delegate, Francis Satolli, who represented the Pope at the Chicago World's Fair in 1892 and then took up residence in Washington, D.C., in 1893.[38] The impact was akin to the visit of Archbishop Bedini in 1854. There appeared to be a real fear that the ideas of Justin Fulton's *Washington in the Lap of Rome* were coming to fruition.

Of course, it should be noted that while many Protestants felt uneasy about Catholicism, they did not join any of the anti-Catholic groups of the period. Many Americans continued to believe that Catholics could be made to respond to the American sense of freedom and pointed to the emergence of the liberal Catholic element in America.[39] Other Americans would also continue to oppose any restrictions on immigration in the 1890s.[40]

However, it is apparent that many Americans of the 1880s and 1890s had legitimate grievances which they came to lay at the doors of Catholics and immigrants. In the minds of many these terms were synonymous.

Thus, in 1887, when Henry Bowers, the Clinton lawyer, called Arthur and Jacob Walliker and the others to a meeting, he was acting reasonably.[41] On that Sunday afternoon in March, these men drew up a constitution for a secret fraternal society similar to the Know-Nothings. The order was committed to battle political Romanism, and thereby to protect America. It was to be a secret group, since the members felt that they were in a war and in a war one does not reveal one's plans to the enemy.[42]

The organization set up an annual national convention during which there would be an address by the president and a report by the secretary. This would provide the apex of leadership. Each state would have its own annual convention. Its officers could be removed by the supreme president of the organization. The officers of the state Superior Council represented the local units at the annual national convention. A local unit required at least twenty-five people. There was an initiation fee of one dollar, plus one dollar annual dues.[43]

In order to become a member of the APA, an application had to seconded by two members. The applicant would then swear to maintain the secrecy of the order. Several oaths were taken. They bound the initiate to prevent Catholics from becoming members of the order, to employ Protestants whenever possible, to avoid giving aid to the Catholic church, never to quarrel with Catholics about the APA, never to support Catholics for public office, and never to cooperate with Catholics in any strikes.

In the early years, the order spread slowly throughout Iowa and the neighboring states. The first national convention was held at Belle Plaine, Iowa, in December, 1889. In September, 1891, a Women's American Protective Association auxiliary was established. In 1895, a Junior APA was organized to reach those between the ages of fourteen and twenty-one. The word *Amorean* was generally viewed by contemporaries to be the secret name of the APA. But, as Kinzer points out, various groups called themselves *American Orders*. If you join the first two letters of *American Orders* you have the word *Amoreans*.[44]

Why did the American Protective Association become the most successful of the American orders? A number of explanations can be provided. First, there was the continuing school controversy which emphasized for many the supposed hostility of Catholics to the common schools. Second, there was the eventual cooperation—some thought of it as a merger—among the various nativist groups which came to be dominated by the American Protective Association. And, finally, the APA was eager to engage in politics. It employed certain political techniques to advantage, especially the tactics of offense rather than defense, concentration on local issues, and the use of existing parties, usually the Republican party, rather than the establishment of a third party.[45]

Many Americans came to agree with one APA member who could not understand why an intelligent, patriotic Protestant would object to fighting against the "spirit of the Catholic Church." The best means available, he insisted, were the principles and platform of the APA.[46]

What was the platform of the APA? The second president of the APA, the Canadian-born William J. H. Traynor provided the aims of the order in 1894. It advocated immigration restriction, knowledge of the English language as a prerequisite for naturalization, as well as a lengthening of the waiting period for naturalization. It also continued to oppose the election of Catholics, a position that was changed in 1897, but by that time the movement was speedily declining.[47]

Anti-Catholicism was the basic theme of APA propaganda, some of it true, some of it false. In the Indian-school controversy, the APA in 1889 endorsed the efforts of the Reverend Thomas J. Morgan, the Indian Commissioner in President Benjamin Harrison's administration and a former professor of church history at the Baptist Union Theological Seminary in Chicago, to end predominantly Roman Catholic denominational schools on the Indian reservations. When Grover Cleveland was elected president in 1892, the APA regarded it as a triumph of "political Romanism." Morgan was replaced as Indian Commissioner and became a prominent member of the APA.[48]

Whatever the truth of the matter in the Indian-schools controversy, the APA did make use of some false documents. Many of the members of the APA, seriously and sincerely alarmed at the Catholic menace, found little trouble in accepting them. One such document was a forged "Pastoral Letter" from the American Bishop of the Roman Catholic church calling for the formation of a Catholic political party. Still another forgery, and one that was frightening, was a set of papal "Instructions to Catholics," circulated in 1892, which called upon Catholics to exterminate all heretics on the Feast of St. Ignatius of Loyola, on July 31, 1893.

Then, too, the APA coupled its anti-Catholicism with antiradicalism, as already noted. Members of the APA were forbidden to join with Catholics in any strikes. When Pope Leo XIII's encyclical *Rerum Novarum* was issued in 1891, it was viewed by the APA as part of the Catholic conspiracy to control labor, just as the church was alleged to control voters.[49] After all, the APA could point to the fact that Terence Powderly, the leader of the Knights of Labor, was a Catholic.[50]

The APA played a significant role in the election of 1892 as the defender of Morgan and the opponent of the Catholic menace. It had shown solid strength in the Midwest, particularly in Wisconsin and Illinois, where the compulsory school attendance laws, which also demanded teaching in the English language, had won both support and abuse. Mainly, they won support from the Republican party and abuse from the Democratic party.[51]

Just as the APA was emerging as a significant political force with the concomitant publicity, it also emerged as the leading spokesman for the xenophobic orders that had proliferated in the eighties and nineties. In 1889, Henry Baldwin, descendant of Simon Baldwin, who had been one of the founders of the Order of United Americans had called for a meeting in New York of all the "patriotic" anti-Catholic groups, to consolidate their efforts in the fight against the Catholic menace.[52] Not too much came of this effort. The following year, with the help of William O. McDowell, founder of the Sons of the American Revolution, Baldwin called for another meeting to be held in February, 1891, in Chicago. This time the societies founded on principles of heredity, as well as the nativist orders, were invited to attend. But again outright opposition from the latter groups and from the GAR, with its heavy German and Irish enrollments, prevented any significant merger of the orders' efforts.[53] Still, a National American Patriotic Union was established, and two APA members were chosen as officers: Henry Bowers was chosen as a vice president and William Traynor, publisher of the *Patriotic American*, as treasurer.

While the APA had not been included in the 1889 call, it was invited to the Chicago meeting in 1891.[54] Soon it would have its initials applied to the whole nativist drive.[55]

In 1893, the APA clearly became the dominant organization in the nativist movement. At its annual convention of that year, it chose a new supreme president, the ambitious William James Henry Traynor of Detroit. Born in Ontario, Canada, in 1845, he moved to Michigan in 1867. He published a number of papers in the Detroit area. The *Patriotic American* was the most notable of his publications. He had been a member of a number of anti-Catholic groups, including the Loyal Orange Institution. Under this new leadership, the APA moved out of the Midwest and spread from coast to coast.

The APA was the beneficiary of the growing tide of opinion

which called for a curb on immigration.[56] Nevertheless, because of its support by the Midwestern Scandinavians, especially the Swedes, the order never pushed very vigorously for immigration restriction, though it could and did condemn Catholic immigrants.[57] The APA's forgeries, especially the one which called for the assassination of heretics, brought the APA to the attention of the public. And its identification with the Republican party made it a natural target for Democrats trying to control their voters, especially in the "hard times" of 1893–95 when a Democratic president ruled the country.[58] The panic of 1893 really increased the membership roles of the APA as well as the other nativist groups.

While the APA had considerable support among the working class during the years under Henry Bowers's direction, its chief strength was located in the Midwestern cities in Wisconsin, Illinois, Ohio, Minnesota, and Michigan. Its greatest appeal was to the residents of the Western states who had recently moved into the urbanized and industrialized areas that were in a period of rapid growth.[59] These areas, not surprisingly, suffered from the social tensions generated by an influx of newcomers, increase in status for some and a decline in status for others. It is understandable that some Americans, particularly in the working and middle classes, found a sense of security in belonging to the APA and its kindred groups.[60]

The panic of 1893, however, granted the new leadership of the order the opportunity to expand. Some APA leaders exploited the panic by suggesting it was part of the Catholic plot to destroy the economic viability of the nation. While they consistently denied that they favored a boycott of Catholic stores and workers, nevertheless, countless Catholics found themselves subjected to such "un-American" pressure.[61] The economic distress of the period lent some credence to these charges in the minds of many Protestants. Candidates endorsed by the APA captured control of the city governments of Detroit, Milwaukee, and Kansas City. In all these cases, Catholic officials were fired from local government.[62]

While the APA enjoyed some success on the East Coast, its more notable achievements were made in the West. It had little success in the South, where most Protestants viewed it as a ploy of the Republican party. Since it welcomed Negro support, there was little chance to use the racial arguments that might have appealed to the South. And many industrial leaders of the South hoped to encourage immigrants to come into the South. Traynor made special efforts to win Southern support, even abandoning the religious issue and substituting antiliquor and antigambling pronouncements.[63] The APA was strong in some Massachusetts cities, namely, Springfield, Boston, Worcester, Fitchburg, Cambridge, Brockton, Somerville, Chelsea, Haverhill, Lowell, Lawrence, and Northampton.[64]

Just how much strength did the order have nationwide? At its peak, 1894–95, it claimed a membership of 2,500,000.[65] Most authorities accept the fact that this figure was more a hope than a reality. Donald Kinzer believes the order had no more than 100,000 dues-paying members, while John Higham places the figure at 500,000.[66] It is probable that the 2,500,000 figure represented the peak influence of the APA, those who were members of allied societies, and those who were willing to listen to their speakers and read their literature. But since it was a secret society, there is no accurate way of determining the actual number of enrolled members.

The organization had little lasting national influence, no matter what its membership was. Like many politicians in the Know-Nothing movement, politicos used the APA for their own reasons and once in office ignored its principles and platforms. Except for its success in terminating the Indian-school denominational contracts, it enjoyed little national success.[67] Its efforts to alter the immigration and naturalization laws were ineffectual. Although it claimed to have elected nearly one hundred congressmen—actually less than two dozen—it could rely on only one Republican, Congressman William Linton of Saginaw, Michigan, a former lumber dealer and onetime mayor of Saginaw.[68]

While the APA was at its peak, the seeds of its decline began to appear. Internal factionalism, quarrels over funds with charges of corruption, and the outbreak of violence at some APA functions marred its reputation. Then, too, many Protestants began to shy away from the excesses of the APA rhetoric. One major issue that increasingly divided the order was

President Traynor's desire for political independence from
the Republicans, while many of the state leaders favored the
continued support of the Republicans.[69] Between the years
1894–96, this issue clearly became divisive. Traynor and his
supporters in 1894 condemned Governor William McKinley
of Ohio because some of his friends were Catholics. Thus
the split became permanent when McKinley received the
Republican nomination in 1896. One wing of the order, led
by Traynor, refused to support McKinley; another element
did endorse him.[70] Traynor favored Congressman Linton for
the Republican nomination. During the campaign, however,
he endorsed the Democrat, William Jennings Bryan.

This internecine warfare intensified when allegations of
fiscal irresponsibility came to light. Traynor was asked what
had happened to the dues money that had been collected.[71]
It became apparent in 1895 that the organization was close
to bankruptcy. Much of the responsibility for this state of affairs
was laid at the doors of President Traynor, who was now clas-
sified as an "autocrat, a despot and a veritable czar."[72]

Violence also marred the reputation of the APA.[73] There
were three religious riots in the years 1894–95. One took place
in Butte, Montana, on July 4, 1894, when two deaths occurred.
A second riot, in Kansas City, Missouri, which occurred during
the local elections, resulted in several deaths. But the third
brawl, in Boston on July 4, 1895, was by far the most damaging
to the APA.[74] The trouble broke out over a float provided by
one of the patriotic societies, wherein a lady was dressed in
an orange dress; the Catholics reacted to this Protestant
symbol, and a melee followed in which one man was killed
and a number injured.

While the APA was not directly responsible for the riot,
many publications placed the blame on the order, since it
had organized the parade. The *New York Times* condemned
the Catholics for their "Irishness" and the anti-Catholics for
their "Orangeism." The paper hoped that both could be submerged in Americanism.[75] Some Protestant clergymen began
to berate the order for its extremism.[76]

The decline of the APA intensified after the July, 1895, riot.
More and more prominent Americans attacked the order. Even

the American press became much more critical of the movement.[77] By October, 1896, Traynor had to suspend publication of his own paper, the *Patriotic American*.[78] He had been replaced as supreme president by John Warnock Echols at the convention of 1896.

The new president, a lawyer from Atlanta and a lifelong Democrat, had come into the APA movement via the Scotch-Irish Society of America.[79] It was hoped that he could heal the rift in the order and increase the chances of success in the South. He was the supreme president who led the APA forces into the 1896 campaign and into relative obscurity following the election of McKinley. As a matter of fact, McKinley's designation of the Catholic trade unionist, Terence Powderly, as his Commissioner of Immigration, was a symbol, if one were needed, that the APA was no longer considered a power in national politics.[80] In 1898, Bowers returned to the presidency of the order and kept the organization going as his own personal vehicle. It had no power after 1896.[81]

The APA, like the Know-Nothings, had a short national existence. Its national prominence rested on its ability to utilize the wave of anti-Catholicism of the 1890s. Catholic efforts to gain public funds for parochial schools alarmed many Protestants. Then, too, the panic of 1893 and the unemployment that followed led many workers to believe that Catholic immigrants were taking their jobs. The forgery of documents which suggested that Catholics were waiting to slaughter Protestants and other heretics could stimulate to feverish pitch the emotions of the Protestants, but it was a difficult pitch to maintain. Then, again, the APA was able to appear as a reform group—to end the municipal corruption of Catholic-controlled cities. Like the Know-Nothings, it was able to make use of the temperance issue.

But despite temporary successes, the APA failed. It is one thing to claim two or three million members, but if those members do not exist, or if they do not pay their dues, financial problems will ensue.[82] But though the APA declined, anti-Catholicism did not disappear from the American scene, as we shall see in both the pre- and post-World War I period.

Although a heightened fear of Romanism failed to keep the

APA in the national spotlight, the anti-immigration propaganda that helped the APA to flourish did not die with the national aspirations of the movement. Some Protestant clergymen saw a far greater menace to America in the immigrants of Southern and Eastern Europe than in the Irish Catholics. In 1894, the Immigration Restriction League of Boston was organized to combat this threat. It eschewed the secrecy and overt bigotry of the APA movement. This attitude was well summed up by the elitist Philadelphia lawyer, Sydney G. Fisher. "The modern movement against immigration," he wrote, " . . . will avoid the absurdity of being a secret organization and the absurdity of recommending that the foreign-born shall never hold office. It will be entirely free from attacks on the Roman Catholics and all violence and bitterness which that involved."[83]

CHAPTER VIII

Restriction and Americanization

EVEN WHILE THE ANTI-CATHOLIC APA MOVEMENT began its crusade against the papists, some Americans were alarmed at what they considered a more basic threat to the nation, the racial character of the immigration of the 1880's and 1890's. In 1888, for example, one Pennsylvania Protestant clergyman reported:

I have stood near Castle Garden [debarkation area in New York City] and seen races of far greater peril to us than the Irish. I have seen the Hungarians, and the Italians and the Poles. I have seen these poor wretches trooping out, wretches physically, wretches morally, and stood there almost trembling for my country, and said, what shall we do if this thing keeps on? In the name of God, what shall we do if the American race is to receive a constant influx of that sort of thing, with such a history as they had had.[1]

This stress on Josiah Strong's Anglo-Saxon argument coupled with anti-Romanism did have an impact on the national legislature. Congress passed the Immigration Act of 1891, which called for certain exclusionary policies. The first of them enlarged and strengthened the pauper-exclusion provisions of the Immigration Act of 1882, which was aimed at the aged and the infirm. Now in 1891, immigration inspectors could deny entry to able-bodied men who might be unable to find employment and thus become public charges. Polygamists, criminals, idiots, the insane, and those suffering from a contagious disease were also barred. Another exclusionary section denied admission to immigrants whose passage had been paid for by individuals or organizations abroad.[2] Such immigrants were to be detained to ascertain that they were not in violation of the contract labor law (1885), or liable to become public charges. The act did not forbid residents of the United States from sending passage money for a relative abroad.[3]

This act of 1891 increased the barriers against immigration and was followed in 1893 by another immigration act, which, however, did not raise the barriers any higher.[4] But neither the acts of 1891 or 1893 satisfied the restrictionists.

More and more Americans were accepting a theory of the changing character of immigration which separated the "newer" from the "older" immigrants. These invidious comparisons between the immigrants of Southern and Eastern Europe and those from Northern and Western Europe were based on the idea of race. Of course, as we have seen, many Protestants emphasized the undesirability of people who persisted in their Catholicism.[5] In this racial argument, a number of subthemes stressing anti-Semitism again surfaced. Significantly antialienism went hand in hand with antiradicalism and anticorruption in city politics.

The largest number of immigrants from Eastern Europe were Jews. Though anti-Semitism was not a major thread in the fabric of the xenophobia of the late nineteenth century, it existed in high and low places. Henry Adams, descendant of two American Presidents, believed that American society had changed—a love of money had been substituted for a love of country. For Adams, *Jewish* became a pejorative adjective; it was synonymous with greed and materialism.[6] Not all patricians were anti-Semitic. Some retained their disdain for the Irish. John Hay, Lincoln's former private secretary, though he was a personal friend of Henry Adams, detested the Irish and the Italians, but he was clearly not anti-Semitic.[7]

Even the working classes engaged in anti-Semitic outbursts. Jew-baiting was a common characteristic of life in the urban slums of the 1890s.[8] This religious xenophobia was also noted by foreign travelers to America in this period: the old signs "No Irish Need Apply" had been replaced by "No Jews Allowed."[9] This hostility to the Jews was initially social as we have seen earlier. Now it began to take on economic overtones.

Two major groups were concerned over economic grievances—the Knights of Labor and the Populists. Were they anti-Semitic? In 1891, the Knights of Labor clearly disassociated itself from the anti-Semitic attitudes of some of its members.[10] In its official publication, its only editorial on the subject (1891) during the years 1880–1900 condemned anti-Semitism.[11] Moreover, it did endorse, in 1892, a proposal to restrict immigration in order to lessen job competition.

On the other hand, the free-silverites—Greenbackers, Greenback Labor—who merged with the Populist party, indulged in a more prolific outburst of anti-Semitic statements. Though individual Populists did give vent to anti-Semitic statements, most historians accept the idea that anti-Semitism was not part of the official Populist ideology.[12]

Of course, even the Populists' national leadership tried to rid itself of the label *anti-Semitic.* William Jennings Bryan in a widely quoted remark during the 1896 campaign insisted, "We are not attacking a race; we are attacking greed, and avarice which knows no race or religion."[13]

What was the point made by the Populists in their anti-Semitic utterances? In a series of publications, reinforced by a number of speeches, the charge was made that Wall Street Jews, symbolized by Baron Rothschild, and the English had subverted the American free coinage of silver by the "Crime of '73" which demonetized silver.[14] Another Populist also referred to the Jew as a Shylock.

The term *Shylock* was also used by other authors in their attacks upon the Jewish bankers and their financial allies.[15] Jewish bankers were subjected to constant criticism by other free-silverites. When Mary E. Hobart wrote *The Secret of the Rothschilds,* she did not preach a hatred of Jews. She did reinforce, however, the stereotypes of the Jews as monied men.

The wisdom of the ancients seems always to have been the inheritance of the Jews," she wrote, "and while they have no country and are scattered among many nationalities, where often they are not permitted to own land, yet so well do they understand the power of money when loaned that we seldom ever see a Jew who is either a tramp or a pauper. Acting upon this ancient knowledge, the House of Rothschild, with a few co-religionists, conspire to own the world.[16]

Other Populist authors picked up the theme of the Roth-schild conspiracy. One author contended that there was a world alliance between the wise men of the Hebrew race and the aristocracy of the gentiles in opposition to the masses of the people. He called this the Rothschild–Great Britain Alliance.[17] This author denied that he was an anti-Semite: "The writer is not a Jew baiter by any means, but he is a lover of Gentiles, and all mankind, and would seek to have the mask of inferiority removed from the Gentiles."[18]

These protestations were part of the Populist line. Ignatius Donnelly, running on the Populist ticket for governor of Minnesota in 1894, was charged with anti-Semitism when he made a very emotional speech against the Jewish moneylenders. He protested the charge, declaring: "No, No, we would not persecute the Jews.... We are fighting Plutocracy, not because it is Jewish or Christian, but because it is Plutocracy.... We have lots of Christian money sharks in western Minnesota who would drive Shylock to hang himself out of shame."[19] Donnelly's novel, *Caesar's Column* (1889), was also charged as being anti-Semitic because the book accepted the Shylock stereotype.[20] A quarter of a million copies were sold in the United States by the turn of the century.

Other authors also used the Shylock image to denote the Jew and blamed much of the financial distress in the United States on the Rothschilds. William "Coin" Harvey presented these themes in two books. In *Coin's Financial School,* he analysed the Panic of 1893 and offered a solution. He insisted that the repeal of the Sherman Silver Purchase Act was responsible for the crash. His prose and logic were effective; his academic theory became a kind of patent medicine for many free-silverites.[21] The book became a best seller. In a novel, *Tale of Two Nations,* Harvey depicts the story of how Baron Rothe (i.e., Rothschild) secured the passage of the "Crime of '73'" and the corruption of Congress by money supplied by Rothe.[22]

In the election of 1896, a number of anti-Semitic statements were made, most notably by a German Jew-baiter, Dr. Herman Ahlwardt, who had been preaching anti-Semitism before the Bryan campaign. Ahlwardt joined the free-silverites. He proclaimed: "By restoring silver, the Nation will put a stop to the present system of robbery by the Shylocks who own and control the output of gold. The Jews have made McKinley their tool."[23]

Another Bryan campaigner, Mary E. Lease, of "raise more hell and less corn" fame addressed an election meeting in Cooper Union Hall in New York on August 10. The redhead from Kansas stirred her audience for two hours with her tirade against England and foreigners. She saved her major salvos for the Rothschilds and the Jews: "Redemption money and interest bearing bonds are the curse of civilization. We are paying tribute to the Rothschilds of England, who are but agents of the Jews. With free coinage of silver, the price will rise to $1.29 an ounce here and in England."[24]

None of the Populists advocated any hostile legislation aimed at the Jews. Nevertheless, it is safe to say that the use of the Shylock stereotype in the Populist literature and rhetoric did nothing to facilitate the acceptance of Jewish immigrants. By the turn of the twentieth century, Jews were seen in one of two ways: as part of a prosperous international banker conspiracy and, ironically, as competitors for work and housing in the urban slums.[25]

Perhaps the best explanation for this phenomenon appeared in the *Reform Advocate,* a Jewish organ published in English.

Most of us lapse into a lamenting mood [the editorial declared], which soon changes to one of protest against and complaint at the injustice of things. Either individual rascality or organized wickedness is held to account for the perversion of the national state. None is our superior, yet the neighbor has risen above us! He has wealth, fame—we lack these distinctions. He must have passed us on the road because he was in league with the powers of sin or was one of the band of wicked conspirators. Semitism is spun on this loop.[26]

Certainly the Populists fostered the Jewish stereotype. Formal organized anti-Semitism, however, would not arise until the Ku Klux Klan movement. Still the Immigration Act of 1891 had certain exclusionary features that seemed to be aimed at Jewish immigrants.

The Baron de Hirsch fund in Europe had been financing the emigration of Jews from Europe.[27] This act restricted that activity by preventing the admission of immigrants where passage had been paid by an overseas group. Then, too, the enforcement of the measure seemed to be aimed at Russian Jews in particular.[28] Others aimed shafts at the Baron de Hirsch fund. One Protestant journalist charged in 1892 that many of the Russian Jews aided by the fund would enrich themselves by the exploitation of others in this country.[29] He called for their restriction.

Within the immigration restriction movement, efforts were made to limit the influx of Jews. But the attacks could never be labeled anti-Semitic; they were couched in arguments applied to most of the "new" immigrants. Soon a new xenophobic organization, the elitist Immigration Restriction League would create additional stereotypes: Poles, Italians, and other Eastern and Southern Europeans.

Opposition to immigrants because of their supposed racial inferiority preceded the formation of the Immigration Restriction League. The Know-Nothings of the 1850s had ridiculed the Poles for their "odd appearance, gestures, costumes and manners."[30] This hostility to the Poles persisted. One commentator noted in 1886 the propensity of the Poles for violence even in church. "In any Polish church congregation," he wrote, "a free fight, or a riot with bludgeons and firearms, may be expected at any moment.... If the spiritual teachers of these people are to be judged by the fruits of their teaching, they have little reason to boast."[31] The image of the Poles and other Slavic people placed a good deal of emphasis on their unruliness. They were socialists and anarchists.[32] One contemporary blamed them for much of the labor conflict, political corruption, vice, and crime in America.[33] The Poles and the Slavs were lumped together with Southern and Eastern Europeans; they were all considered racially inferior and nonassimilable.[34]

But if there were no specific stereotypes for the Poles and the Slavs, the Italians throughout the nineteenth century suggested violence in the minds of the nativists. Not only were their language and customs different, but they brought with them the idea of the Mafia and the vendetta.[35] In 1890, this idea was exemplified in the New Orleans Italian community. Two factions of Italian dockworkers were struggling for control of the piers. Trying to stem the warfare between these two groups, the superintendent of police, David Hennessy, was murdered by a gang of six men. Before he died, Hennessy is supposed to have reported, the "Dagoes did it." The result was a hysterical mass arrest of Italians. Finally, nine were selected to stand trial. But much to the chagrin of the authorities, six were acquitted and three were given a mistrial.[36]

As a result, an angry mob, convinced by the local press that the jury had been bribed, marched on the jail and slaughtered the nine. Congressman Henry Cabot Lodge, already a restrictionist, wrote that this incident was proof of the Italian danger. He provided a lurid picture of the unassimilable "Dagoes." They drank to excess, they lived in filth, and at the slightest provocation, they went for the stiletto. The remedy was simple: keep them out![37]

The lynchings were not condoned, except in the South, but many Americans felt that New Orleans represented a lesson that the Italian criminals would understand. It reinforced the popular belief that some form of restriction was in order. The New England Brahmin, Prescott Hall, was convinced that the Italian government was dumping its criminal element on the United States.[38]

Mob violence against Italians broke out periodically: in 1890, a group of miners in Colorado lynched an Italian. In Louisiana, in 1899, five Italian storekeepers were lynched. These attacks on Italians continued into the twentieth century.[39]

The economic nature of much of the hostility directed against the Italians is apparent. Native workers and older immigrants became convinced that their employers were using the Italians and other Southern and Eastern European immigrants to beat down wages.[40] There were often clashes along ethnic lines over jobs. For example, one coal miner in the Midwest declared, "I tell ye, sir, the Italians and Hungarians is spoil'n' this yere country fur white men; n'I do'n see no prospect for

hits be'n' better till they get shoved out uv't."[41] Working-class
Americans thus came to accept the racial inferiority of the
Italians and the other Southern and Eastern Europeans.
However, the racial argument was not proposed by working-
class Americans. It was a product of the upper-class intellectuals, the press, and business elites. American historians writing
at this time viewed the immigrant impact on America nega-
tively. While the Germans and the Scandinavians—essentially
Protestant and rural—came off not too badly, the Irish and
the Southern and Eastern Europeans—essentially non-
Protestant and urban—were treated harshly by the historians.[42]

Even before the 1890s, however, the Italians were held in
low esteem in the United States. As early as 1835, the diarist
Philip Hone noted that as bad as the Irish were the Italians
were even worse, a sentiment that was echoed in the 1890s.
One Protestant editor commented, "An Irish Catholic is prefer-
able to an Italian Catholic, an Irish shillalah to an Italian
knife."[43]

Other social scientists also emphasized the reputed racial
inferiority of the Italians and other immigrants of Southern
and Eastern Europe. The sociologist, Professor Franklin Henry
Giddings of Columbia University, wrote that only Northern
and Western Europeans were possessed of that intangible
something that provided these "races" with Nordic supremacy.[44] He also believed that ethnic rivalries were instinctive,
much as the modern-day ethnologists believe that aggression
and territoriality are basic instincts.[45] Perhaps the leading
nativist sociologist was Edward A. Ross.[46]

Even the business communities, while somewhat ambivalent on immigration restriction, did accept the nativist
stereotypes of the Southern and Eastern Europeans. In many
instances, especially in the 1890s, American businessmen
aided and abetted the nativist impulse that was moving toward
a white racism.[47] Generally, it was not unknown for employers
to play off the "wop" against the "hunkie" to preclude either
the unionizing of workers or, in particular instances, to prevent
the laborers from presenting a united front.[48]

In the South, there developed a feeling that somehow the
darker skins of some Southern and Eastern Europeans were

a sign of Negroid blood. Some Southern authors blended a form of white racism with some form of immigration restriction. They opposed the idea of America as an asylum for the oppressed. "Our institutions," one nativist insisted, "have cost too much and are too valuable to be vandalized thus."[49] In discussing the race problem in 1890, Wade Hampton, Confederate hero and former governor of South Carolina, also lumped together Negro suffrage with citizenship and suffrage for "the Anarchist, the Communist, the Nihilist, and all the other scum of European nations."[50] But, even more extreme was one Southerner's radical solution to the question: not only exclude aliens, but expel all alien races from the country.[51] But as already noted, the Southern economic leadership favored immigration to the South in the 1880s and 1890s. Still, these ideas would provide the basis for the reemergence of the Ku Klux Klan in the twentieth century.

While many of the leading American magazines did try to provide a balanced coverage of the Italian immigrants in particular, and Southern and Eastern Europeans in general, the bias was distinctly against the newer immigrants.[52]

Even the Irish-dominated Catholic church in America at times accepted the stereotype of the Italian and the other newer immigrants. Though both the Italians and the Poles were predominantly Roman Catholic, some churchmen often proved to be as insensitive to the needs of these Christians as their more nativistic neighbors.[53] While much of this castigation of the racial inferiority of the Southern and Eastern European immigrants continued, there were groups organized to help speed the assimilation of the immigrants through programs for Americanization. This process involved more than the naturalization of the foreign-born through education; it also included the imposition of American ideals and standards upon these newer immigrants.[54] Some of the hereditary and patriotic societies became interested in the early 1890s in educating the immigrant to play a constructive role in American society.[55] Very often this teaching led to some critical evaluations of the immigrants.

Other groups, such as the American Institute of Civics (1886), for example, tried to reform governments and end corruption through an emphasis on unselfishness in government.[56] Generally, what seemed to happen here was again a kind of racist assumption that Anglo-Saxon, middle-class Protestants—usually Yankees and Scandinavians—were motivated by the public interest, while the lower-class immigrant culture, i.e., Polish, Italian, and Irish Catholics placed their own personal gain first.[57] The aim of the Institute of Civics was to establish clubs throughout the country based on this idea of high ideals in citizenship and government.

In New York City in 1891, the Patria Club was one such group that was established under the aegis of the Institute. It drew its membership from the upper-class business elite.[58] Most of the organizers were also members of the hereditary societies.[59]

But whatever the stated aims of the club, the subject matter always seemed to be the problem of immigration. Former Republican congressman from Utica, New York, Ellis H. Roberts, assistant treasurer of the United States, addressed the group in the spring of 1892 on the "Perils to the Republic."[60] The major menace was not so much the number of foreigners flooding America's shores, as it was the "character of those who came to the country. Disease, ignorance, pauperism and crime were foes of the Republic and laws to keep them out were more necessary than forts and ships against hostile invasions."[61] This theme was hammered home time and time again at the club meetings.[62]

How would the Patria Club bring about changes? It attempted to instill patriotic feelings in the young by erecting statues to great men of America's past who had performed great deeds. It also advocated the teaching of patriotism; it published a manual for use by teachers in inculcating patriotism in the young.[63]

At about the same time that the Patria Club in New York and the Massachusetts Society for Promoting Good Citizenship were operating with many other such groups from under the umbrella of the American Institute of Civics, there emerged a group of Boston Brahmins who became convinced of the need for a more direct assault upon free, unrestricted immigration. They established, in 1894, the Immigration Restriction League.

It is obvious that the Immigration Restriction League did not create the climate which led religious leaders, the press, labor, and business to question the worthiness of the so-called newer immigrants. But for almost three decades it remained a potent pressure group that persisted in advocating the necessity of restricting the numbers and kinds of immigrants who came to America. These men questioned whether immigration was beneficial; whether the new immigrants were assimilable; whether any efforts should be made to facilitate their assimilation.[64]

General Francis A. Walker, president of the Massachusetts Institute of Technology and former superintendent of the Census of 1870, provided the premise for the league's work: he crystallized the difference between the old and the new immigrants.[65] In 1891, Walker warned that the immigrants were changing the character of America's population stock. Native Americans were reducing their birthrate, while the newer immigrants increased theirs. The result was the decline of the Anglo-Saxons in America. Why did the Anglo-Saxon Americans have fewer children? Was it a case of the survival of the fittest? No, said Walker. He declared that the increased immigration brought about a decline in wages. Rather than reduce their standard of living, the Americans reduced the size of their families.[66]

Walker and others, including Richmond Mayo-Smith, Professor of Political Economy at Columbia University, agreed that the United States could no longer accept the disparate people who flooded our shores in the 1890s in ever-increasing numbers.[67] These restrictionists denied that they were bigots. Their arguments were presented with an impressive array of statistics and a lengthy catalog of evils that had befallen America: strikes, crime, corruption, and poverty among the most prevalent. They placed the blame on the immigrants.

This fear that the character of America was changing made it appear that the social health of the community was in danger.[68] To end this threat, a group of New England Brahmins organized the Immigration Restriction League, with two young Harvard University graduates dominating the group: Prescott Hall and Robert DeCourcy Ward.[69] Prescott Hall had been graduated from Harvard in 1889 and three years later from the Harvard Law school. At the age of twenty-six, he was deeply concerned about the threat posed by the immigrant. Robert DeCourcy Ward had also received a Harvard degree, in 1888, and had spent a couple of years in graduate science studies. He was older than Hall. Both men came from the first families of New England.

The arguments of Walker and Mayo-Smith made a good deal of sense to Hall and Ward. Like their anti-immigrant predecessors, they were concerned with the growing political strength of the foreign-born in urban areas. They also emphasized the differences between the older and newer immigrants. Hall, for example, wrote that "before 1870, immigration was chiefly of races kindred in habits, institutions and traditions to the original colonists."[70] The Germans, he believed, were thrifty and industrious; the Italians, however, did not readily learn English, they were clannish, and they were criminals.[71] Ward concurred in these views.[72]

Initially, the league had intended to become a national organization. By 1895, it had 531 members in 14 states. But rather than continue to expand the organization, Hall, the secretary of the group, and Ward, decided to restrict not only immigration, but also the size of the society.[73] Concentrating their energies on the Boston group, they continued to call on their friends for financial support. In 1901, for example, the league raised $6,000 and hired Charles D. Edgerton, formerly with the United States Industrial Commission, as assistant secretary of the league. He was to be stationed in Washington, D.C., and help gain passage of the literacy-test legislation.[74]

Hall and Ward were not the originators of the idea of the literacy test, but from 1894 to 1917 it was their major device for restricting immigration. Publicly they tried to avoid a negative image; they did not emphasize any hostility to immigrants because of their religious beliefs; they wanted to make the ability to read and write the criterion for admission to the United States. If Hall and Ward had their way, they would have thrown up the gates and halted all immigration from Southern and Eastern Europe. They recognized that this approach was not entirely feasible. It was far better to insist upon the literacy test.

As a pressure group, the league presented its message to the formulators of public opinion. In its first six months, it disseminated almost 40,000 pamphlets and documents. Most of these went to newspapers and legislators.[75] By the opening of the twentieth century, it broadened its efforts. It now contacted the various boards of charity throughout the country as well as the more than 3,000 chambers of commerce in the nation. It strove for their support for the education test as a means of reducing the numbers of immigrants likely to become paupers.[76] By 1900, over 150,000 pamphlets had been distributed.[77]

The league came close to success within the first year of its establishment. In 1895, the United States Senator from Massachusetts, Henry Cabot Lodge, introduced into the Senate the literacy-test proposal.[78] The bill was aimed at excluding "undesirable" immigrants from Southern and Eastern Europe—Poles, Italians, Greeks, and the various Slavic groups —who, it was thought, were illiterate and thus would be excluded. The measure would not interfere with immigration from Northern and Western Europe, where such illiteracy was rare. Because of the fear generated by the still powerful American Protective Association, the measure had a good deal of support and very little vocal opposition. Also there was much support for a somewhat similar measure introduced into the House of Representatives by another Boston Republican, Samuel McCall. The McCall literacy act was passed by the House of Representatives in May by the lopsided margin of 195 to 26.

The Senate, however, was more deliberative. It delayed action until after the November presidential election. Then the Senate duplicated the lopsided House margin, 52 to 10.[79] A conference committee met in December to iron out the differences in the two measures. The league's work, it seemed, would soon be over.

The conference committee, however, released a bill with anti-Semitic overtones. Whereas the original bills had called for exclusion of those who could not read or write English or some other language, the conference bill stipulated that it would deny admission to those immigrants who could not read or write English or the language of their native or resident country. This measure appeared to be aimed at the Yiddish-speaking Jews. Prescott Hall and Robert DeCourcy Ward wanted to admit only those who could read and write English.[80] The bill caused a furor.[81] It was eventually submitted to a second conference committee report and the "some other language" phrase was reinserted in the measure. It then passed both houses of Congress and was sent to the lame-duck president Grover Cleveland for his signature.

President Cleveland provided the first of the four presidential vetoes of the measure over the next twenty years. In the course of his lengthy comments on his motives for the veto, the president pointedly remarked that "if any particular element of our illiterate immigration is to be feared for other causes, they should be dealt with directly, instead of making illiteracy a pretext for exclusion."[82] Cleveland retained the old democratic faith that the illiterate immigrants would be assimilated and become good Americans.[83]

Undaunted, the Immigration Restriction League and Senator Lodge prepared for the next congressional session when the Democrat Cleveland would be replaced by the Republican McKinley, who had run on a platform of some immigration restriction. But the decline of the APA, the foreign-born voters' support of the Republicans in 1896, and the improvement of economic conditions, coupled with organized opposition, especially among the Germans, spelled difficult days ahead for the literacy test.[84] These factors help explain not only the failure of Congress to override the veto, but also some of the league's future difficulties.

Despite the Immigration Restriction League's assurances, opposition to the Lodge-McCall bill now became widespread among the immigrant groups from Northern and Western Europe.[85] These groups came to believe that the education test was the first step toward a more drastic move against all immigration. The Jews, too, for the most part, gave up their ambivalent feelings and became firm opponents of the literacy test.[86]

Thus while both Lodge and the Immigration Restriction League felt certain that the McKinley years would witness the success of their efforts to impose a literacy test on immigrants, their efforts were frustrated. In both the Fifty-fifth and Fifty-sixth Congresses, Lodge's bill won some support, but not enough to gain enactment.[87] The Immigration Restriction League publicly explained these legislative failures by placing the blame on the Spanish-American War. The war distracted these two congresses from other domestic legislation.[88]

The league did believe that it had one outstanding success in the 1890s: it lobbied successfully for an endorsement of the Lodge bill at the American Federation of Labor convention at Nashville in December, 1897. The measure was carried by a vote of 1,858 to 352.[89]

The league also pushed its pet program vigorously before the Federal Industrial Commission, which was studying the impact of urbanization and industrialization on American life.[90] But much more important to the restrictionists was President McKinley's assassination in 1901 by the anarchist Leon Czolgosz, who, though native-born, was still considered a foreigner. This unfortunate event brought a new president, Theodore Roosevelt, who was more sympathetic to immigration restriction and gave rise to a new wave of antialien and antiradical feelings among native Americans.[91]

But though the league lobbied strenuously, it was unable to get the literacy test accepted as part of the Immigration Act of 1903. This act was aimed at the radicals: it excluded anarchists from entrance to the country, doubled the head tax on immigrants, and extended to three years the period during which an immigrant could be deported if he was found to be an anarchist. Yet, though the literacy test had been included in the House of Representatives version and was being supported by Southerners and Westerners, the Senate rejected this amendment because it felt the literacy test would jeopardize the whole measure, including the antianarchist provisions.[92] The bill, without the literacy test, was approved by both houses of Congress and signed by the president on March 3, 1903.

What was now apparent was that though the league had as president of the United States a man who would support a literacy test, the opposition to it had grown among many of the older as well as the newer immigrant organizations,

so much so that President Roosevelt never did get the opportunity to sign the literacy test into law.[93] Then, too, the Immigration Act of 1903 was the first serious effort to restrict immigrants because of their beliefs and associations.[94] Both major
political parties strove for the votes of naturalized citizens.
Besides, important elements in the business community continued to press for an open-door immigration policy.

Still, if the league's efforts on behalf of the literacy test
were not immediately successful, there were some changes
in personnel in the immigration service that did meet with
the support of the league. In 1902, the appointment of William
Williams, a staunch old-line New Englander, as commissioner
of immigration at the port of New York augured well for restriction. Williams was firmly opposed to an open-door policy; he
favored a radical restrictionist policy whereby no immigrants
would be admitted unless they would be of immediate benefit
to the United States.[95] Prescott Hall, on behalf of the league,
commended Williams for his strict enforcement of the public-
charge section of the Immigration Act of 1891.[96]

Not only was Williams a restrictionist, but the head of the
service, Frank P. Sargent, the commissioner general of immigration, was another. However, while Williams was almost
a complete restrictionist, Sargent welcomed the "older" immigrants, but wanted to bar the "newer" immigrants, from Southern and Eastern Europe.[97]

The restrictionist movement did not die with the failure
of 1902–1903. Prescott Hall and Robert DeCourcy Ward continued their endeavors. They believed—sincerely believed
—that in order to save the future of the nation, the number
of newer immigrants must be reduced. In 1905, Ward, for
example, spoke before groups of social workers who had
become interested in immigration restriction.[98] Still, many
social workers—notably Jane Addams and Grace Abbott—were
more concerned with aiding the integration of the immigrants
into American society.[99]

But addressing social workers was not the major function
of the league. It continued to press for congressional action.
In 1906, another determined effort to gain the literacy test
was mounted by Senator Lodge and his son-in-law, Con-

gressman Augustus P. Gardiner of Massachusetts. In 1906 Senator William Dillingham had introduced an immigration bill to raise the head tax from two to five dollars, to add to the excluded classes those of poor physique; to establish a Division of Information in the Immigration Service in order to help immigrants locate jobs in less densely settled areas of the country, and to set up a commission to study the impact of immigration on the nation. To this measure, Senator Lodge appended an amendment embodying the literacy test. These provisions were approved by the Senate.[100]

In the House, Representative Gardiner took up the cudgels on behalf of the literacy test. Sentiment for it was strong. Its defeat could be ascribed to one man, the Speaker of the House, "Uncle" Joe Cannon.[101] The result of that opposition was a House version of Gardiner's bill that excluded the literacy test and also returned the head tax to its original two-dollar level. It passed in June, 1906.

Lodge and his colleagues in the Senate remained adamant, however. They insisted on the literacy test. Cannon, for his part, was equally firm. After eight months, President Roosevelt intervened. He requested Lodge to give way on the literacy test since the president was interested in having the legislation restrict the Japanese from coming to the States via Hawaii. Lodge agreed.[102]

The bill that Roosevelt signed into law on February 20, 1907, called for no literacy test, but for prohibition of Japanese immigration from Hawaii, a doubling of the head tax to four dollars, the establishment of the Division of Information and the organization of a commission—the Dillingham Commission—to investigate the problem of immigration.[103]

The league and its secretary, Prescott Hall, were disappointed by the Immigration Act of 1907. The failure of the literacy test and the establishment of the Division of Information were considered setbacks.[104]

However, the establishment of the Dillingham Commission, with a definite prorestriction membership, gave the league another chance.[105] The league was glad to supply approximate data to the commission. Its arguments now began to stress the eugenics aspects of immigration.[106] Both Hall and Ward had become active members of the American Breeders Association and there emphasized the need to utilize science not only in the breeding of animals, but also to preserve the American race.[107] The way to retain the racial purity of the Americans, according to Hall and Ward, was to limit the influx of peoples endowed with inferior "blood."

In January, 1911, after three years of compiling information, the Dillingham Commission released its findings. The majority report endorsed the literacy test as the best way to restrict undesirable immigration.[108] It emphasized the need to restrict immigration as a form of protection for the American workingman.[109] The report could have been written by Hall or Ward. The commission *Reports* were supported by American Labor, and its foreign-born president, Samuel Gompers.[110] As a matter of fact, the *Reports,* which were the result of more than three years of work and one million dollars in expenditures, were accepted by most Americans as a fair analysis of the immigration issue.[111]

Now the congressional restrictionists moved to put into law the recommendations of the commission. In 1911–1912, both the House and Senate discussed two literacy-test bills, the Burnett and Dillingham bills. Both measures passed their respective houses in 1912. The Conference Committee reconciled the differences in the two measures and the Dillingham-Burnett bill was speedily passed by both Houses in January and February, 1913.

President William Howard Taft, however, vetoed the bill. He refused to accept the literacy test, since it violated the traditional open-door policy of America.[112] But, though the Senate overrode the veto, the House narrowly sustained it.[113] Once again, the league and the literacy test were rejected. Still, the vote was very close. The Immigration Restriction League had almost succeeded in having its cherished idea legislated into law. It would try again.

The election of 1912 saw all political parties striving to sway the immigrant voters to support their candidates. Even Woodrow Wilson, who as a scholar, had written disparagingly about the immigrants, shifted his viewpoint as a politician.[114]

Yet, Hall and Ward persisted. Their cause was reinforced

by the recession, 1913–1914, the outbreak of World War I, and the interest of the hyphenated Americans in winning support for their homelands. These efforts conflicted with the supposedly neutral stance of the government. More and more citizens began to question the wisdom of permitting the large influx of immigrants to continue.

This climate gave the league and its twin pillars, Hall and Ward, hope that restriction of immigration would be achieved. Thus the movement for the imposition of a literacy test persisted.[115]

The war, and the fear that hyphenated Americans might be disloyal, brought success to the league's efforts in 1915. The literacy-test bill was passed. But once again Wilson vetoed it. He emphasized the American tradition of asylum and the fact that the literacy test would violate that principle. Then, too, his campaign promises of 1912 were quite clear: he opposed restriction.[116] The veto was again upheld, but again only by a slender margin in the House of Representatives.[117]

The restrictionists both in the league and in Congress were spurred on by the loyalty issue of the hyphenated Americans and the increased emphasis on American nationalism during the course of World War I. Restriction and self-protection from foreigners and the war became synonymous in the minds of many Americans. Thus the process of Americanization with its emphasis on "one hundred percent Americanism" and restriction walked hand in hand in some quarters. The goal was Americanization of the aliens already here and restriction against any additional arrivals.[118]

Throughout the congressional session of 1916, the literacy-test bill was again discussed and again passed. The major argument offered on its behalf was the need to limit the number of immigrants who would flee from war-ravaged Europe after the end of World War I. Once more it was subjected to a Wilson veto. This time, though, the House and Senate overrode the veto on February 1, 1917.[119]

The Immigration Restriction League, after twenty years of struggle, had finally witnessed the passage of the literacy test. A large segment of the American people had expressed their view, through their legal representatives, that restriction was necessary. But the literacy test proved of no great value in reducing the flow of immigrants.[120]

The Immigration Restriction League's success in effect brought restriction to its high point. During its fight for the literacy test, the league had benefited from Anglo-Saxonism, anti-Catholicism, anti-Semitism and antiradicalism. But the success of its restrictionist efforts did not end xenophobia in America. The apparent limited value of the literacy test as a barrier to immigration led to renewed demands for further restrictions. Anti-Catholic, anti-Semitic and antiradical outbursts culminated in yet another xenophobic secret society, the Ku Klux Klan.

CHAPTER IX

The Ku Klux Klan

THE LITERACY TEST DID NOT TERMINATE LARGE SCALE immigration. The war, however, drastically curtailed the inflow of foreigners, so that many in the Immigration Restriction League considered their work successful. Yet with the return of peace there was a fear of an upsurge in immigration that would rival that of the prewar years. Thus, Prescott Hall and the league continued to lobby for the restriction of the "racially unfit."[1]

Those who had insisted on the idea of Americanizing the immigrant via a campaign of one hundred percent Americanism were also aware of their failure. Instead of speeding assimilation, this program, before, during, and after the war, appeared to increase the ethnic awareness of the immigrants and their children.[2] Thus the supporters of the American crusade, many of them Progressives, came to doubt the immigrants' capacity to assimilate.

The Progressives' attitude toward the immigrant was ambivalent. Edward A. Ross, as we have seen, was hostile to the newer immigrant groups; he accepted the notion of their racial inferiority. Others, notably social workers like Grace Abbott of the Immigrant Protective League, believed that immigrants had a positive contribution to make.[3] But despite the success of Israel Zangwill's play, *The Melting Pot* (1908), it became more and more apparent that the Progressive reformers were coming to a point of agreement with the restrictionists that there was a need to limit immigration.

Aiding this movement was the changing attitude of the South which came to regard immigrants in the same racial light as blacks—they were inferior.[4] By 1905, the Southern congressional delegations had moved solidly in support of all the restrictionist efforts. They and the Western congressional delegations remained the firm advocates of restriction until the quota legislation of the 1920s was passed.[5] These congressmen represented, by and large, the viewpoints of their constituents who continued to feel that immigrants were Catholics, Jews, or radicals, or combinations of these undesirables. Anti-Catholicism did not die with the APA. Anti-Semitism and antiradicalism were also very much alive in the first two decades of the twentieth century.

A number of factors clearly revealed anti-Catholic hostility. When President Theodore Roosevelt received delegations of Roman Catholic clerics at the White House, an almost certain chorus of criticism followed—usually from Protestant sources.[6] One of his critics was the former Army chief of staff (1895), General Nelson Appleton Miles. Miles had won the Congressional Medal of Honor for his services in the Civil War, where he had been wounded four times. He was reprimanded by President Roosevelt in 1902 for his remarks during a naval court-martial proceeding. This led to his retirement the following year.[7]

Miles's anti-Catholicism and anti-immigrant views led him into a number of patriotic societies. In 1911, he helped organize the secret society, the Guardians of Liberty. Like its Know-Nothing predecessor, it was opposed to Catholics and immigrants as candidates for political office, since, it was argued, they would either take their orders from Rome, if Catholic, or ignore the best interests of the country, if foreign-born. The organization, supported by other former military leaders, remained a genteel group; it never had the political clout of the earlier Know-Nothings. The Guardians had their greatest strength in the rural counties of upstate New York.

However, there did appear in the same year as the Guardians an anti-Catholic propaganda organ, the *Menace*, which reached a circulation of over one and a half million in 1914–1915.[8] This publication found its greatest support among rural readers. The efforts of the Catholic church to remove the *Menace*'s mailing privileges on the grounds of obscenity—the alleged immorality of the Catholic Church was graphically portrayed—were not sustained by the courts.[9]

Other anti-Catholic periodicals were also maintaining a steady stream of anti-Catholic propaganda, but without the success of the *Menace.* Tom Watson, the frustrated Georgia Populist Leader—the Populist presidential candidate in 1904 and 1908—was one of the leading anti-Catholic editor-publishers of the period. His *Tom Watson's Magazine* had been in existence before the *Menace,* but by the time the latter appeared, Watson's publication was no longer a national organ of great vitality. It provided a steady diet of anti-Catholic propaganda, however, with an emphasis on the Catholic immigrant conspiracy idea first presented by Samuel F. B. Morse in the 1830s, and subsequently developed by the APA in its forged orders from Pope Leo XIII.[10] By 1914, there were sixty-one anti-Catholic papers in America. Three years later, all but two or three had disappeared.[11]

Unlike the earlier anti-Catholics these antipapal crusaders enjoyed their greatest successes in the rural areas. The census of 1920 made factual what most Americans had sensed by mid-decade, that the rural-agrarian nature of America had given way to a new urban-industrial life-style. Many rural Protestants were completely unhappy with the transformation. The alleged power of the Jews in America, clearly enunciated by some of the Populists, also reappeared in the prewar and postwar years. Tom Watson and Henry Ford were among those involved in this rural-oriented movement.

Watson was not only an outstanding anti-Catholic propagandist, he also became known as an outstanding anti-Semite. His notoriety was a result of his reactions to the Leo Frank case.[12] Frank was a wealthy Georgian Jew accused of murdering Mary Phagen, a fourteen-year-old girl. Emotions were stirred. Most members of the community were incensed at the murder. There were anti-Semitic mutterings when Frank was arrested. He was convicted, but his sentence was commuted.

Watson saw this commutation as part of a gigantic conspiracy. His reaction was an emotional anti-Semitic outburst. He reminded his readers of the value of vigilantes and lynch law when justice seemed to have been subverted. When Frank was taken out and hanged August 16, 1915, Watson applauded the action.[13] Once started on this anti-Semitic theme, Watson persisted in his attacks upon the Jews. What was clearly evident in his writings was a blurring of the distinction between native-born Catholics and Jews and their foreign-born coreligionists.

Henry Ford, a folk hero of rural America, was a symbol of the Horatio Alger myth, a self-made man. The family-owned business had no Wall Street ties. He condemned bankers, intellectuals, Catholics, and Jews, groups already unpopular in rural areas.[14] He became a popular foe of finance capital and its alleged concomitant, "international Jewry."

His magazine, the *Dearborn Independent* had an average yearly readership of close to half a million in the 1920s. Its main staple between 1920 and 1922 and in 1924 was a virulent anti-Semitism. Although he was a supporter of the one hundred percent Americanism campaign during World War I, Ford had generally been considered an enlightened, liberal supporter of Wilsonian idealism. But his emphasis shifted in 1920. Where formerly he condemned the witch-hunts that sought out Bolsheviks, now his *Dearborn Independent* began to equate Jews with Bolsheviks. What triggered this dramatic shift? Probably his financial troubles and his disillusionment with the postwar world acted and interacted to produce this traumatic change.

Ford was hard hit economically by the postwar slump in 1920. Despite his hostility to bankers, he had been forced to borrow $75,000,000 in 1919 in order to take complete control of the business from his partners. Ford was not happy about this loan. He came to see all bankers as the dominant influence in America's business. These bankers, he believed, were part of the Jewish international conspiracy, a plot propagandized by the Populists a generation earlier. As his business declined—car sales fell precipitously—his optimistic forecasts for the future also soured.[15]

He was particularly disillusioned with the postwar world. Why had his efforts on behalf of peace failed? Why had America failed in its international peace efforts? Why had the League of Nations failed to win approval? Ford's answer was simplistic: the Jewish conspiracy was behind it all.

While John Foster Fraser's *The Conquering Jew* (1916) may

have been the first openly anti-Semitic book in America, Ford certainly became the most consistent and most famous anti-Semite for a two-year period, 1920–22. The columns of the *Dearborn Independent* were transformed subsequently into pamphlets with titles such as *The International Jew, Jewish Influences in American Life,* and *Aspects of Jewish Power in the United States.*

Ford also gave wide-scale publicity to the forgeries "The Protocols of the Elders of Zion," which came to the United States in 1918.[16] These Protocols had initially been an attack on Napoleon III. The Protocols declared that there was an international Jewish conspiracy. In fact, they asserted that there continued to be a secret government in Israel, which had been there since the year 2,000 B.C. Although the Protocols were proved to be forgeries in August, 1921, Ford persisted in using them in the *Independent.*

Because some Jews were leaders of the Bolshevik Revolution, Ford began to equate the two. Then when some Jews became involved in the Communist putsches in Germany and Hungary in the 1920s, Ford became convinced that anti-Semitism and antiradicalism were synonymous terms.

Ford's activities did win some support. He was considered a leading candidate for the presidency of the United States, in 1923 and 1924. William Randolph Hearst, for example, endorsed his candidacy. Certainly Ford's greatest support came from the rural areas of the South and the West, the same regions in which Watson's anti-Catholic and anti-Semitic crusades found their greatest appeal.

Still, not one major politician endorsed the Watson-Ford harangues. Nor did any appreciable support come from members of the Immigration Restriction League or various patriotic societies which were now clamoring for some form of immigrant restriction.[17] Still Watson's and Ford's anti-Catholicism and anti-Semitism did reinforce the Anglo-Saxon racial argument first introduced nationally by the Reverend Josiah Strong in *Our Country.* This racial argument would also win support as a result of World War I, and the antiradicalism campaign that merged into an antialien campaign.

While many Americans quietly acquiesced into Ford's campaign, their support for antiradicalism became quite vocal. The Ku Klux Klan, under the guise of reform, benefited from all the major antialien, pro-Nordic racial arguments. But they would also condemn immigrants as Catholics, Jews, and radicals. These were their major ingredients; their hostility to blacks was submerged under these older xenophobic manifestations.

The Ku Klux Klan was organized in Atlanta, Georgia, in October, 1915, by the self-styled "Colonel" William J. Simmons, a former preacher and professional organizer of patriotic and fraternal groups. Two factors appear to have turned Simmons's attention to the need for a second Klan. First, the excitement generated by the Leo Frank Case, and secondly, the success of the film, *The Birth of a Nation.*

Tom Watson, in one of his tirades against Frank, had called for a new Ku Klux Klan.[18] *The Birth of a Nation*, a highly fictionalized account of the first Klan, had widespread appeal. Even Woodrow Wilson and some Congressmen applauded the film.[19] The picture, based on the Reverend Thomas Dixon's novel *The Clansman,* saw Reconstruction as an effort to Africanize the ten ex-Confederate states.[20] The Ku Klux Klan was presented as the patriotic group that saved the Southern nation.

Simmons, influenced by these events, and the stories told him by his father, a small-town doctor, millowner, and ex-Klansman, set up the second Ku Klux Klan.

His father's economic failure made it difficult for young Simmons to study medicine. Then he became a clergyman and rode the circuit during the years 1900–1912, delivering lectures on "Women, Weddings, and Wives," "Red Heads, Dead Heads, and No Heads," and "Kinship of Kourtship and Kissing." In 1912, the Alabama Conference of Methodists denied him the use of the pulpit because of his inefficiency and moral turpitude.[21]

Simmons's Klan was a patriotic and fraternal organization which initially stressed one hundred percent Americanism and the supremacy of the white race. The ritual of the secret society was contained in *The Kloran.* The KKK was similar to the Know-Nothings in that there was a hierarchy, though the officers of the national organization were all appointed by the leader, the Imperial Wizard; only the officers of the local units, the klaverns, were elected. The Wizard could not only appoint national officers, but he could remove them. He could also establish local units, or disband them as he saw fit. He could establish new offices if he so desired. The KKK was considered the Invisible Empire. All members took an oath never to betray the secrets of the order. The Imperial Empire was divided into eight domains, a domain consisted of a group of states, and each domain was presided over by a Grand Dragon. Beginning in 1922, there were national conventions of the Klan, called klonvokations. The Klan had paid recruiters, known as kleagles, to facilitate the growth of the organization.

The order, as indicated, required an oath. Only white, native-born Protestants could take the oath. Before initiation, the prospective member paid a fee of ten dollars. He also bought his white hood and robes, to guarantee that his own member-ship in the order would remain hidden.

During America's involvement in World War I, Simmons and the Klan joined in the effort of coercing conformity from the citizens of Georgia and Alabama, where the Klan had some strength. The Klan members, masked and robed in their white garments, intervened in a Mobile shipyard strike in the name of patriotism. It hunted draft dodgers and marched in patriotic parades.[22]

The Klan lent its support to the Immigration Act of 1918. This act was aimed at radical aliens. It provided for the deporta-tion of aliens who belonged to radical groups; in a way it supported the idea of guilt by association. The measure was aimed at the Industrial Workers of the World, the Wobblies, who were suspected of being anti-American because they refused to support the war, and because of their strikes and activities in Seattle.[23]

A number of factors aided the Klan's growth. First, there was the publication of a number of racist books which sup-posedly supported the notion of the racial inferiority of the newer immigrants. Madison Grant's *Passing of the Great Race*, though originally published in 1916, found its largest audience after the end of World War I. It pointed to the dangers posed by Italians and other newer immigrants, who were mongrelizing the American race. Lothrop Stoddard, a disciple of Grant's, was worried over the increase in the population of the colored races of the world. In 1920, he published *The Rising Tide of Color*, which emphasized the danger of these yellow and brown peoples to the Nordic whites. Other authors also utilized this Nordic theory. By far the most widely read was the novelist Kenneth Roberts, who provided a series of articles, 1920–22, for the mass circulation weekly, the *Saturday Evening Post*, on the dangers of the newer immigrants.[24]

The results of the United States's armed forces testing programs for army recruits tended to support the racist assumptions of Grant, Stoddard, and Roberts. These tests seemed to indicate that Southern and Eastern European immigrants were inferior because they scored lower than those from Northern and Western Europe. Italians, Poles, and Negroes were heavily represented at the bottom of the test results. Of course, no weight was given to the differences in backgrounds and education of those taking the test.[25] But it did appear to give scientific support to the Nordic supremacy idea, and the Klan used the test data in its propaganda.[26]

The American feeling of unease was intensified by the outbreak of the influenza epidemic of 1918, which took almost a half a million lives. The blame for this disaster was placed by some on the presence of undesirable immigrants. But of far greater benefit to the Klan recruiters were the apparent failure of the prohibition law enacted in 1919, the outbreak of the Red scare in 1919 and 1920, and the beginning of the exodus of blacks from the South into the Northern cities to take advantage of wartime job opportunities, which exacerbated racial relations. These happenings coupled with the economic recession of 1920, which had helped transform the thinking of Henry Ford, as we have already seen, aided the Klan to become not only a rural Southern phenomenon but a national organization that had strength in both urban and rural centers.

Some Protestant Americans had placed great hope in the Volstead Act to transform the moral character of America. They hoped it would reinvigorate the older American ideals and religion, or at least bring back the older, traditional values. The Volstead Act was too often ignored by both the American people and the law-enforcement agencies. One reason why the Klan was often endorsed by the local Protestant minister was that it provided an action group that would coerce conformity by threatening the police and destroying the stills of the bootleggers.[27]

The movement of black Americans out of the rural areas of the South into the cities of the North and the South, which began in 1915, led to outbreaks of racial violence that provided fertile ground for the subsequent Klan recruiters in these urban areas. In 1917, over forty racial confrontations took place. The most serious were in Saint Louis and Houston. In East Saint Louis, thirty-nine blacks and nine whites were killed in a particularly vicious racial outburst. That same year in Houston, black troops were badgered so constantly that the black soldiers took their weapons and set upon their white tormentors. Twelve whites and at least five blacks were killed.[28]

In 1919 these racial outbursts—the black scare—were linked to the Red scare. The riots of 1917 and 1919 usually involved the black reaction to white-initiated attacks, either physical or verbal.[29]

Nevertheless, the outburst of violence between May and September, 1919, in Charleston; Longview, Texas; Washington, D.C.; Knoxville; Omaha; Chicago; Phillips County, Arkansas; and thirteen other, smaller localities led many whites to connect these black-white conflicts with the Red scare which frightened many Americans.[30] Though whites initiated these outbursts, public reaction was to blame the radicals. Congressman James F. Byrnes of South Carolina inisted that this "Negro subversion" was the result of the radical, Bolshevik propaganda among the blacks.[31] Many Americans agreed with Byrnes. This type of thinking provided fertile ground for the Ku Klux Klan kleagles.

But by far the most obvious manifestation of uneasiness in America was the Red scare of 1919–20 with its antiradicalism and antialienism. America seemed to have lost faith in the ability of democracy to overcome the small groups of radicals in the nation.[32] Why this antiradicalism?

Most Americans had been genuinely alarmed over the supposed success of the Wobblies, especially in the Lawrence strike of 1912. The Wobblies' opposition to World War I intensified this alarm.[33] Then when other radicals, some of the Socialists and the Communists, for example, also opposed the war, the American public clamored for some form of suppression via state and national espionage and sedition acts.[34] By 1920, thirty-five states had some form of antianarchist and antiradical legislation.[35]

The success of the Bolshevik Revolution in Russia magnified these American fears. When the year 1919 witnessed some 3,600 strikes involving over 4,000,000 workers, many Americans were ready to ascribe these strikes to the revolutionary activities of the Bolsheviks and Wobblies.[36] The rash of bombings, and the attempt on the life of the attorney general, A. Mitchell Palmer, led many to believe that a band of revolutionary leaders were out to subvert America. And since the overwhelming majority of these radical leaders—some 90 percent —were foreigners, many Americans felt that the deportation of these aliens would provide the solution to the radical menace.[37]

The Ku Klux Klan and some ambitious politicians—Attorney General A. Mitchell Palmer and General Leonard Wood, for example—made use of this theme of anti-American conspiracy and thus increased the tension.[38] The existing unease culminated in the Palmer raids, an arrest of some ten thousand radicals in January, 1920.[39] The failure of the courts to deport these aliens emphasized to many Americans the need for new immigration laws that would permit the deportation of such people from America. Congress responded to this pressure with the passage of the antianarchist Immigration Act of 1920, which made it a deportable offense to possess radical literature, and to advise people to join radical groups that advocated the violent overthrow of the government. Even a financial contribution to any of these groups could result in deportation.[40] But this legislation came at the end of the Red scare. By then Americans had regained some sense of balance.

The Ku Klux Klan and its activist efforts furnished support against those dissidents. And, of course, the Red scare did increase the demand for some form of immigration restriction. By the end of the war, the idea of America as a haven for the oppressed had been pretty well put to rest. Now the demand was for restriction.

The willingness to restrict not only radical immigrants, but all immigrants, became apparent during the Sixty-sixth Congress. The House of Representatives passed a measure which called for a fourteen-month suspension of immigration.[41] The Senate, however, refused to go along; employers objected because it would reduce their labor supply. It substituted Senator Dillingham's quota idea, that is, a plan to limit the number of immigrants to five percent of the numbers of each foreign-born group in the United States as of the census of 1910. The Senate accepted this plan.[42] The House then went along with the Senate version, though it reduced the percentage from five to three percent.[43] The act was to last one year. In May, 1922, the measure was extended for an additional period of two years.[44]

What was most striking about the debates over this quota bill was the almost universal feeling that some form of restriction was necessary. The Ku Klux Klan did not lead this particular restrictionist movement; rather, they benefited from it.

The Ku Klux Klan not only gained from factors beyond its control, but new leadership, willing and able to take advantage of these postwar economic upheavals and disillusionments promoted the growth of the Klan. In 1920, Simmons turned active control of the Klan over to the Southern Publicity Association. This was the name used by Edward Young Clarke and Mrs. Elizabeth Tyler for their fund-raising activities. They were to receive 80 percent of all future initiation fees; the other 20 percent would go to Simmons.[45] Clarke and Tyler shifted the full emphasis of the organization to one hundred percent Americanism with all its ramifications.

Thus the Klan expanded. Its organizers, recruited from among the Protestant clergy and the other fraternal organizations, especially the Masons, were instructed to offer the Klan as a solution to the various worries hanging over many communities. Their message was that one hundred percent Americans should be concerned about Jews and Catholics, blacks and Orientals, bootlegging and corruption.[46] As a result, the Klan gained over 100,000 members by the middle of 1921. Its membership would increase even more dramatically to over two million by 1925—because of the publicity it received in the New York City press and the congressional hearings on its activities caused by this airing in the press.

In 1921, both the *New York World* and *New York Journal-American* portrayed the internal workings and the violence used by the Klan. The *World* articles indicated that the morality of the Klan was itself suspect. Clarke and Mrs. Tyler, the story went, had been found drunk and disorderly in a house of prostitution in 1919.[47] The charges were weakly explained away. But because of the additional charge of failure to pay income taxes, the House of Representatives agreed to hold hearings to investigate the Klan. The investigation did nothing to damage the Klan. In fact, the publicity increased the prestige of the group.

Who joined the Klan? And why? Originally, the Klan recruiters and members came from native-born American Protestants who could trace their ancestry back several generations in the United States. They were protesting the alien character of the new urbanized and industrialized America. They felt that they had a grievance: they wanted America for Americans.

They were also disgruntled at the increased power of Roman Catholicism, which they believed was made up almost completely of immigrants or descendants of recent immigrant groups.[48] Conservative estimates in the 1920s judged that only 42 percent of the people in the United States were descended through both their parents from the old colonial stock.[49] Klan members believed that every immigrant replaced a son or daughter of native stock.[50]

Thus the Klan found its greatest success in those areas where the largest percentage of the Old American stock lived: the South, Southwest, Oregon, and the Midwest. But as these groups, or at least their children, moved to the growing urban centers, the Klan also made tremendous inroads in the cities.[51] Over half of its membership came from city areas.

The rationale for Klan membership was not too difficult to

understand: the Klan had a positive program as well as a negative outlook. It stood for Protestantism as opposed to the alien creeds of Catholicism and Judaism. The Klan campaigned against moral laxity and in defense of prohibition. And it stood for one hundred percent American patriotism.[52] It would "save America from the invading hordes of alienism."[53] It denounced aliens, liberals, trade unions, and strikes as subversive.[54]

Its main fear was disunity. One Klan leader wrote:

We are seeing in America the workings of this law of disunity through alienism. Our councils are divided, our progress checked, our spirit weakened. . . . We are drifting away from national unity, in fact, we are carefully and deliberately driven away from it by alien ideas. . . . The Klan . . . believes the whole tendency must be stopped and that control of the nation must return, and remain in, the hands of men with the character and spirit of pioneers . . . .[55]

World War I, Klan propagandists insisted, had proven the disloyalty of the hyphenated American.[56]

The Klan did not believe in the assimilation of immigrants. The second Imperial Wizard, Dr. Hiram Wesley Evans, the Dallas dentist, declared, "We Know that the Melting Pot has failed. . . ."[57] This attitude as we noted earlier, was evident in many of the Progressives—they felt that the aliens refused to "melt." They were no longer assimilating. And as Madison Grant had suggested, the racial character of the United States was changing.

But the greatest themes in Ku Klux Klan propaganda was the antialien character of Catholicism and Judaism. "Protestantborn," they insisted, "is an essential part of Americanism. . . . Roman rule would kill it. It is more than a religion. It is the expression in religion of the same spirit of independence, self-reliance and freedom which is the highest achievement of the Nordic race. Its destruction is the deepest purpose of other peoples."[58] The Roman Catholic Church and its immigrant supporters are "the chief leaders of alienism, and the most dangerous alien power with a foothold inside our boundaries."[59]

The Jew, on the other hand, while not ignored, did not

appear to be a major target of the Klan during the height of its power, 1920–25. Imperial Wizard Evans, writing in 1925, asserted: "The Jew the Klan considers a far smaller problem. For one thing, he is confined to a few cities, and no problem at all to the rest of the country. For another thing, his exclusiveness, political activities and refusal to become assimilated are racial rather than religious, based on centuries of persecution. They cannot last long in the atmosphere of free America.[60] Still many Klan members went along with Ford's anti-Semitic crusades. Reprinting "The Protocols of the Elders of Zion" from the *Dearborn Independent,* the Klan declared that the Jews added nothing to human welfare; they were good for nothing.[61] They insisted that Jews were really not white at all—they were Asians.[62]

The Klan's success led it into the political arena, where its support went to those candidates who stood for one hundred percent Americanism. It elected United States senators and congressmen, governors and state legislators, sheriffs, mayors and local officials. But despite the success of the Klan, the order began to lose its vigor. Internal bickering, the moral decadence of many of the Klan leaders, and the passage of the Immigration Act of 1924 were forces that brought about its decline.

In 1922, Simmons had been induced by trickery to accept the new lifetime title of Emperor of the Klan. He relinquished the leadership of the Klan to a new Imperial Wizard, Hiram Wesley Evans. But Simmons refused to remain retired. He attempted to win back control; he even seized the headquarters when Evans was away. Court fights followed. It became apparent that some of the Klan leaders were interested in their own personal welfare. Most important, some of the Klan's klaverns supported Simmons; others supported Evans.[63]

The charges of immorality brought against Clarke and Mrs. Tyler were but the beginnings of a number of such charges brought against Klan leaders. By far the most damaging was the trial and conviction for rape and second-degree murder of the Indianapolis Klan's Grand Dragon, David C. Stephenson, in 1925.[64] He was sentenced to life imprisonment, but expected to be freed by the Klan Governor of Indiana, Edward

Jackson. When no pardon was forthcoming, Stephenson released his files, showing payoffs between the Klan and politicians. It created a national stir.[65]

Then, too, the violence of the Klan proved a drawback. As with the American Republicans and the Know-Nothings, the Klan's violence led most Americans to view the Klan with disapprobation. It should be said that over 90 percent of the Klan membership never engaged in these violent outbursts. As a matter of fact, more often than not, the Klan was the victim of violence.[66] Nevertheless, all Klan members were tarred with the same brush.

Finally, the passage of the Immigration Act of 1924 appeared to remove one of the major threats to one hundred percent Americanism. The Klan, itself, was given some credit for the passage of the 1924 statute.[68] The Congress passed the Quota Act of 1924, which reduced European immigration to 150,000 per year. The immigrants would be chosen on the basis of the 1890 census figures rather than those of 1910, and the quota percentage was reduced from three to two. This plan would be in operation until 1927, when the quota would be based on the national origins of the entire American population of 1920. President Calvin Coolidge, a restrictionist, signed the measure, though he was opposed to the complete restriction on Japanese immigration, since it appeared to abrogate unilaterally the Gentlemen's Agreement of 1908 between Japan and the United States.[69]

The Klan, which may have had two to three million enrolled members, probably also spoke for many others when they condemned the changes they saw around them. Like the secret societies that preceded them, the Know-Nothings and the APA, the KKK represented a basic fear of change, a change induced by a fundamental transformation of American life from a lifestyle that was rural, agrarian, and Protestant to one that was urban, industrialized, and secularized. To add to their anxiety, the nation now numbered among its residents millions of Catholics and Jews.

As we have indicated earlier, one can understand their fears and sympathize with them. Most of the KKK members looked upon the Klan as a refuge. But to believe that the Klan could reverse the trends of the twentieth century was not reasonable.

The Klan declined because of the internecine conflicts, the shallow moral leadership, and the violence that came to be associated with its night riders. Although it started as a law and order organization that stood for one hundred percent Americanism, its actions and activities came to represent definite un-American tendencies. The Klan continued to exist, but by 1929 it had lost its basic middle- and lower-middle-class support. Where it had formerly represented Americanism, it now became the haven for bigots. Its program after 1929 was entirely negative, and its membership became completely Southern. The election of 1928, with the Catholic Democrat Al Smith of New York running for the presidency of the United States, gave the Klan a chance for its last national hurrah.[70]

The decline of the KKK did not terminate xenophobic outbursts in the United States. But the Klan does appear to have been the last such group to win a national audience. Other groups arose that were opposed to aliens and immigration, but they rarely found extensive support.

CHAPTER X

Epilogue

FOR MOST AMERICANS, THE QUOTA LEGISLATION OF THE 1920s provided the solution to the immigration problem. Restrictionists, though, continued to press for further limitations. No Congressional session from 1925 to 1940 was complete without some legislative efforts to reduce the quotas or terminate all immigration to the United States. These efforts ended in failure.[1] They were supported generally by the American Federation of Labor, the Allied Patriotic Societies, the American Eugenics Society, the American Legion, and other organizations with a much more xenophobic stance.

The American Federation of Labor's opposition to immigration remained fairly constant. During the 1920s, it made special efforts to end the job competition of the Mexican immigrants. It charged employers with using the Mexicans as strikebreakers and wage depressors.[2] In the 1930s, the AFL continued to fear any additional immigration because of the great depression and its high unemployment rates.

The Allied Patriotic Society, in its support for further restriction, emphasized the need to Americanize the immigrants already in the country. It, too, pointed out, in the 1930s, the need to protect the jobs of the workers who were here, rather than to jeopardize these employment opportunities with the addition of new workers. The American Eugenics Society again questioned the genetic benefit of any additional immigrants.[3]

The American Legion was also a forceful advocate of immigration restriction. It viewed immigrants as potential enemies—borers from within. The legion favored the deportation of two groups of immigrants: immigrants who refused to serve in the American armed forces in World War I and those who were radicals.[4] In the legion's anti-immigration stance in the

1920s and 1930s, there was definite anti-radicalism and a disparaging note of racism, that is, the belief that certain national groups, especially those from Eastern Europe, could not readily be assimilated.

These restrictionists came close to succeeding in having the quotas reduced by ninety percent in 1930. But just as Speaker Joe Cannon had been instrumental in thwarting the restrictionists earlier in the century, so now, the delaying tactics were provided by Senator David I. Walsh of Massachusetts. Though the reduction measure had passed the House readily, Walsh prevented the measure from coming to a vote in the upper house.[5]

While there was some support for restriction during the 1930s, the clamor by and large was muted. The reason was simple: there was a net loss of immigrants in the 1930s; more aliens left the country than entered it.[6]

There was one problem, however, that did cause some concern, that is, the efforts to rescue the Jews of Germany after the Nazis passed the infamous Nuremburg Laws of 1935, which took away the citizenship of all Jews in Germany. With the abrogation of citizenship all political and civil rights for Jews came to an end. This law also applied to the Austrians after the Anschluss of 1938.

As a result of this action in Germany, efforts were made in the United States to have some twenty thousand German Jewish children admitted to the United States in 1938 and 1939. The Congress took up this legislation, but the opposition to it was intense. In their appearances before the Congressional committees, the spokesmen for the American Legion and the various other patriotic and restrictionist groups emphasized the economic argument: we had enough children to care for here in America, and these Jewish children would subsequently become job competitors when they grew older.[7]

The refugee problem in the 1930s was a difficult one. It may well be that the 1930s was the most anti-Semitic decade in the history of the United States. The fears and frustrations caused by the great depression provoked the age-old allegations that the Jews were a "race" with vast power and wealth and little interest in the deprivations of Americans.[8] Thus the

Jewish refugees became victims of the anti-Semitic crusade by the more militant Christians, though the American Legion, the Daughters of the American Revolution, the Allied Patriotic Society, and other such groups were all quite careful to avoid utterances that could be construed as anti-Semitic.

Others, however, were not so careful. A number of small xenophobic groups organized in the 1930s. The Black Legion, the Defenders of the Christian Faith, the Christian Protective League were all anti-Semitic and anti-Catholic. They were also pronounced opponents of aliens. The Silver Shirts and the National Union for Social Justice, on the other hand, broke with the normal pattern of American nativism: they were predominantly anti-Semitic. Except for the National Union for Social Justice (1934), organized by the Canadian-born Father Charles E. Coughlin, all were local organizations with limited membership, though it appears that every section of the country had some sort of national group opposed to Jews.

In the 1930s, organizations such as the Black Legion, with its Klanlike oath and its black hoods and robes, were anti-Semitic and anti-Catholic and not embarrassed to make their positions known. The Black Legion was also anti-Negro and anti-trade-union. Its appeal was mostly to white Protestant Southerners of the unskilled and semiskilled classes who had moved to the Northern cities, especially Detroit.[9] It was also antialien because aliens tended to be Catholics or Jews. But the Black Legion also feared the job competition of the aliens. The group had a short existence. It was never very large, but whatever power it had ended when seven of its members were tried and convicted of murder in 1936.

The Defenders of the Christian Faith were established by the Reverend Gerald B. Winrod of Kansas in 1933. Winrod set up the group to attack President Franklin Delano Roosevelt as an agent of Communism. After a trip to Germany, he became a pronounced anti-Semite. His publication, the *Defender*, indicated that Jewry, Jesuits, and Communists were all part of the same plot to subvert America. He gave wide publicity to the "Protocols of the Elders of Zion."[10] His main thrust was anti-Communist, and he and his Defenders were part of the antiradical tradition, though he was also anti-Semitic, anti-

Catholic, and antiblack. His failure to win the Kansas Republican nomination for United States senator in 1938 signaled the decline of this rural, small-town–supported movement.

The Silver Shirts, another nativist group, was organized in 1933 by William Dudley Pelley. The son of an itinerant Methodist preacher, Pelley called for the establishment of a Christian commonwealth. Unlike other nativist societies, Pelley and the Silver Shirts, for the most part, tried to ignore the Catholics as a threat to America. But from time to time, the anti-Catholic oratory of the Silver Shirts was apparent, though Pelley himself applauded the work being done by the radio priest of Detroit, Father Coughlin. The Silver Shirts, a fascist group that emulated their Nazi counterparts in Europe, had the base of their support on the West Coast.

Pelley was a poor leader. He was accused of being a racketeer engaged in mulcting thousands of dollars annually from his fanatical and misled followers.[11] He proposed in a book, *No More Hunger* (1939), an economic program which would be run on the principles of Christian economics rather than on alien Communism and Socialism. The outbreak of World War II and America's sympathies for the Allies brought about the decline of the Silver Shirts, who were never very numerous to begin with. Their one stock in trade was a virulent anti-Semitism. By and large, the group was antialien and definitely opposed to the admission of any additional Jewish immigrants.

The Christian Protective League was also quite vocal in condemning the efforts to admit the German Jewish refugees in 1938 and 1939. It saw the plan as part of a Jewish plot to bring more Jews to America.[12]

But the organization that signaled a change in the caliber and membership of the xenophobic movements in the 1930s—a change that has persisted into the 1970s—was the establishment of the National Union for Social Justice (1934) and an offshoot, the Christian Front (1938). Now, instead of a basic anti-Catholicism, the groups often tolerated Catholics, and occasionally were led by Catholics.[13] The chief target of the new nativism was no longer the alien Catholics, but the alien ideology, Communism. At times, this anti-Communism took on anti-Semitic overtones, especially among some of Father Coughlin's supporters.

Father Coughlin had been speaking over the radio on religious subjects as early as 1920. He had begun his radio talks because of a flaming cross left at his church by the Ku Klux Klan. Father Coughlin hoped to remove the bigotry that was based on ignorance of Catholicism.[14] But in 1930 his emphasis shifted to the economy and politics.

An early supporter of Roosevelt and the New Deal, he became highly critical of the president for his failure to nationalize the banks and remonetize silver.[15] He placed the responsibility for this failure at the doors of the Jewish bankers.[16]

He had a national audience for his Sunday afternoon radio addresses that ran into the millions. In 1934, he established the National Union for Social Justice. In 1936, Coughlin and the National Union published a weekly newspaper, *Social Justice*, which presented a Populist view within the framework of the papal social encyclicals.

By 1938, his anti-Semitism had brought him to the point of reprinting in his weekly, "The Protocols of the Elders of Zion." In 1938 and 1939, he praised Hitler and placed full responsibility for the war on the Jews.[17]

The Coughlinites were not anti-immigrant. The bulk of Coughlin's support came from urban Catholics, usually unskilled and semiskilled workers frightened at what was happening to America. The depression had scarred them, and Father Coughlin had an explanation for it. It was the fault of the bankers and the Jews. The Jews were also accused of being Communists.

In 1941, *Social Justice* was banned from the mails as seditious, and Father Coughlin was silenced by his bishop. As a result, the National Union came to a close.

In 1938, an offshoot of the Coughlinite movement in New York City appeared: the Christian Front. It emphasized the link between Communists and Jews.[18] This group, too, ended with America's growing involvement in the war.

Who supported these groups? By and large, they were more likely to find support among Catholics and Lutherans. Many Catholics listened to Coughlin; Lutherans approved of his sympathy for Germany. The members of the National Union were most often found to be among the less well to do, the working classes of the urban areas. The National Union found adherents as well among farmers and small-town residents and among older people. Geographically, the areas of greatest support were the Midwest and the South, perhaps because of the anti-Catholicism still prevalent in these areas. The Christian Front members in New York City were mainly workers and union members, though the leaders were priests and lawyers.[19]

What is apparent, however, was the support by Catholic immigrants for Coughlin. Catholics could now join in the antiradical xenophobia which condemned Jews and Communists, often one and the same thing in the minds of the Coughlinites. What was the reason for this shift? Again, dismay at the changes in America. For many of the Catholic Coughlinites, America's economic crisis was a bitter pill to swallow. Why had their hopes changed? Like the native-born xenophobes of earlier days, they saw a conspiracy, one that linked Communism with some of its Russian supporters who were Jewish. These people, they believed, were trying to destroy America.

Of course, not all the Coughlinites were immigrants. But the same fears motivated the actions of the native-born. By and large, xenophobes are frightened, unhappy people, seeking an answer to the cause of their dilemma. Initially, they had been afraid of the Catholic immigrants. Now, ironically some Catholics joined with other Americans, very often natives, whose fear was focused on the Communists, especially in the post–World War II era.[20]

But while xenophobic outbursts against the immigrants have diminished, the focus of hostility has shifted. The migration of millions of rural peoples into America's urban centers is still in progress. The new element of hostility is closely allied to another rural shift—the black exodus, which began in 1915. The blacks, and the Puerto Ricans and other Hispanic peoples of Mexico and Latin America, are the new "culprits of change" and the new objects of hostility.

Notes and References

CHAPTER I

1. J. Mervyn Jones, *British Nationality Law and Practice* (Oxford, 1947), pp. 34–39. See idem., *British Nationality Law* (Oxford, 1956), p. 58.

2. Walter Blake Odgers, *Nationality and Naturalization* (London, 1916), pp. 24–25.

3. For the positive side of the colonial policy, that is, the moves to encourage immigration, see Erna Risch, "Encouragement of Immigration as Revealed in Colonial Legislation," *Virginia Magazine of History and Biography*, XLV (January, 1937), 1–10; Edward Hoyt, "Naturalization under the American Colonies: Signs of a New Community," *Political Science Quarterly* LXVII (June, 1952), 248–66. For the ambivalence of the colonists and its persistence in America's history, see Cecil D. Eby, "America as an 'Asylum': A Dual Image," *American Quarterly* XIV (Fall, 1962), 483–89; and Philip Gleason, "The Melting Pot: Symbol of Fusion or Confusion?" Ibid., XVI (Spring, 1964), 20–46.

4. Munro S. Edmonson et al., *Nativism and Syncretism* (Publication 19, Middle Atlantic Research Institute, Tulane University, 1960), pp. 183–84.

5. This paragraph and those that follow lean heavily on Emerson Edward Proper, *Colonial Immigration Laws: A Study of the Regulation of Immigration by the English Colonies in America* (New York, 1900), esp. pp. 1–76.

6. Charles P. Daly, *Naturalization. The Past History of the Subject and Present State of the Law in the Countries of the World* (New York, 1860), p. 15.

7. The South Carolina Reconstruction legislature (1868) removed from the state's new constitution the requirement to take an oalth on the Bible. See Jacob M. Ross, "An Historical Study of the Elimination of the Religious, Civil and Political Disabilities of the Jews in the Thirteen Original States from Their Earliest Days to

the Present" (Ph.D dissertation, New York University, 1914), p. 84. Parliament allowed Jewish naturalization in 1740, but Jews could still not be English officeholders or Privy Council members. A. H. Carpenter, "Naturalization in England and the American Colonies," *American Historical Review* IX (January, 1904), 293–94.

8. For other instances of anti-Semitism, see Louis Wirth, *The Ghetto* (Chicago, 1928), pp. 131–51. Jews were granted citizenship rights in Rhode Island, New York, and Georgia, but they were excluded, nevertheless, from voting and holding office. Hoyt, "Naturalization," p. 256.

9. J. Mervyn Jones, *British Nationality Law*, p. 75

10. Proper, *Colonial Immigration Laws*, p. 76.

11. Marcus Hansen, *The Atlantic Migration, 1607–1860: A History of the Continuing Settlement of the United States*, (Torchbook ed., New York, 1961), p. 46. But even in South Carolina, where the Huguenots had a good deal of political power, they found themselves harassed especially between the years 1692–1706. See Arthur Henry Hirsch, *The Huguenots of South Carolina* (Durham, 1928), pp. 106–30.

12. Maldwyn Allen Jones, *American Immigration* (Chicago, 1960), p. 44.

13. Maldwyn Allen Jones, *American Immigration*, p. 45. Henry Jones Ford, *The Scotch-Irish in America* (Reprint ed.; Hampden, 1966), pp. 221–25; James G. Leyburn, *The Scotch-Irish, A Social History* (Chapel Hill, 1962), pp. 238–39. Wayland F. Dunaway, *The Scotch-Irish of Colonial Pennsylvania* (Chapel Hill, 1944), pp. 37–38. Dunaway also mentions the opposition of the New Englanders to the Scotch-Irish, op. cit., p. 48.

14. Ford, *Scotch-Irish in America*, pp. 264–68; Leyburn, *The Scotch-Irish*, pp. 191–93.

15. Albert Bernhardt Faust, *The German Element in the United States with Special Reference to Its Political, Moral, Social and Educational Influence* (Boston, 1909), I, 128–29. Davie places the figure at approximately 70,000. Maurice R. Davie, *World Immigration with Special Reference to the United States* (New York, 1939), p. 21.

16. Glenn Weaver, "Benjamin Franklin and the Pennsylvania Germans," *William and Mary Quarterly*, Series III, XIV (October, 1957), pp. 5–36.

17. Franklin to Parker, March 20, 1750, cited in Weaver, p. 539.

18. Franklin to Collinson, May 9, 1753, cited in Weaver, p. 539. For a defense of the Germans, see Faust, *The German Element*, pp. 130, 146–8.

19. Cited in Weaver, p. 549.
20. Proper, *Colonial Immigration*, p. 53.
21. Maldwyn Allen Jones, *American Immigration*, p. 44
22. See Winthrop Jordan, *White Over Black: American Attitudes Toward the Negro, 1550–1812* (Chapel Hill, 1968), passim, but esp. pp. 91–98.
23. Alexis De Tocqueville, *Democracy in America*, trans. Henry Reeve (New York, 1961), I, 304–9.
24. The best analysis is James Morton Smith, *Freedom's Fetters: The Alien and Sedition Laws and American Civil Liberties* (New York, 1956), passim. For a defense of the acts, see Page Smith, *John Adams* (New York, 1962), II, 975–78. For Federalist fears of the Irish, see Edward C. Carter, "A 'Wild Irishman' under Every Federalist's Bed: Naturalization in Philadelphia, 1789–1806," *Pennsylvania Magazine of History and Biography*, XCIV (July, 1970), 331–46.
25. Samuel Eliot Morison, *The Life and Letters of Harrison Gray Otis, Federalist, 1765–1848* (Cambridge, 1913), I, 107.
26. Ibid.
27. Smith, *Freedom's Fetters*, p. 24.
28. James M. Banner, Jr. *To The Hartford Convention: The Federalists and the Origins of Party Politics in Massachusetts, 1789–1815* (New York, 1970), p. 90.
29. Broadus Mitchell, *Alexander Hamilton, The National Adventure 1788–1804* (New York, 1962), pp. 513–14. Six years later, Gulian C. Verplanck, Richard Varick, and Isaac Sebring, all from New York City, organized a semisecret benevolent society. It did serve as a Federalist propaganda agency but made no special efforts to win support from the naturalized citizens. See Robert W. July, *The Essential New Yorker: Gulian Crommelin Verplanck* (Durham, 1951), pp. 18–25.
30. David Hackett Fischer, *The Revolution of American Conservatism: The Federalist Party in the Era of Jeffersonian Democracy* (New York, 1965), p. 163.

CHAPTER II

1. J. Hector St. John de Crèvecoeur, *Letters from an American Farmer* (London, 1782), p. 73.
2. See Catherine Crary, "The Humble Immigrant and the American Dream: Some Case Histories, 1746–1776," *Mississippi Valley Historical Review*, XLVI (June, 1959), 46–66, and Cecil D. Eby, "America as an 'Asylum': A Dual Image," *American Quarterly*, XIV (Fall, 1962), 483–89.

3. Ralph Linton, "Nativistic Movements," *American Anthropologist*, XLV New Series (April–June, 1943), 230–40.

4. Yeshoshua Arieli, *Individualism and Nationalism in American Ideology* (Baltimore, 1966), pp. 20–27.

5. David Brion Davis, "Some Themes of Counter Subversion: An Analysis of Anti-Masonic, Anti-Catholic and Anti-Mormon Literature," *Mississippi Valley Historical Review*, XLVII (September, 1960), 205–24. Seymour Martin Lipset and Earl Raab, *The Politics of Unreason: Right-Wing Extremism in America, 1790–1970* (New York, 1970), pp. 14–17, also emphasize the conspiracy theory in their discussion of extremist groups, among which they number the xenophobic nativist movements.

6. Davis, "Some Themes of Counter Subversion," p. 206 see idem., "Some Ideological Functions of Prejudice in Ante-Bellum America," *American Quarterly*, XV (Summer, 1963), 115–25 and the brilliant and concise analysis of prejudice in Jean Paul Sartre, *Anti-Semite and Jew*, trans. Henry J. Becker (New York, 1960), passim. The above works place emphasis on the irrational element in the prejudiced mind.

7. Immigration Statistics are not always reliable. For a critique of the figures from 1819 to 1850, see George Tucker, *Progress of the United States in Population and Wealth in Fifty Years As Exhibited by the Decennial Census from 1790 to 1840* (New York, 1855), pp. 80–88. Another criticism centers not on the number of immigrants that arrived, but how many remained. See Bernard Axelrod, "Historical Studies of Emigration from the United States," *International Migration Review* 6 (Spring, 1972), 32–49. For the official figures of the years 1820–1930, see ibid. Table 5, p. 45.

8. For the organization of the North American Association of the United States (1837) with its headquarters in Washington and the role of Ellis as President of the Missouri Native American Organization, see William Darrell Overdyke, *The Know Nothing Party in the South* (Baton Rouge, 1950), pp. 4–5.

9. While Lipset and Raab, in *The Politics of Unreason*, passim, emphasize the irrational nature of the nativists, Professor John Higham, in "Another Look at Nativism," *The Catholic Historical Review*, XLIV (July, 1958), 147–58, believes there is a reasonable ground for the nativists' prejudice: that is a loss of status.

10. For the reasons for Irish immigration, see William Forbes Adams, *Ireland and the Irish Immigration to the New World from 1815 to the Famine* (New Haven, 1932), and Cecil Woodham-Smith, *The Great Hunger: Ireland, 1845–1849* (New York, 1962); for the Germans, see Hansen, *The Atlantic Migration, 1607–1860*, pp. 220–

41, and Mack Walker, *Germany and the Emigration, 1816–1855* (Cambridge, Mass., 1964), pp. 71–73.

11. Max Berger, "The Irish Emigrant and American Nativism," *Pennsylvania Magazine of History and Biography*, LXX (April, 1946), 150–54.

12. For an explanation of this opposition to the Irish, see Thomas J. Curran, "Assimilation and Nativism," *The International Migration Review*, III (Spring, 1966), 15–25.

13. For example, this was the case in New York. See Ray Burdick Smith, ed., *History of the State of New York, Political and Governmental* (Syracuse, 1922), II, 5. Professor Dahl notes the same change in New Haven, Connecticut. See Robert A. Dahl, *Who Governs? Democracy and Power in an American City* (New Haven, 1961), p. 20. For similar changes in Pennsylvania, see Charles McCool Snyder, *The Jacksonian Heritage: Pennsylvania Politics, 1833–1848* (Harrisburg, 1958), p. 105.

14. For the increase in voter participation, see Chilton Williamson, *American Suffrage from Property to Democracy, 1760–1860* (Princeton, 1960), passim.

15. Frederick W. Dallinger, *Nomination for Elective Office in the United States*, (Harvard Historical Studies, vol. iv, New York, 1897), p. 29. Professor McCormick sees the year 1840 as the election year when the new democracy participated as widely in national elections as it did in local and state elections. Richard P. McCormick, "New Perspectives on Jacksonian Politics," *American Historical Review*, LXV (January, 1960), 296.

16. Clifford S. Griffin, *Their Brothers' Keepers: Moral Stewardship in the United States, 1800–1860* (New Brunswick, 1960), pp. 140, 208–09; Ray Allen Billington, *The Protestant Crusade, 1800–1860: A Study of the Origins of American Nativism* (New York, 1952), passim.

17. Thomas T. McAvoy, "The Formation of the Catholic Minority in the United States, 1820–1860," *Review of Politics*, X (January, 1948), 24.

18. Allan Nevins, ed., *Diary of Philip Hone, 1828–1851* (New York, 1927), I (November 27, 1835), 190. Hereafter cited as Hone, *Diary*.

19. *The Crisis: An Appeal to Our Countrymen on the Subject of Foreign Influence in the United States* (New York, 1844), p. 5. Hereafter cited as *The Crisis*.

20. Lewis C., Levin, *A Lecture on Irish Repeal, in Elucidation of the Fallacy of Its Principles, and in Proof of its Moral, Religious and Political Aspects* (Philadelphia, 1844), p. 15. For an explanation

of Levin's career, see Henry Stuart Foote, *Casket of Reminiscences*, (Washington, D.C., 1874), pp. 65–71. Senator Foote first met Levin in 1832. They served in Congress together in the 1840s. For a more recent assessment, see John A. Forman, "Lewis Charles Levin: Portrait of an American Demagogue," *American Jewish Archives*, XII (October, 1960), 150–94.

21. "Address to My Fellow Citizens," a draft in the William Prall Papers, New-York Historical Society.

22. *The Crisis*, p. 5. See also a later nativist appraisal of the Irish Protestants who had a great "longing for the true principles of our liberty." Anna Ella Carroll, *The Great American Battle: Or the Contest Between Christianity and Political Romanism* (New York, 1856), p. 177. The author was the daughter of the former Governor of Maryland (1829–30).

23. Hibernicus, *"What Brings So Many Irish to America!" A Pamphlet Written by Hibernicus: One Part of Which Explains the Many Causes of Irish Immigration: The Other the Consistency of American Nativism As It Is* (New York, 1845), p. 37.

24. The Leopoldine Foundation provided over $170,000 to the Church in America from 1829–39. It had no political motives. Theodore Roemer, "The Leopoldine Foundation and the Church in the United States (1829–1839)," *United States Catholic Historical Society Monograph Series*, XIII (1933), 148–49. Nativism provided an emotional release to Morse from his personal and professional frustrations. Oliver W. Larkin, *Samuel F. B. Morse and American Democratic Art* (Boston, 1954), 122–23.

25. [S. F. B. Morse], *Imminent Dangers to the Free Institutions of the United States through Foreign Immigration and the Present State of the Naturalization Laws: A Series of Numbers Originally Published in the New York Journal of Commerce Revised and Corrected with Additions* (New York, 1835), passim. The *New York Journal of Commerce* was controlled by another brother, Richard Morse.

26. "The Protestant Vindicator is designed solely to assert the purity of Christian truth against Papal tradition and corruption: the simplicity of gospel institutes against the imperious and superstitious ceremonies of Romanism; and the claims of liberty, knowledge, morality and refinement, which are inseparable from Popery." *Protestant Vindicator*, August 20, 1834, p. 3, col. 5.

27. Brownlee's paper had been embarrassed by Father John Hughes, the future Bishop of New York, when Hughes submitted a series of scurrilous attacks, the "Cranmer Letters," to the new publication. When the *Protestant* published them, Father Hughes unmasked himself as the author. Paul J. Foik, *Pioneer Catholic Journalism* (New York, 1930), pp. 31–32.

28. Marian Gouveneur, *As I Remember: Recollections of American Society During the Nineteenth Century* (New York,1911), pp. 86.

29. For one Protestant's reaction, see Henry Van Der Lyn's Diary, III (April 23, 1835), 309. New-York Historical Society.

30. Maria Monk's mother asserted that she was a wild girl who had injured her brain as a child. Billington, *Protestant Crusade*, pp. 99–101. Maria Monk's own daughter, Mrs. L. St. John Eckel, wrote *Maria Monk's Daughter: An Autobiography* (New York, 1874). It was the story of her conversion to, and a staunch defense of, the Catholic faith. Not all Protestants accepted the story. Michael Floy, Jr., the devout young Methodist and Secretary of the New York Anti-Slavery Society wrote on January 26, 1836: "I believe it to be a lie from beginning to end.... I fear and tremble when I consider what needless and mischievous rumors are circulated concerning the Catholics. I may be thought a croaker, but I fear the rash proceeding of Brownlee...." Yet even he noted that tens of thousands of copies had been sold and "a great excitement is already caused." Richard Albert Edward Brooks, ed., *The Diary of Michael Floy, Jr.: Bowery Village, 1833–1837* (New Haven, 1941), p. 216. Hereafter cited as Floy, *Diary*.

31. For example, Morse edited in 1836 *The Proscribed German Student Being a Sketch of Some Interesting Incidents in the Life and Death of Lewis Clausing; to Which Is Added a Treatise on the Jesuits, a Posthumous Work of Lewis Clausing*, and the following year he presented *The Confessions of a French Priest, to Which Are Added Warnings to the People of the United States*. Francis J. Connors, "Samuel Finley Breese Morse and the Anti-Catholic Political Movements in the United States," *Illinois Catholic Historical Review*, X (October, 1927), 99.

32. Billington, *The Protestant Crusade*, p. 168.

33. Philip L. White, *The Beekmans of New York in Politics and Commerce, 1642–1877* (New York, 1856), p. 579.

34. Anson Phelps Stokes, *Church and State in the United States* (New York, 1950), I, 831.

35. Milo Milton Quaife, ed., *The Diary of James K. Polk During his Presidency, 1845–1849* (Chicago, 1910), I, 408–10. Polk did not want the Mexicans fighting with the fervor of crusaders.

36. Ted C. Hinckley, "American Anti-Catholicism During the Mexican War," *Pacific Historical Review*, XXXI (May, 1962), 121–37, and esp. 125.

37. *Proceedings of the Public Demonstrations of Sympathy with Pope Pius IX and with Italy in the City of New York on Monday, November 29, A.D. 1847* (New York, 1847). This support was tem-

porary. Cardinal Mastai-Ferretti, as Pope Pius IX, was the liberal and democratic successor to the more autocratic Gregory XVI. Pope Pius IX had inaugurated a series of reforms in Rome after his elevation in July, 1846. Austria intervened in the Piedmont in July, 1847. But the outburst of violence in the 1848 revolution brought an end to his liberalism. He became as autocratic as his predecessor and is now most noted for his Syllabus of Errors, a most reactionary document. See also Alexander De Conde, *Half Bitter, Half Sweet: An Excursion into Italian-American History* (New York, 1972), p. 43.

38. Hone, *Diary*, II (December 22, 1847) 831–32.

39. For an analysis of the election, see R. Riker to Campbell P. White, April 21, 1834, Campbell P. White Papers, New-York Historical Society. White was a wealthy merchant and a Jacksonian Congressman. Philip Hone noted, "on Thursday, April 10, the last day of the election, dreadful riots between the Irish and Americans have again disturbed the public peace." Hone, *Diary*, I (April 10, 1834), pp. 122–37.

40. Cornelius Lawrence, former congressman and wealthy merchant, was the Democratic candidate. Gulian C. Verplanck, former Jacksonian congressman turned Whig as a result of the Jackson war on the Bank of the United States was the Whig candidate. Lawrence received 17,575 votes to Verplanck's 17,394. Complete election returns are available in the *Courier and Enquirer*, April 14, 1834, p. 2, col. 1.

41. Roy V. Peel, *The Political Clubs of New York City* (New York, 1935), p. 32; Floy, *Diary*, p. 76.

42. First reports of the riot are in the *Courier and Enquirer*, March 16, 1835, p. 2, col. 2. Brownlee's explanation appeared on March 19, 1835, p. 2, col. 3.

43. Carleton Mabee, *The American Leonardo: A Life of Samuel F. B. Morse* (New York, 1943), pp. 168–69. The Irish press saw the effort as anti-Democrat as much as anti-Irish. *The Truth Teller*, June 27 and August 8, 1835.

44. *New York Evening Post*, April 17, 1835, p. 2, col. 4. This election, unlike the previous mayoralty campaign, was relatively quiet.

45. *Spirit of the Times*, July 27, 1835, p. 3, col. 2.

46. The seat had been held by Campbell P. White, the wealthy Jacksonian merchant whose business interests demanded all of his attention. The Whig alderman and cousin of the former president James Monroe was nominated and endorsed by both the natives and the Whigs.

47. Monroe was beaten by a little more than 1,100 votes; *Courier and Enquirer*, November 6, 1835, p. 2, col. 2.

48. *Spirit of '76*, September 15, 1835, p. 2, col. 1. Watson was also a supporter of the Equal Rights movement. A mechanic, he eventually became a Van Buren Democrat. Leo Hershkowitz, "The Native American Democratic Association in New York City, 1835–1836," *New-York Historical Society Quarterly*, XLVI (January, 1962), 52. Bacheler had been the editor of the Boston *Anti-Universalist*, a Protestant weekly which had a shaky existence. See *Anti-Universalist*, August 5, 1829, p. 2, col. 4. For an example of his anti-Catholic views, see ibid., p. 4, col. 2–3; September 2, p. 12, col. 1–2; and September 15, 1830, p. 83, col. 2. The paper ceased publication in September, 1830.

49. *Native American Citizen and Brooklyn Evening Advertiser*, Vol. II (March 17, 1836), p. 2, cited in Nicholas Kramer, "A History of the Know Nothing Movement" (Ph.D dissertation, University of Southern California, 1936), p. 69.

50. Both Philip Hone, the former mayor, and Gulian C. Verplanck, the unsuccessful Whig candidate for the post in 1834, declined the nomination.

51. *Courier and Enquirer*, April 11, 1836, p. 2, col. 1.

52. The Whig candidate was Seth Geer, a building contractor.

53. *Spirit of '76*, April 31, 1835, p. 2, col. 1; Hone, *Diary*, I (October 5, 1835), 179; James L. Crouthamel, "James Watson Webb and the New York *Courier and Enquirer*, 1827–1861" (Ph.D dissertation, University of Rochester, 1958), p. 477.

54. Edward Pessen, "The Wealthiest New Yorkers of the Jacksonian Era: A New List," *New-York Historical Society Quarterly*, LIV (April, 1970), 166.

55. Actually Clark received more votes in 1839 than he had in either 1837 or 1838, but there was a larger turnout in 1839. *New York Evening Post*, April 17, 1839, p. 2, col. 3.

56. Hone, *Diary*, 1, 327.

57. John Moses, *Illinois Historical and Statistical Comprising the Essential Facts of the Planting and Growth as a Province, County, Territory, and State* (Chicago, 1889), I, 444.

58. Gustave Koerner, *Memoirs of Gustave Koerner, 1809–1896: Life Sketches Written at the Suggestion of His Children*, ed. Thomas J. McCormack (Cedar Rapids, Iowa, 1909), I, 426.

59. William H. Condon, *Life of Major-General James Shields, Hero of Three Wars and Senator from Three States* (Chicago, 1900), p. 126.

60. Moses, *Illinois*, I, 445.

CHAPTER III

1. Van Der Lyn Diary, V, March 28, 1842 and VI, August 29, 1843.

2. Thomas D'Arcy McGee, *A History of the Irish Settlers in North America, from the Earliest Period to the Census of 1850* (Boston, 1852), p. 142.

3. See, for example, the entry for October 11, 1840, in Nicholas B. Wainwright, ed., "The Diaries of Sidney George Fisher, 1839–1840," *Pennsylvania Magazine of History and Biography*, LXXVII (January, 1853), 94, and Nicholas B. Wainwright, ed., *A Philadelphia Perspective: The Diary of Sidney George Fisher Covering the Years, 1834–1871* (Philadelphia: The Historical Society of Pennsylvania, 1967), October 20, 1844, p. 177. Hereafter cited as Fisher, *Diary.*

4. Frederick W. Seward, ed., *Autobiography of William H. Seward from 1801 to 1834 with a Memoir of His Life and Selections from His Letters, from 1831 to 1846* (New York, 1877), pp. 462–63.

5. For the Whig reaction, see Harriet Weed, ed., *Autobiography of Thurlow Weed* (Boston, 1883), I, 484, and for the Democrats' reaction, see Albany *Argus Extra*, January, 1840, p. 3. See also Glyndon G. Van Deusen," Seward and the School Question Reconsidered," *Journal of American History*, LII (September, 1965), 317, and Vincent P. Lannie, *Public Money and Parochial Education* (Cleveland, Ohio, 1968), passim.

6. James Kelley to William H. Seward, November 28, 1840, Seward Papers, Rochester University Library.

7. *The Beacon Light*, March 20, 1841, New York Public Library.

8. Mabee, *The American Leonardo*, pp. 176–77.

9. Frederick A. Tallmadge to Seward, October 23, 1841 (Tallmadge was Recorder of New York State and a supporter of the Native Americans in 1835); Richard M. Blatchford to Seward October 28, 1841 (Blatchford was a prosperous banker and lawyer); David M. Nagle to Seward October 28, 1841 (Nagle was a minor Irish Whig politician in New York City); Seward Papers. All of the above were in on the scheme.

10. Hone, *Diary*, II (October 30, 1841), 571. See also the comments of Charles H. Haswell, *Reminiscences of New York by an Octogenarian (1816–1860)* (New York, 1896), p. 375. The full ticket, ten Democrats and five Whigs, is given in the *New York Herald*, October 30, 1841, p. 2, col. 1.

11. Alonzo Johnson to Weed, November 21, 1841, Weed Papers, Rochester University Library.

12. Bishop John Hughes to W. G. Read, November 6, 1841 (copy), Hughes Papers, Archives of the Archdiocese of New York, Dunwoodie, New York. The Carroll Hall ticket drew between 2,422 and 2,521 votes. *Whig Almanac,* 1843, p. 39.

13. Seward, ed., *Autobiography,* p. 536; Joseph J. McCadden, "Bishop Hughes Versus the Public School Society of New York," *Catholic Historical Review,* L (July, 1964), 206–7.

14. Allan Nevins and Milton Halsey Thomas, eds., *Diary of George Templeton Strong* (New York, 1952), I (April 13, 1842), 177–78. Hereafter cited as Strong, *Diary.* Professor Graham has noted the paradox in the American capacity for riot and violence compared with the continued social stability of American institutions. It is apparent that the New Yorkers were protecting rather than rebelling. Hugh Davis Graham, "The Paradox of American Violence: A Historical Appraisal," *American Academy of Political and Social Science Annals,* 391 (September, 1970), 75–76.

15. Seth C. Hawley to Seward, October 18, and November 2, 1842, Seward Papers.

16. John R. Hassard, *Life of the Most Reverend John Hughes, D.D., First Archbishop of New York with Extracts from His Private Correspondence* (New York, 1866), p. 250.

17. Strong, *Diary,* I (June 4, 1843), 204–5.

18. Hugh John Nolan, *The Most Reverend Francis Patrick Kenrick, Third Bishop of Philadelphia, 1830–1851* (Philadelphia, 1948), pp. 293–95.

19. For the Bible controversy in Philadelphia, see Michael Jay Feldberg, "The Philadelphia Riots in 1844: A Social History" (Ph.D dissertation: University of Rochester, 1970), ch. II. Less satisfactory is Sister M. St. Henry, "Nativism in Pennsylvania with Particular Regard to Its Effects on Politics and Education, 1840–1860," *Records of the American Catholic Historical Society of Philadelphia,* XLVII (1936), 18.

20. Sister Loyola Harney, "The Defensive Action of Rt. Rev. Benedict J. Fenwick, S. J., to Anti-Catholicism in New England, 1829–1845," (Ph.D dissertation: Boston College, 1936), passim.

21. Billington, *Protestant Crusade,* p. 182; Handlin, *Boston's Immigrants,* pp. 128; and Carleton Beals, *Brass Knuckle Crusade; The Great Know Nothing Conspiracy: 1820-1860* (New York, 1960), pp. 25–27.

22. Barbara M. Cross, ed., *The Autobiography of Lyman Beecher* (Cambridge, Mass., 1961), II, 342–43.

23. Rev. Alfred G. Stritch, "Political Nativism in Cincinnati, 1830–1860," *Records of the American Catholic Historical Society,* XLVIII (1937), 258 and 262. For the role of the Protestant ministers, see ibid., 242.

24. Billington, *Protestant Crusade,* pp. 143 and 157.

25. Whitney R. Cross, *The Burned-Over District: The Social and Intellectual History of Enthusiastic Religion in Western New York, 1800-1850* (Ithaca, N. Y., 1950), p. 83.

26. William G. Bean, "Puritan and Celt: 1850–1860," *New England Quarterly,* VII (March, 1934), 71–72.

27. For example, the Democrats had a habit of naturalizing immigrants before the election. They also discharged prisoners before their terms expired, and had them vote. Robert Taylor, a Whig police judge, condemned the practice in April, 1842. Diary of Robert Taylor, February 5, 1846, New York, Public Library. For Ketchum, see Griffin, *Their Brothers' Keeper,* p. 215.

28. Carroll, *Great American Battle,* pp. 264–65; *Congressional Globe,* 29th Congress, 1st Session, p. 107.

29. James C. N. Paul, *Rift in the Democracy* (New York, 1961), pp. 42–43.

30. *Address of the General Executive Committee of the American Republican Party of the City and County of New York to Their Fellow Citizens, December 23, 1843* (n.p.d.), passim.

31. *Arguments Proving the Inconsistency and Impolicy of Granting to Foreigners the Right of Voting* (n.p.d.), p. 5.

32. Joseph Tinker Buckingham, *Golden Sentiments: Being an Address to the Native Americans of New York* (Boston, 1844), pp. 3–4.

33. *New York American Republican,* July 8, 1844, p. 2, col. 1.

34. Ibid., July 20, 1844, p. 2, col. 1.

35. Ibid., July 8, 1844, p. 2, col. 4.

36. *Philadelphia Native American,* July 9, 1844, p. 2, col. 1–2.

37. For example, see "Observations on the Census," in *United States Census,* 1860, IV, p. ix.

38. For a discussion of the idea of labor scarcity see Peter Temin, "Labor Scarcity and the Problem of American Industrial Efficiency in the 1850's," *Journal of Economic History,* XXVI (September, 1966), 227–98 esp. p. 295.

39. *Philadelphia Daily Sun,* May 14, 1844, p. 2, col. 1.

40. The municipal reform aspects of the party in New York have been emphasized by Ira M. Leonard in "The Rise and Fall of the American Republican Party in New York City, 1843–1845," *New-York Historical Society Quarterly,* L (April, 1966), 151–92, esp. p. 162,

and in Carl Franklin Siracuse, "Political Nativism in New York City," (Master's thesis: Columbia University, 1965), pp. 27–28.

41. For New York, see General Executive Committee Minutes, February 9, 23, and March 22, 1844, William Prall Papers, New-York Historical Society. For Philadelphia, see American Republican Locust Ward Association Minutes, February 27 and March 12, 1844, New York Public Library.

42. They polled 8,711 votes in the election for state senator. The Democrats won with 14,325 votes: the Whigs polled 14,291. *Whig Almanac*, 1844, p. 44.

43. Thomas Mc Elrath to James Harper, March 25, 1844, Harper Papers, New-York Historical Society. Mc Elrath, an editor on the Whig organ, the New York *Tribune* was also the leader of the Whig party in New York City.

44. General Executive Committee Minutes, February 23 and March 1, 1844, Prall Papers.

45. Ibid., March 29, 1844.

46. Ibid., April 1, 1844, and John Finch to the General Executive Committee, July 18, 1844, ibid.

47. Strong, *Diary*, I, (April 10, 1844), 228.

48. Contemporary opinion was that at least one out of every three Democrats voted for Harper, while in some wards three out of every four Whigs voted for the nativists. Francis William Grimes, "The New York City Municipal Elections of 1844, 1845, and 1846 as Reported in the Local Press" (Master's thesis, New York University, 1961), p. 31. Rank order correlation between the Whigs and the nativists is +0.84 which reflects a strong relationship between the Whigs and the nativists. Siracuse feels that while the rank order correlation between the Democrats and the American Republicans was only +0.488, which indicates little relationship between them, he does believe that the nativists had some success with the Democrats. He points out that the American Republicans were successful in the former strongholds of the Democrats, the 11th and 13th wards. Siracuse, "Political Nativism", pp. 102–03.

49. In Pennsylvania, Philadelphia and Lancaster counties successfully organized a nativist party. Sister M. Theophane Geary, *A History of Third Parties in Pennsylvania, 1840–1860* (Washington, D.C., 1938), p. 104.

50. Margaret B. Tinkcom, "Southwark, A River Community: Its Shape and Substance," *American Philosophical Society Proceedings*, CXIV (August, 1970), 327–42, esp. the summary on p. 342, which distinguishes the changes that afflicted Kensington but which bypassed Southwark.

51. Henry A. Fay to U.S. Senator William L. Archer of Virginia, June 15, 1844, Prall Papers. For a view that sympathizes with the Catholics, see Billington, *Protestant Crusade,* pp. 220–34. The nativist side is presented in Levin's *Philadelphia Daily Sun,* May 8, 1844, p. 2, col. 1–2, and May 15, 1844, p. 2, col. 1. For all of the relevant document, see Raymond H. Schmandt, "A Selection of Sources Dealing with the Nativist Riots of 1844," *Records of the American Catholic Historical Society of Philadelphia,* LXXX (June–September, 1969), 68–200. For a view of the social composition of the rioters, see Feldberg, "Philadelphia Riots", ch. 3.

52. Fisher, *Diary,* (May 12, 1844), p. 165, and (May 15, 1844), p. 167; Schmandt, "A Selection of Sources", pp. 86–87.

53. Ibid., p. 68.

54. Address of the American Republicans of the City and County of Philadelphia to Their Fellow Citizens," in *Philadelphia Daily Sun,* May 14, 1844, p. 2, col. 7.

55. Hone, *Diary,* II (May 8, 1844), 700–701.

56. Bishop Kenrick placed part of the responsibility for the riot on the shoulders of the pastor of St. Philip's, Rev. John Patrick Dunn. The Irish-born Dunn denied that there were any armed men in the church; he claimed he was never asked if the church had any arms. He was ordered out of Philadelphia by Bishop Kenrick. See Schmandt, "A Selection of Sources", pp. 110–11.

57. This account is drawn from Fisher, *Diary* (July 24, 1844), p. 174.

58. Henry R. Mueller, *The Whig Party in Pennsylvania* (New York, 1922), p. 109.

59. *Philadelphia Sun,* July 30, 1844, p. 2, col. 1.

60. Fisher, *Diary* (October 20, 1844), p. 177. Philadelphia *Spirit of the Times,* October 9, 1844, p. 2, col. 1.

61. Oscar Handlin, *Boston's Immigrants: A Study in Acculturation,* rev. ed. (New York, 1969), p. 190.

62. Albert P. Langtry, ed., *Metropolitan Boston: A Modern History* (New York, 1929), I, 229.

63. Justin Winsor, *The Memorial History of Boston Including Suffolk County, Massachusetts, 1630–1880* (Boston, 1881), III, 250.

64. Ibid.

65. Report of the Committee on the Organization of the State of New York, June 10, 1844, and "Proceedings of the American Republican State Convention, September, 1844," Prall Papers; for Pennsylvania, see *Proceedings of the Native American State Convention Held at Harrisburg, February 22, 1845* (Philadelphia, 1845), passim.

66. Handlin, *Boston's Immigrants,* pp. 190–91.

67. For the Pennsylvania alliance, see Snyder: *The Jacksonian Heritage*, p. 185.

68. *American Advocate*, October 14, 1844, p. 2, col. 1., and October 21, 1844, p. 2, col. 1.

69. Hone, *Diary*, II (November 5, 1844), 719.

70. W. W. Dibblee to Hamilton Fish, December 3, 1844, Fish Papers, Library of Congress.

71. Hone, *Diary*, II (November 8, 1844), 719; Simeon Baldwin to his father [Simeon Baldwin, Sr.], November 23, 1844, Baldwin Family Papers, Yale University Library. Baldwin Sr. had been a Congressman from Connecticut, and another son was elected governor of Connecticut in 1844; see also Whitney, *A Defence of American Policy*, p. 253.

72. Dudley Seldon, former Jacksonian Congressman was the Whig candidate. Andrew M. Barber to Weed, October, 1845, Weed Papers.

73. Benomi Rose to Thomas Betts, April 17, 1845, Betts Papers, New-York Historical Society.

74. Strong, *Diary*, I (April 9, 1845), 258.

75. Bishop John Hughes to Dr. Paul Cullen, January 24, 1845, Hughes Papers.

76. *Declaration of Principles Comprised in the Address and Resolutions of the Native American Convention Assembled at Philadelphia, July 4, 1845, to the Citizens of the United States*, revised and corrected by one of the committee (New York, 1845), passim. For Dearborn, see Daniel Goodwin, Jr., *The Dearborns; A Discourse Commemorative of the Eightieth Anniversary of the Occupation of Fort Dearborn, and the First Settlement at Chicago* (Chicago, 1884), pp. 33–38.

77. Especially notable in New York in 1845 and 1846. See Louis Dow Scisco, *Political Nativism in New York State* (New York, 1901), pp. 56–60; Robert Taylor Diary, February 18 and April 2, 1846.

78. Bishop John Hughes to Bishop Anthony Blanc, December 15, 1844 (copy), Hughes Papers; Fisher, *Diary*, p. 174; James M. Hoerner, *The Rights of Adopted Citizens and the Claims of the "Natives": Illustrated and Set Forth* (New York, 1844), pp. 15, 17.

79. Levin's sallies were quoted often with laughter. See, for example, *Congressional Globe*, 29th Cong., 1st sess. p. 74; 31st Cong., 1st sess., p. 12.

CHAPTER IV

1. Charles W. Ferguson, *Fifty Million Brothers: A Panorama of American Lodges and Clubs* (New York, 1937), pp. 7–8; Rowland

Bertoff, "The American Social Order: A Conservative Hypothesis," *American Historical Review* LXV (April, 1960), 507, and Rowland Bertoff, *An Unsettled People: Social Order and Disorder in American History* (New York, 1971), pp. 270–73, 288–89.

2. Simeon Baldwin to his father [Simeon Baldwin, Sr.], November 23, 1844, Baldwin Family Papers.

3. OUA, November 18, 1848, p. 4, col. 3; Whitney, *A Defense of American Policy*, p. 261.

4. I have been unable to find any information on George Phelps Parker, William Atkinson, T. B. Minor, George W. Parson, and E. D. Root, who were also members of the Alpha Chapter.

5. Baldwin to Edward L. Baldwin, June 6, 1844, Baldwin Family Papers.

6. Alfred B. Ely, *American Liberty—Its Sources—Its Dangers —Its Preservation* (New York, 1855), p. 9. A Republican congressman from New York, Ely was taken prisoner by the Confederates at the first battle of Bull Run, 1861.

7. OUA Scrapbook, New York Public Library. This book contains pamphlets and letters written by the various chapters of the OUA.

8. *Resolutions, Ordinances and Decisions of the Chancery of the State of New York from Its Organization to January 13, 1851* (New York 1851), p. 3.

9. *Constitution of the Order of United Americans, and Laws of Arch-Chancery and Chancery of the State of New York. By-Laws and Rules of Order of Ethan Allen Chapter Number 20, City of Williamsburg* (Williamsburg, 1853), pp. 5–8.

10. Carroll, *Great American Battle*, p. 258; Jacob Broom, *An Address Pronounced before the Order of the United Sons of America at Philadelphia on the Twenty-Second Day of February,* A.D. *1850* (Philadelphia, 1850), p. 17.

11. Whitney, *A Defense of American Policy*, pp., 312–15.

12. John Thomas Scharf and Thompson Wescott, *History of Philadelphia, 1609–1884* (Philadelphia, 1884), III, 2075.

13. Whitney, *A Defense of American Policy*, p. 316; Scharf and Wescott, *Philadelphia*, III, 2075.

14. *The Republic*, I (July, 1851), 44–46; Whitney, *A Defense of American Policy*, pp. 271–72.

15. *O.U.A.*, December 16, 1848, p. 40, col. 1.

16. Ibid., April 14, 1849, p. 173, col. 1.

17. Ibid., April 21, 1849, p. 180, col. 1.

18. A. B. Ely, *American Liberty*, p. 27.

19. O.U.A. Scrapbook.

20. Corporation Council: Whigs 20,909, Democrats 18,779;
    Street Commissioner: Whigs 20,974, Democrats 18,684;
    Comptroller: Whigs 21,344, Democrats 17,684.

21. For the Union Safety Committee, see Philip S. Foner, *Business and Slavery: The New York Merchants and the Irrepressible Conflict* (Chapel Hill, 1941), pp. 49–51.

22. *Congressional Globe*, 34th Cong., 1st sess., Appendix, pp. 955–57. The referendum of 1849 was resubmitted to the electorate a second time in 1850 as a result of the opposition of the Roman Catholics and some owners who feared an increase in taxes for the use of the schools. Harold Reynolds, Jr., "Some Historical Considerations of the Free School Controversy in New York State Leading to the Free School Referendums of 1848 and 1849" (Master's thesis, Cornell University, 1953), p. 69.

23. *The Republic*, I (February, 1851), 91.

24. This view differs somewhat from Billington's. He states that with the Compromise of 1850, the years 1850–54 were a time when the American people forgot the slavery controversy and turned their attention to the Catholic immigrant menace. Billington, *Protestant Crusade*, pp. 262–64.

25. Arthur Charles Cole, *The Whig Party in the South* (Gloucester, Mass., 1962), pp. 182–84.

26. The committee initially wanted to set up a bipartisan presidential ticket with Henry Clay and Lewis Cass as their candidates. Clay was willing, but Cass and several other Democrats rejected the idea. Foote, *Casket of Reminiscences*, pp. 83–86.

27. Louis Dow Scisco, *Political Nativism in New York State*, pp. 72–73. Scisco's work is invaluable because he had access to the minutes of the Grand Executive Committee, the political arm of the OUA.

28. Sam C. Crane, *Facts and Figures for Native-Born Americans* (Ithaca, N. Y., 1856), p. 3.

29. Scisco, *Political Nativism in New York State*, p. 80.

30. *The Republic*, II (November, 1851), 229.

31. Ibid.

32. Ibid., I (June, 1851), 183; IV (July, 1852), 52; IV (October, 1852), 219.

33. Ibid., III (June, 1852), 311.

34. Charles O. Paullin, "The National Ticket of Broom and Coates, 1852," *American Historical Review*, XXV (July, 1920), 689; *The Republic*, IV (August, 1852), 99; (December, 1852), 328.

35. Paullin, "The National Ticket of Broome and Coates," 690.

36. The party platform is summarized in the *New York Herald,* August 3, 1853, p. 4, col. 4. Whitney was enthusiastic in his support of the platform. *The Republic,* IV (August, 1852), 96.

37. John W. Latson to Seward, April 22, 1852, Seward Papers. Latson was a minor Whig politician. He had been an unsuccessful candidate for the Whig state convention at Syracuse in 1851. Ninth Ward Whig Election, September 5, 1851, Mott Family Papers.

38. Latson to Seward, April 22, 1852; J. Ely Sherwood to Seward, June 4, 1852, Seward Papers.

39. Paullin, "The National Ticket of Broom and Coates, 1852," 690. Broom was elected to Congress by the Know-Nothings in 1854.

40. It received 1,670 votes in Pennsylvania, 831 in New Jersey, and 184 in Massachusetts. Ibid. The party did have a program for New York City in 1853; a party platform, the work of Thomas Whitney, appeared in the *New York Herald* on August 3, 1853. Some historians have erroneously concluded that this platform indicated the party was actively functioning in 1853. This was not so. Though Whitney still spoke of the party as late as December, 1852, even he ran in 1852 as the unsuccessful Whig candidate for the First District to the State Assembly. Again in 1853, he and Erastus Brooks, both recognized nativists, were elected to the state senate on the Whig ticket. There was no American party endorsement. It was obvious, however, that the nativists had a voice in choosing candidates for the Whig party of New York City. *The Republic,* IV (December, 1852), 318.

41. I have been unable to determine what kind of agent Allen was, insurance, marine, stock or shipping. I have searched through the commercial registers, but with no success. He had an office in the Astor Hotel.

42. C. B. Allen to the Editor, *Newport News,* July 26, 1855, printed in the *Herald,* July 29, 1855, p. 4, col. 3. Allen came to New York in 1835 and worked first as a clerk, then as an agent. Strangely enough, after he formed the new order, he married a young German immigrant who arrived in this country in 1849. County Clerk of New York, New York Manuscript Census Returns, 4th Election District, 21st Ward, 1855.

43. I have leaned heavily upon Georg Simmel's explanation of secrecy and the nature of secret societies. Kurt H. Wolff, ed., *The Sociology of Georg Simmel,* Trans. Kurt H. Wolff (London, 1950), pp. 307–76.

44. Thomas R. Whitney, *An Address Delivered by Thomas R. Whitney Esq. December 22, 1851, at the Hope Chapel New York City on the Occasion of the Seventh Anniversary of Alpha Chapter. Order of United Americans.* (New York, 1852), p. 6.

45. Van Der Lyn Diary, VI, March 15, 1853.

46. John Lawrence, *Plain Thoughts on Secret Societies*, 3rd ed. (Circleville, Ohio 1852), pp. 39–40, 58; See also Herbert Vivian, *Secret Societies, Old and New* (London, 1927), p. 18.

47. See a summary of Reverend Edward Stiles Ely, D.D., arguments presented in his *Vindication of the Sons of Temperance*, which is in Lawrence, *Plain Thoughts*, pp. 208–209.

48. Charles Marden, "Secret Societies," in Joseph S. Roucek, ed., *Social Control*, 2nd ed. (Princeton, New Jersey, 1956), p. 301. The Baptists' war on the Masons continued. See *American Baptist*, February 25, 1868. Gerrit Smith wrote an article for this publication condemning the Masons. The same year there was a meeting of the National Christian Convention Opposed to Secret Societies. Harlow, *Gerrit Smith*, p. 472.

49. New York *Tribune*, November 16, 1853, p. 4, col. 5.

50. Whitney, *A Defense of American Policy*, p. 282.

51. C. B. Allen to the Editor, *Newport News*, July 26, 1855, printed in the *Herald*, July 29, 1855, p. 4, col. 3.

52. Whitney reported the membership at less than 50. Whitney, *A Defense of American Policy*, p. 280. *New York Herald*, December 20, 1854, p. 1, col. 2.

53. Whitney, *A Defense of American Policy*, p. 299. At least one nativist author, Anna Carroll, thought this "investigation" caused the birth of Know-Nothingism, because it then became known among the nativists of the nation. Carroll, *Great American Battle*, pp. 267–71. So, too, did Bayard Clarke, Know-Nothing Congressman in the 34th Congress. *Congressional Globe*, 34th Cong., 1st sess., Appendix, p. 957.

54. There was a great deal of sentiment for a reform league that would stand above party politics and bring order to a disorganized municipal government. William A. Brewer asked for a "dismemberment of the old parties...." He wanted the serious-minded citizen to join in reforming the government. [William A. Brewer], *A Few Thoughts for Tax Payers and Voters in the City of New York* (New York, 1853), pp. 48–49. *The Journal of Commerce* noted with indignation the city's increased tax payments: from $3,000,000 in 1852 to $5,000,000 in 1853. *Corruption of City Government: Reprints from the New York Journal of Commerce, of Unanswered Editorials Showing Deep Abuses in the New York City Government* (New York, 1853), p. 1. Neither publication blamed the immigrant voters.

55. New York *Tribune*, November 16, 1853, p. 4, col. 5.

56. *Syracuse Standard*, November 21, 1851, p. 2, col. 4; Brother Basil Jerome Dewhurst, "The Nativist Movement in Brooklyn,"

(Master's Thesis, Manhattan College, Graduate Studies, 1954), p. 77; Billington, *Protestant Crusade*, pp. 289–314.

57. Edwin B. Morgan to Seward, January 27, 1852. Seward Papers. Morgan was elected congressman by the Cayuga County Whigs in 1853.

58. Herbet Alan Johnson, "Magyar-Mania in New York City: Louis Kossuth and American Politics," *New-York Historical Society Quarterly*, XLVIII (July, 1964), 237–49.

59. Charles Rogers to John H. Boyd, December 15, 1851, Boyd Papers, New York State Library. Boyd represented Washington County in the 28th Congress.

60. *Freeman's Journal and Catholic Register*, December 27, 1851, p. 1, col. 1–5, p. 2; col. 1–2, p. 4; col. 1, p. 5; col. 5, Foik, *Pioneer Catholic Journalism*, pp. 200–201.

61. Nathan Sargent, *Public Men and Events from the Commencement of Mr. Monroe's Administration, in 1817 to the Close of Mr. Fillmore's Administration in 1853* (Philadelphia, 1875), pp. 381–82.

62. *Republic*, III, 155; IV, 43 and 267.

63. Archbishop John Hughes to Cardinal Giacome Antonelli, January 16, 1852 (copy), Hughes Papers; Antonelli was the last layman elevated to the position of Cardinal (1847). Johnson, "Magyar-Mania in New York City: Louis Kossuth and American Politics," p. 240.

64. Bishop John Timon to Bishop Francis P. Kenrick, July 10, 1852 (copy), Hughes Papers.

65. Geary, *History of Third Parties in Pennsylvania, 1840–1860*, p. 65.

66. Williams James to Seward, March 25, 1852, Seward Papers.

67. Maunsell Van Rensselaer to Beekman, February 28, 1852, Letterbook No. 2 (February–March, 1852), Beekman Papers. Van Rensselaer was pastor of St. Peter's Episcopal Church, Albany. In 1859, he became president of De Veaux College, Niagara.

68. William H. Neilson to Beekman, March 9, 1852, Letterbook No. 2 (February–March 1852), Beekman Papers.

69. Peter Guilday, "Gaetano Bedini: An Episode in the Life of Archbishop Hughes," *United States Catholic Historical Society Records and Studies*, XXII, (1933), pp. 99–100.

70. Alessandro Gavazzi, *Lectures in New York: Also the Life of Father Gavazzi Corrected and Authorized by Himself*, 3rd ed. (New York, 1853), passim.

71. Ibid., p. 78.

72. *New York Times*, November 15, 1853, p. 4, col. 1.

73. Strong, *Diary*, II (December 15, 1853), 140.

74. *New York Tribune,* December 12, 1853, p. 5, col. 3; *New York Herald,* December 15, 1853, p. 8, col. 1–2; Strong, *Diary,* II (December 15, 1853), 140.

75. Archbishop John Hughes to Bishop Anthony Blanc, February 3, 1854 (copy), Hughes Papers. Specifically, Archbishop Hughes held the refugees from Germany, France, and other countries of Europe responsible for the outburst of Know-Nothingism. It was they who "communicated *their* secret of organization to the first founders of Know Nothingism." This explanation of nativism was somewhat nativistic. (Bishop John Hughes to Reverend Bernard Smith, *Sacra Congregazione de Propaganda Fide,* March 23, 1858 (copy), Hughes Papers. Browne, ed., "A Memoir of Archbishop John Hughes, 1838–1858," loc. cit., p. 178.) It was not necessary to borrow from *Carbonari* the secret nationalist societies of Italy organized in 1815. Secret political societies were already known in New York. As early as 1808 Gulian C. Verplanck had helped organize the semisecret Washington Benevolent Society on behalf of the Federalist cause. Harlan H. Ballard, "A Forgotten Fraternity," *Collections of the Berkshire Historical and Scientific Society,* III (1913), p. 290. The temperance movement of the 1830s and 1840s and the Anti-Renters of the 1840s also employed secret societies.

76. John Denig, *The Know Nothing Manual, or Book for America No. 1 in Which the Native American Platform and Principles as Adopted by the Know Nothings Are Set Forth and Defended: Together with a Dissertation on Romanism* (Harrisburg, Pa., 1855), p. 17.

77. Archbishop John Hughes to Reverend Bernard Smith, *Sacra Congregazione de Propaganda Fide,* March 23, 1858 (copy), Hughes Papers. Browne, ed., "A Memoir of Archbishop John Hughes, 1838–1858," p. 152.

78. E. B. Washburne to Seward, September 17, 1852, Seward Papers.

79. Truman Smith to Weed, September 19, 1852, Weed Papers. Of course, there were Whigs who felt there might be a Protestant backlash. See Robert Leif Martin to Webb, March 12, 1852, Webb Papers.

80. Robert B. Minturn to Alfred Pell, February 19, 1853, Daniel E. Sickles Papers, New York Public Library. Minturn, wealthy Whig merchant of New York, was opposed to foreign paupers invading New York. Robert Minturn to James W. Beekman, April 11, 12, 1851, Beekman Papers.

81. Warren F. Hewitt, "The Know Nothing Party in Pennsylvania," *Pennsylvania History,* II (April, 1935), 73.

82. Patrick Byrne to Hendrick B. Wright, October 30, 1853, Hendrick B. Wright Papers, Wyoming Valley Historical and Geological Society. Wright was the congressman and Democratic boss of Luzerne County, Pennsylvania.

83. The appellation *barnburner* derived from the charge that these radical Democrats wished to burn the program of state works in order to be rid of the abuses connected with the work. Herbert D. A. Donovan, *The Barnburners: The Study of the Internal Movements in the Political History of New York State and of the Resulting Changes in Political Affiliation, 1830–1852*, (New York, 1925), pp. 32–33 and 72.

84. Holman Hamilton, *Prologue to Conflict: The Crisis and Compromise of 1850* (Lexington, Ky., 1964), pp. 46–47.

85. Ibid., pp. 33–34.

86. They are described in ibid., pp. 58–59.

87. Marquis James, *The Raven: A Biography of Sam Houston* (New York, 1929), pp. 377–78.

88. Hamilton, *Prologue to Conflict*, pp. 135–43.

89. Gary C. Lott, "New York State Whig Convention, 1850" (Master's thesis: Columbia University, 1960), pp. 74–75. For the origins and developments of the feud, see Harry J. Carman and Reinhard H. Luthin, "The Seward-Fillmore Feud and the Crisis of 1850," *New York History*, XXIV (April, 1943), 163–84. See also Lee H. Warner, "The Perpetual Crisis of Conservative Whigs: New York's Silver Grays," *New-York Historical Society Quarterly*, LVII (July, 1973), 213–36.

90. Henry B. Stanton, *Random Recollections* (New York, 1887), p. 180. See also Henry J. Carman and Reinhard Luthin, "The Seward-Fillmore Feud and the Disruption of the Whig Party," *New York History*, XXIV (July, 1943), 335–57.

91. Robert J. Rayback, *Millard Fillmore: Biography of a President* (Buffalo, 1959), p. 384; George W. Thurlow to Daniel Ullman, September 14, 1853, Ullman Papers, New-York Historical Society. Also Lyman A. Spalding to Weed, August 3, 1854, Weed Papers.

92. *Rochester Democrat*, October 22, 1853, p. 2, col. 4.

93. *Whig Almanac*, 1854, p. 41.

CHAPTER V

1. C. B. Allen to the Editor, *Newport News*, July 26, 1855, printed in the *Herald*, July 29, 1855, p. 4, col. 3; Carroll, *Great American Battle*, p. 269.

2. The Allen group was given the right to grant charters to those wigwams north and east of New York, while the Barker group could

establish councils for those areas south and west of New York. James W. Barker, President, to the Grand Council, February 13, 1855, in *New York Times,* March 8, 1855, p. 8, col. 3; *New York Herald,* December 20, 1854, p. 1, col. 2.

3. Carroll, *The Great American Battle,* p. 270.

4. Ibid., p. 271. A copy of the constitution with the amendments of November, 1854, and February, 1855, National Councils can be found in Michael W. Cluskey, ed., *The Political Text-Book or Encyclopedia,* 12th ed. (Philadelphia, 1860), pp. 57–61. A copy of the ritual, reproduced from the *New Orleans Delta* and the *Philadelphia Register,* is in the *New York Tribune,* March 25, 1854, p. 6, col. 4. Additional details on the Know-Nothing numerical codes are in the *New York Herald,* September 25, 1854, p. 2, col. 5. The new constitution was supposedly the work of Ned Buntline. Jay Monaghan, *The Great Rascal: The Life and Adventures of Ned Buntline* (Boston 1952), pp. 208–9.

5. Overdyke, *The Know Nothing Party in the South,* p. 127; Monaghan, *Great Rascal,* p. 124.

6. For the various explanations of Douglas's motives, see Roy Franklin Nichols, "The Kansas-Nebraska Act: A Century of Historiography," *Mississippi Valley Historical Review,* XLIII (September, 1956), 187–212.

7. Eric Foner, *Free Soil, Free Labor, Free Men: The Ideology of the Republican Party Before the Civil War* (New York, 1970), p. 95.

8. John Marsh, *Temperance Recollections, Labors, Defeats, Triumphs: An Autobiography* (New York, 1866), p. 265.

9. Washington Hunt to Weed, October 21, 1854, Weed Papers. Hunt was the Whig Governor of New York, 1851–53. Francis Granger to Ullman, November 14, 1854, Ullman Papers.

10. Joseph R. Gusfield, *The Symbolic Crusade: Status Politics and the American Temperance Movement* (Urbana, 1963), p. 51.

11. *Cyclopedia of Temperance and Prohibition* (New York, 1891), p. 129.

12. Diary of Henry Van Der Lyn VII, June 17, 1855, New-York Historical Society. For Van Der Lyn, see Thomas J. Curran, ed., "Diary of Henry Van Der Lyn," *New-York Historical Society Quarterly,* LV (April, 1971), 119–52.

13. For a fuller explanation of the Know–Nothings' failure, see Thomas J. Curran, "Seward and the Know Nothings," *New-York Historical Society Quarterly,* LI (April, 1967), 141–59.

14. Seward to Weed, March 13, 1855, Weed Papers.

15. John P. Hale to Weed, February 2, 1855, Weed Papers; Millard

Fillmore to Edward Everett, April 7, 1855, Everett Papers, Massachusetts Historical Society.

16. William G. Bean, "An Aspect of Know Nothingism—The Immigrant and Slavery," *South Atlantic Quarterly*, XXIII (1924), 322.

17. A. R. Caulfield (Indianapolis, Indiana) to Seward, April (n.d.) 1855, Seward Papers. A. Walcott Hackley, editor of the *Dubuque Tribune*, wrote from Iowa, " 'Sam' [Know-Nothings] is *everywhere*, is directed by his anti-slavery friends, and is a good fellow." A. W. Hackley to Weed, February 16, 1854, Weed Papers. Italics in the original.

18. Anthony C. Brown to Weed, February 11, 1855, Weed Papers; Overdyke, *Know Nothing Party in the South*, p. 292.

19. Rayner to Ullman, May 8, 1855, Ullman Papers. Italics in the original.

20. N. Darling to Weed, May 30, 1850, Weed Papers.

21. *New York Times*, June 16, 1855, p. 1, col. 2; and in Cluskey, *Political Text-Book*, pp. 55–56.

22. See Ernest A. McKay, "Henry Wilson: Unprincipled Know Nothing," *Mid-America*, XLVI (January, 1964), 29–37.

23. *New York Times*, June 15, 1855, p. 1, col. 1.

24. Geo. E. Baker to Seward, April 19, 1855, Seward Papers.

25. [William Knapp], *I Died a True American: Life of William Poole, with a Full Account of the Terrible Affray in Which He Received His Death Wound, Containing Also a Sketch of Tom Hyer, James Sullivan and John Morrisey* (New York, 1855), p. 7.

26. Strong, *Diary*, II (March 13, 1855), 214–15.

27. For an unfavorable character sketch of Law, see Matthew H. Smith, *Sunshine and Shadow in New York* (Hartford, 1869), pp. 421–22.

28. Vespasian Ellis to Ullman, October 22, 1855, Ullman Papers. Ellis, an attorney, had been the publisher of the xenophobic *Native American Bulletin* in St. Louis, Missouri, in 1841. Ellis to Fillmore, July 31 and November 7, 1856, Fillmore Collection.

29. V. Ellis to Ullman, August 3, 1855, and October 27, 1855, Ullman Papers.

30. V. Ellis to Ullman, November 11, 1855, Ullman Papers.

31. V. Ellis to Ullman, October 27, 1855, and October 28, 1855. ibid.

32. Ibid. Ellis was interested in having the meeting take up his suggestion made at the June Convention that no slave state be admitted to the Union, north of 36° 30′, and that states below that line would decide to be slave or free as they wished. (*New York Times*, June 14, 1855, p. 1, col. 2) Robert C. Winthrop could not

make the secret meeting in New York. He promised to keep the secret but was sure that the *Herald* would somehow get the details. Robert C. Winthrop to Edward Everett, December 3, 1855, Everett Papers.

33. F. W. Prescott to Amos A. Lawrence, December 17, 1855, Lawrence Papers.

34. *New York Times*, December 14, 1855, p. 4, col. 5.

35. James Elliott (Cincinnati) to Weed, November 27, 1855, Weed Papers.

36. *Congressional Globe*, 34th Cong., 1st sess., Appendix, p. 1220.

37. *Congressional Globe*, 34th Cong., 1st sess., Appendix, p. 1000. Plan for organizing the House of Representatives contained in a circular in Daniel Ullman Papers. See also Fred H. Harrington, *Fighting Politician: Major General N. P. Banks* (Philadelphia, 1948), p. 31.

38. *Congressional Globe* 34th Cong., 1st sess., Part I, p. 337.

39. Ibid., Appendix, p. 1000. The charge was leveled on August 2, 1856.

40. Henry W. Taylor to Seward, January 3, 1856, Seward Papers.

41. *New York Times*, February 19, 1856, p. 1, col. 6. A former Democrat, Bartlett had replaced Barker, whose support of Law had antagonized many in the order. Bartlett's father had been in the Kentucky state legislature for almost two dozen years. See *American Organ*, June 26, 1855, p. 2, col. 2.

42. *New York Times*, February 21, 1856, p. 1, col. 2.

43. Circular, *Platform and Principles of the American Party*. Adopted by the National Council Philadelphia. (Philadelphia, 1845).

44. Crane, *Facts and Figures*, p. 2.

45. Carroll, *Great American Battle*, p. 177; Denig, *Know Nothing Manual*, p. 17. "Justice, however, demands that the distinction that exists should be made, as between the Irish of the lower classes being by far the most lawless, aggressive and objectionable of naturalized citizens the whole class of foreigners that migrate to our shore." Dex [pseud.], *The Know Nothings* (Abstract from the *National Standard*), p. 7.

46. *Congressional Globe*, 34th Cong., 1st sess., Appendix, p. 957. Other reasons he gave for joining the Know-Nothings were the dangers of the "Jesuit mind," the Catholic priests' "war on the Bible" and "the political societies of foreigners." Ibid.

47. *The Crusader*, October 14, 1854. Saul W. Johnson to Ullman October 24, 1854; S. Z. Lathrop to Ullman, November 18, 1854; Robert Chandler to Ullman, December 4, 1854; and A. D. [?] Pettengell to Ullman, December 4, 1854, Ullman Papers.

48. Irish invited Ullman's comments in a note written on a broad-

side announcing the formation of the new group. Charles G. Irish, Jr., President, to Daniel Ullman, March, 1855, ibid.

49. American Party, New York, *Principles and Objects of the American Party* (New York, 1855), p. 21.

50. Overdyke, *Know Nothing Party in the South*, p. 222.

51. Robert C. Reinders, "The Louisiana American Party and the Catholic Church," *Mid-America*, XL, new series XXIX (October, 1958), 219, 227.

52. Leon Cyprian Soule, *The Know Nothing Party in New Orleans: A Reappraisal* (New Orleans, La., 1961), p. 52.

53. Overdyke, *Know Nothing Party in the South*, pp. 128–30.

54. Rayner to Ullman, August 21, 1855, Ullman Papers. Italics in the original.

55. Jos Legar [?] to Ullman, May 31, 1855, ibid.

56. *New York Times*, February 20, 1856, p. 1, col. 3.

57. Benoni Thompson to Ullman, July 6, 1855, Ullman Papers. Dr. William B. Clancy of Middletown, Connecticut, wrote to his friend, James W. Beekman, after the Know-Nothings' display of strength in the election of 1854 that he favored altering the naturalization laws, but he wanted to do it openly. "I don't fancy 'foreigners,'" he said, "but then I don't like *secret* combinations against them." William B. Clancy to Beekman, November 8, 1854, Beekman Papers. Italics in the original.

58. S. H. Hammond to Ullman, April 20, 1855, Ullman Papers; *New York Express*, May 30, 1855, the order had gone to fantastic lengths to preserve the secrecy of its ritual. When one member, James Elliott of New York City, indicated he was going to release the contents of the ritual, Charles B. Allen, Dr. Wilkinson Sleight, and Benjamin P. Morris broke into his house one night in May, 1854, and stole the ritual from him. The three were acquitted, since no one could or would absolutely identify them as the thieves. Chauncey Shaffer was their attorney. (*New York Times*, May 18, 1854, p. 8, col. 1. Ibid., May 19, 1854, p. 8, col. 2–3) Again at the Syracuse Grand Council meeting in May, 1855, a Madison County member had been condemned for releasing a report of the business of the Grand Council to the press. Ambrose Stevens denounced him for it. *New York Times*, May 11, 1855, p. 1, col. 1.

59. Millard Fillmore to A. H. Stuart, January 15, 1855, Fillmore Papers.

60. John M. Clayton to Ullman, June 26, July 11, 1855; and T. L. Smith to Ullman, April 4, 1855, Ullman Papers. Webb in the *Courier & Enquirer*, May 12, 1855, condemned secrecy as "unmanly." Cited in Crouthamel, "James Watson Webb," p. 586.

61. "Secret Societies—the Know Nothings," *Putnam's Magazine*, V, (January–July, 1855), p. 95. The magazine was owned and edited by George William Curtis, who was a member of the radical wing of the Republican party. Gordon Milne, *George William Curtis and the Genteel Tradition* (Bloomington, 1956), pp. 64, 104.

62. Monaghan, *The Great Rascal*, p. 215.

63. William Swinson, *An Expose of the Know Nothings, Their Degrees, Signs, Grips, Pass Words, Charges, Oaths, Initiations: Together with Their Objects, Tendencies and Increase* (Philadelphia, 1854), p. 4.

64. *New York Times*, February 20, 1856, p. 1, col. 2, and February 21, 1856, p. 1, col. 1.

65. The delegates chose Ephraim Marsh of New Jersey, president. *New York Times*, February 23, 1856, p. 1, col. 1.

66. Ibid.

67. Ibid., February 24, 1856, p. 1, col. 5–6.

68. Ibid., February 26, 1856, p. 1, col. 1.

69. *Congressional Globe*, 34th Cong., 1st sess., Appendix, pp. 1220–1221; *New York Times*, February 26, 1856, p. 1, col. 2–3.

70. Carroll John Noonan, *Nativism in Connecticut, 1829–1860* (Washington, D.C., 1938), p. 279.

71. C. Edwards Lester, *Life of Sam Houston: The Only Authentic Memoir of Him Ever Published* (New York, 1855).

72. Marquis James, *The Raven: A Biography of Sam Houston*, pp. 377–87.

73. Llerna Friend, *Sam Houston, the Great Designer* (Austin, 1954), p. 291.

74. *New York Times*, February 26, 1856, p. 1, col. 3.

75. Ibid., February 26, 1856, p. 1, coi. 3–4; *Congressional Globe*, 34th Cong., 1st sess., Appendix, p. 1221.

76. The Know-Nothings engaged in strange machinations. At one time they had three tickets in the field: the regular Fillmore-Donelson ticket; the Fremont-William F. Johnston ticket of the North Americans and the North American seceding ticket of Robert F. Stockton and Kenneth Rayner. For the details, check Overdyke, *Know Nothing Party in the South*, p. 141; Fred H. Harrington, "Fremont and the North Americans," *American Historical Review*, XLIV (1938), 842–48, and Fred H. Harrington, *Fighting Politician: Major General N. P. Banks*, pp. 36–38.

77. Thomas M. Monroe to Ullman, June 13, 1856, Ullman Papers.

78. Monroe to Ullman, June 26, 1856, ibid.

79. Rayner to Ullman, June 2, 1856, ibid.

80. H. W. Miller (Raleigh, N.C.) to Ullman, July 9, 1856, and

August 15, 1856; and Thomas M. Monroe to Ullman, July 31, 1856, ibid.

81. David Donald, *Charles Sumner and the Coming of the Civil War* (New York, 1960), p. 298.

82. H. W. Miller (Raleigh) to Ullman, September 6, 1856, Ullman Papers; Overdyke, *Know Nothing Party in the South*, p. 147.

83. N. Sargent to Ullman, July 15, 1856, Ullman Papers. Sargent (1794–1875), a journalist and nonpracticing lawyer, had been appointed to the office of the Register of the Treasury by Fillmore in 1851. With Ullman's help he had also been appointed a clerk in the House of Representatives in 1855. See Nathan Sargent to Ullman, March 18, 1855, Ullman Papers.

84. Samuel C. Busey to Ullman, September 1, 1856, Ullman Papers. Busey was a physician. He became prominent as a practitioner in Washington, D.C., after the Civil War. He was the founder of the District's Medical Society.

85. Weed to Edwin D. Morgan, August 9, 1856, E. D. Morgan Papers. Sammons circulated the story among the Protestant press as an effective campaign device. Sammons to Fillmore, July 24, 1856, Fillmore Collection.

86. Allen Nevins, *Fremont: Pathmarker of the West* (New York, 1955), p. 445. Greeley used the *Tribune* to deny the charge, though he said little against the Know-Nothings. Van Deusen, *Greeley*, p. 208. American electioneering techniques have often used outright falsehood. In the election of 1800, Federalist editors promulgated the false report of Thomas Jefferson's death. See Charles Warren, *Odd Byways in American History* (Cambridge, Mass., 1942), pp. 129–35.

87. Nevins, *Fremont*, p. 446.

88. Strong, *Diary*, II (August 30, 1856), 290.

89. Fillmore to W. W. Corcoran, July 17, 1856 (copy), Fillmore Papers. On July 12, he was not so optimistic. Fillmore to Edward Everett, July 12, 1856, Everett Papers.

90. J. Livingston (New Orleans) to Ullman, July 31, 1856, Ullman Papers.

91. L. Sprague Parsons made known this support when he endorsed a resolution to admit Irish-born Protestants into the order. *New York Herald*, August 26, 1857, p. 1, col. 1–4.

92. Geo. E. Baker to Seward, August 11, 1856, Seward Papers.

93. *New York Times*, September 18, 1856, p. 2, col. 1, and p. 4, col. 2.

94. *Whig Almanac*, 1857, p. 46.

95. E. G. Spaulding to Seward November 24, 1856, Seward

Papers; Hamilton Fish to James A. Hamilton, December 1, 1856, Letterbook P (July 29, 1856–September 6, 1860), Fish Papers.

96. Francis H. Ruggles to Seward, December 11, 1856, Seward Papers.

97. *Message of Simeon Baldwin, Arch Grand Sachem, O.U.A., December, 1857* (New York, 1857), p. 7.

98. Jonathan Pierce, *Valedictory Address of Jonathan Pierce, Arch Grand Sachem, O.U.A. to Arch Chancery, Annual Session, November 15, 1859* (New York, 1859), pp. 3–4.

99. For the Constitutional Union party, see John Burgess Stabler, "A History of the Constitutional Union Party: A Tragic Failure," (Ph.D. dissertation, Columbia University, 1954), passim.

100. For antiabolition sentiment and riots, see Leonard L. Richards, *"Gentlemen of Property and Standing": Anti-Abolition Mobs in Jacksonian America* (New York, 1970), passim.

101. George M. Fredrickson, *The Black Image in the White Mind: The Debate on Afro-American Character and Destiny, 1817–1914* (New York, 1971), pp. 140–42.

CHAPTER VI

1. This positive view of the Civil War can be found in Wallace Fred Tangwell, "Immigrants in the Civil War: Some American Reactions" (Ph.D. dissertation, University of Chicago, 1962), pp. 73–74. For the decline of the nativists, see Maldwyn Allen Jones, *American Immigration* (Chicago, 1960), p. 160; and John Higham, *Strangers in the Land: Patterns of American Nativism, 1860–1925* (New Brunswick, N. J., 1955), pp. 12–13.

2. *New York Times*, June 4, 1863, p. 4, col. 4.

3. For the draft riots, see James McCague, *The Second Rebellion; the Story of the New York City Draft Riots of 1863* (New York, 1968), passim; Albon P. Mann, Jr. "Labor Competition and the New York Draft Riots of 1863," *Journal of Negro History*, XXXVI (October, 1951), 375–405.

4. Allan Nevins, ed., *George Templeton Strong's Diary of the Civil War, 1860–1865* (New York, 1962), July 19, 1863, pp. 342–43. Hereafter cited as Strong, *Civil War Diary*.

5. Tangwell, "Immigrants in the Civil War," p. 52.

6. For Christianity and one of its byproducts, anti-Semitism, see James Parkes, *Antisemitism* (London, 1963), passim, but especially pp. 60–71. See also Charles Y. Glock and Rodney Stark, *Christian Beliefs and Anti-Semitism* (New York, 1966), passim.

7. Washington *American Organ*, November 29, 1854, p. 2, col. 4; May 30, 1855, p. 2, col. 5–6; July 23, 1855, p. 1, col. 6, and p. 2,

col. 1. For Shakespeare's Shylock stereotype, see Morris U. Schappes, "Shylock and Anti-Semitism," *Jewish Currents* (June, 1962), reprint, 3–12.

8. Washington *American Organ*, June 9, 1856, p. 2, col. 2. Belmont was accused of paying the expenses for a group of New York Democrats who supported James Buchanan, the Democratic nominee. For Belmont, see Irving Katz, *August Belmont: A Political Biography* (New York, 1968), passim, but esp. pp. 20, 82, and 143–46.

9. John Y. Simon, ed., *The Papers of Ulysses S. Grant* (Carbondale, Ill., 1970), III, 425 and 360.

10. For Grant's membership in the Know-Nothings, see U. S. Grant, *Personal Memoirs* (New York, 1895), I, 169. For his General Order, see Bertram Wallace Korn, *American Jewry and the Civil War* (Philadelphia, 1951), pp. 158–63.

11. Strong, *Civil War Diary*, November 4, 1864, pp. 508–9.

12. A new explanation for anti-Semitism has appeared recently. It insists that the Jew is discriminated against because he is a deterritorialized man. For Ardrey, the Jew ceases to exist when he becomes reterritorialized. See Robert Ardrey, *The Territorial Imperative, A Personal Inquiry into the Animal Origins of Property and Nations* (New York, 1968), pp. 306–9. For a critique of Ardrey, see M. F. Ashley Montagu, ed., *Man and Aggression* (New York, 1968),

13. Richard J. Gabel, *Public Funds for Church and Private Schools* (Washington, 1937), p. 473.

14. *Congregational Review*, X (1870), 173.

15. See, for example, the *Lutheran Quarterly*, VI (1876), 291–92; and Charles Lewis Sewrey, "The Alleged 'Un-Americanism' of the Church as a Factor in Anti-Catholicism in the United States, 1860–1914," (Ph.D. dissertation, University of Minnesota, 1955), pp. 177–78.

16. James D. Richardson, ed., *A Compilation of the Messages and Papers of the Presidents, 1789–1897* (Washington, D.C., 1898), VII, 356.

17. Sewry, "The Alleged 'Un-Americanism' of the Church," pp. 181–83.

18. The Democratic party under Abraham Hewitt and Samuel J. Tilden was, itself, in the process of reforming the corrupt Tweed ring. See Seymour J. Mandelbaum, *Boss Tweed's New York* (New York, 1965), pp. 132–33.

19. Albert Granger to Daniel Ullman, November 27, 1876. Ullman Papers.

20. Alvin P. Stauffer, "Anti-Catholicism in American Politics, 1865–1900" (Ph.D. dissertation, Harvard University, 1933), p. 60.

21. See Stuart Creighton Miller, *The Unwelcome Immigrant: the American Image of the Chinese, 1785–1882* Berkeley, 1969), passim.

22. Robert McClellan, *The Heathen Chinese: A Study of American Attitudes toward China, 1890–1905* (Athens, Ohio, 1971), pp. 7–8; Gunther Barth, *Bitter Strength: A History of the Chinese in the United States 1850–1870* (Cambridge, Mass., 1964), pp. 35–36, discusses the Californians' first reactions.

23. Barth, *Bitter Strength.* p. 3.

24. Initially (1849–1852) the American Californians were opposed to Hispanic and French miners. Leonard Pitt, "The Beginnings of Nativism in California," *Pacific Historical Review*, XXX (1961), 23–38.

25. Alexander McCleod, *Pigtails and Goldust* (Caldwell, Idaho, 1947), p. 336.

26. Washinton *American Organ*, December 12, 1854, p. 2, col. 3. See also ibid., May 23, 1856, p. 2, col. 1–2. For Marshall, see Mai Flournoy Van Deren, "Humphrey Marshall" (Ph.D. Dissertation, Louisiana State University (Baton Rouge), 1936), and Lawrence A. Schneider, "Humphrey Marshall, Commissioner to China, 1853–1854," *Register of the Kentucky Historical Society*, LXIII (1965), 97–120.

27. *New York Tribune*, September 29, 1854, p. 2, col. 1.

28. These Chinese immigration statistics and those which follow unless otherwise noted can be found in *The Statistical History of the United States from Colonial Times to the Present* Stamford, Conn., 1965), pp. 58–59.

29. Barth, *Bitter Strength*, p. 113.

30. Saxton insists that the response of labor derived from ideological and psychological reasons rather than the economic. Alexander Saxton, *The Indispensable Enemy: Labor and the Anti-Chinese Movement in California* (Berkeley, 1971).

31. McClellan, *The Heathen Chinese*, pp. 20–23, 25, 36–39.

32. Ibid., p. 44.

33. See David R. Weimer, "Myth in the American Federation of Labor, 1881–1914" (Ph.D. dissertation, University of Minnesota, 1954), p. 254, and passim. See also Samuel Gompers, *Seventy Years of Life and Labor: An Autobiography* (New York 1925), I, 216–17, 304–5, and II, 162–69.

34. Theodore Tilton, the abolitionist editor opposed this anti-Chinese movement. See, *Independent*, September 9, 1869.

35. *Brooklyn Daily Union*, June 29, 1870.

36. Ibid., July 1, 1870: John R. Commons, et al., *A Documentary History of American Industrial Society* (Cleveland, 1910), IX, 86–88. See also W. W. Stone, "The Knights of Labor on the Chinese

Question," *Overland Monthly*, 2nd Series, VII (March, 1886), 225–30.

37. Cited in J. Thomas Scharf, "The Farce of the Chinese Exclusion Laws," *North American Review*, 166 (January, 1898), 86. Scharf had been the United States immigration inspector at the Port of New York. He was anti-Chinese. For Stanford's inaugural see Norman E. Tutorow, *Leland Stanford: Man of Many Careers* (Manlo Park, Calif., 1971), pp. 50–51.

38. Act of March 3, 1875, 18 Stat. 477, Sec. 1, U.S.C.

39. See Marion T. Bennett, *American Immigration Policies: A History* (Washington, D.C., 1963), pp. 16–17.

40. Mary R. Coolidge, *Chinese Immigration* (1909; reprint ed., New York, 1969), p. 3.

41. Coolidge, *Chinese Immigration*, pp. 24–25; John Berdan Gardner, "The Image of the Chinese in the United States, 1885–1915" (Ph.D. dissertation, University of Pennsylvania, 1961), pp. 62–91.

42. For the importance of the China trade in the acquisition of California, see Norman A. Graebner, *Empire on the Pacific: A Study in American Continental Expansion* (New York, 1955), pp 63–64 and passim. The Protestant missionary opposition to the exclusion bill is in Elmer C. Sandmeyer, *The Anti-Chinese Movement in California* (Urbana, Ill., 1939), p. 35.

43. Sandmeyer, *The Anti-Chinese Movement in California*, p. 29.

44. See Ted Robert Gurr, *Why Men Rebel* (Princeton, 1970), passim.

45. Ralph Kaver, "The Workingman's Party of California," *Pacific Historical Review*, XIII (1944), 280.

46. For the details of Kearney's life, see Richard Dillon, *Humbugs and Heroes: A Gallery of California Pioneers* (Garden City, N. Y., 1970), pp. 188–93. This account rests heavily on James Bryce, *The American Commonwealth*. See Russell M. Posner, "The Lord and the Drayman: James Bryce vs. Denis Kearney," *California Historical Society Quarterly*, L (September, 1971), 277–84. For a more sympathetic view of Kearney and his movement, see the reformer Henry George's—himself a Sinophobe—article, "The Kearney Agitation in California," *Popular Science Monthly*, XVII (August, 1880), 433–53.

47. Kaver, "Workingman's Party," p. 281.

48. Ibid.

49. Ibid.

50. *Debates and Proceedings of the Constitutional Convention. 1878*, II, 634–704.

51. Ibid., 1519.

52. Kaver, "Workingman's Party," p. 285; Posner, "The Lord and the Drayman," p. 279.

53. Henry George also campaigned for its rejection. He said it was supported by the Grangers and the land and railroad monopolies.

See Charles Albro Barker, *Henry George* (New York, 1955), pp. 261–63.

54. Kever, "Workingman's Party," pp. 286–87.

55. In the summer of 1878, Kearney had gone to Massachusetts to aid the campaign of the Democratic-Greenbacker, General Benjamin Butler. Butler was defeated. But Kearney became an ardent Greenbacker, thereafter. Richard S. West, Jr., *Lincoln's Scapegoat General: A Life of Benjamin F. Butler, 1818–1893* (Boston, 1965), pp. 367–68.

56. See United States Senate, 44th Congress, 2nd Session, *Report of the Joint Special Committee to Investigate Chinese Immigration* No. 689 (1870), passim.

57. Ibid., p. 1062.

58. Harry Barnard, *Rutherford B. Hayes and His America* (Indianapolis, 1954), pp. 447–48.

59. Treaty Between the United States and China Concerning Immigration (1880), 22 Stat. 826, Article 1.

60. George Frederick Howe, *Chester A. Arthur: A Quarter-Century of Machine Politics* (New York, 1957), p. 168.

61. Sandmeyer, *The Anti-Chinese Movements in California*, p. 76.

62. Act of October 1, 1888, 25 Stat. 504, Sec. 1; 8 U.S.C. 270.

63. Act of May 5, 1892, 26 Stat. 5925, Sec. 6, 8 U.S.C.

64. Robert G. Ingersoll and Thomas J. Geary, "Should the Chinese Be Excluded," *North American Review*, 157 (July, 1893), 63–64. In this article, Ingersoll insisted that the Chinese could help the growth of America and that white racial prejudice was the real reason for the law. Ibid., p. 52.

65. Bennett, *American Immigration Policies*, p. 20.

66. See Thomas F. Gossett, *Race: The History of an Idea in Ameria* (Dallas, 1963), pp. 287–310.

67. See Yung Kiung Yen, "A Chinaman on Our Treatment of China," *Forum*, 14 (September, 1892), 86–87.

68. For the beginning of the agitation against the first Japanese immigrants, see Donald Teruro Hata, Jr., "Undesirables: Unsavory Elements among the Japanese in America Prior to 1893 and Their Influence on the first Anti-Japanese Movement in California" (Ph.D. dissertation, University of Southern California, 1970), passim.

69. Prior to 1885, the Japanese had been forbidden to emigrate under penalty of death.

70. Figures are from the *Statistical History of the United States*, pp. 58–59.

71. Richard Hofstadter, *Social Darwinism in American Thought*, rev. ed. (Boston, 1955), pp. 189–190.

72. The anti-Japanese movement can be followed in Roger

Daniels, *The Politics of Prejudice* (Berkeley, 1972), passim. See also the older, but still useful, work by the Protestant minister Sidney Lewis Gulick, *The American Japanese Problem* (New York, 1914), passim.

73. Spencer C. Olin, Jr., "European Immigrant and Oriental Alien: Acceptance and Rejection by the California Legislature of 1913," *Pacific Historical Review*, XXXV (August, 1966), 303–15.

74. Walter MacArthur, "Opposition to Oriental Immigration," *Annals of the American Academy of Political and Social Science*, XXXIV (September, 1909), 239.

75. See for example Madison Grant, *The Passing of the Great Race* (New York, 1916), pp. 70–71; and Lothrop Stoddard, *The Rising Tide of Color* (New York, 1921), p. 232.

CHAPTER VII

1. For Turner's views, see Frederick Jackson Turner, *The Frontier in History* (New York, 1920), passim; and for the "crisis of the eighties," see John Higham, *Strangers in the Land*, pp. 35–67.

2. For a discussion of this transformation, see Robert Wiebe, *The Search for Order, 1877–1920* (New York, 1967), passim.

3. For the transformation of the Protestant churches, see Henry F. May, *Protestant Churches and Industrial America* (New York, 1963), pp. 91–112; Aaron I. Abell, *The Urban Impact on American Protestantism, 1865–1900* (Cambridge, Mass., 1943), passim. See also Samuel P. Hays, *The Response to Industrialism, 1885–1914* (Chicago, 1957), pp. 24–47; and Wiebe, *Search for Order.*

4. Richard Hofstadter, "Manifest Destiny and the Philippines," in Daniel Aaron, ed., *America in Crisis* (New York, 1952), pp. 173–200.

5. Marcus Benjamin, "American Patriotic Societies," *Munsey's Magazine*, XIV (1895), 74. Rowland Bertoff, *An Unsettled People: Social Order and Disorder in American History* (New York, 1971), p. 432.

6. William Evan Davies, *Patriotism on Parade: The Story of Veterans' and Hereditary Organizations in America* (Cambridge, Mass., 1955), pp. 50–61 and passim.

7. E. Digby Baltzell, *The Protestant Establishment* (New York, 1964), p. 115.

8. Lipset and Raab, *The Politics of Unreason*, p. 82.

9. Mary R. Dearing, *Veterans in Politics: The Story of the G.A.R.* (Baton Rouge, 1952), p. 408. Davies, *Patriotism on Parade*, p. 295.

10. Peter Guilday, *A History of the Councils of Baltimore, 1791–1884* (New York, 1932), p. 238.

11. John Tracy Ellis, *American Catholicism* (Chicago, 1956), p. 102.

12. The Catholics received $3,960,00 during the years 1886–1900. The Protestants (Presbyterians, Congregationalists, Quakers, and Episcopalians) were given during the same period only $860,000. Henry E. Fritz, *The Movement for Indian Assimilation, 1860–1890* (Philadelphia, 1963), pp. 104–05.

13. In 1889, Wisconsin passed the so-called Bennett Law, which stated that attendance at some school was compulsory and that all basic subjects must be taught in English. The law was condemned by both Lutherans and Catholics. A similar law, the Edwards Act, was passed in Illinois. Paul Kleppner, *The Cross of Culture: A Social Analysis of Midwestern Politics* (New York, 1970), pp. 158–59; John Higham, *Strangers in the Land*, p. 59.

14. Josiah Strong, *Our Country: Its Possible Future and Its Present Crisis* (New York, 1855), passim.

15. See Evangelical Alliance of the U.S.A. *Conference Proceedings* (Washington, 1887). For the role of the Evangelical Alliance, see Philip D. Jordan, "The Evangelical Alliance for the United States of America: An Evangelical Search for Identity in Ecumenicity during the Nineteenth Century" (Ph.D. dissertation, University of Iowa, 1971). For an abstract of this thesis, see *Church History*, 40 (June, 1971), 201.

16. Charles P. T. Chiniquy, *Fifty Years in the Church of Rome* (New York, 1885). Chiniquy had also published a book which tried to show the political and moral dangers of the confessional. Charles P. T. Chiniquy, *The Priest, the Woman, and the Confessional* (Chicago, ca.1886).

17. Justin H. Fulton, *Rome in America* (Boston, 1887), passim.

18. Justin H. Fulton, *Washington in the Lap of Rome* (Boston, 1888), p. 11.

19. Justin H. Fulton, *Why Priests Should Wed* (Boston, 1888), passim.

20. Margaret Lisle Sheperd, *My Life in the Convent: Marvelous Experience of Margaret L. Sheperd of the Amo's Court Convent, Bristol, England* (Boston, 1893). This book is a new edition of the volume first published in 1887. See also idem., *The Little Mother* (Boston, 1887).

21. Donald L. Kinzer, *An Episode in Anti-Catholicism: The American Protective Association* (Seattle, 1964), p. 24.

22. Isaac J. Lansing, *Romanism and the Republic* (Boston, 1889), passim.

23. Robert P. Sample, *Beacon Lights of the Reformation, or Romanism and the Reformer* (Philadelphia, 1889), passim.

24. James M. King, *Facing the Twentieth Century* (New York: American Union League Society, 1899), passim.

25. Kinzer, *An Episode in Anti-Catholicism*, pp. 56–57.

26. For example, Jeremiah J. Crowley published *The Parochial School: A Curse to the Church; A Menace to the Nation*, and the former superintendent of the Indian Schools, the Methodist clergyman, Daniel Dorchester published a bitter attack on Roman Catholicism. Daniel Dorchester, *Christianity in the United States* (New York, 1890).

27. Daniel C. Eddy, "Immigration," *Baptist Home Mission Monthly*, XI (September, 1889), 247–52.

28. Higham, *Strangers in the Land*, p. 61.

29. For the organization of this militant group, see Hereward Senior, *Orangeism in Ireland and Britain* (London, 1966), pp. 45–46.

30. New York City (1880); and Lawrence (1881) Mass., Lowell (1882) Mass., and Boston (1884), Mass., had elected Irish-Catholics to the office of Mayor.

31. John Higham, "The American Party: 1886–1891," *Pacific Historical Review*, XIX (1950), 37–46.

32. Allan Nevins, *Abram Hewitt: With Some Accounts of Peter Cooper* (New York, 1935), pp. 510–14. Henry Franklin Graff, "A Decade of Nativism as Seen from New York, 1887–1897," (Master's thesis, Columbia University, 1942).

33. Donald Raichle, "The American Protective Association: A Study in Nativism," (Master's thesis, Columbia University, 1947), pp. 11–12.

34. Higham, *Strangers in the Land*, p. 57.

35. The best study of the APA is Donald L. Kinzer, *An Episode in Anti-Catholicism*.

36. Kinzer, *An Episode in Anti-Catholicism*, pp. 36–37. For the controversy over the names of the organizers, see ibid., fn. 16, pp. 271–72.

37. For the alleged un-American character of the Catholic Church, see Charles Lewis Sewrey, "The Alleged 'Un-Americanism' of the Church as a Factor in Anti-Catholicism in the United States, 1860–1914," (Ph.D. dissertation, University of Minnesota, 1955), pp. 177–78.

38. Michael Williams, *Shadow of the Pope* (New York, 1932), p. 98.

39. For the role of liberal Catholicism, see Robert D. Cross, *The Emergence of Liberal Catholicism* (Cambridge, Mass., 1958) passim.

See also R.W. Nary, "Church, State and Religious Liberty: the Views of American Catholic Bishops of the 1890's in Perspective" (Ph.D. dissertation, Georgetown University, 1966). Some Protestant clergymen also opposed the APA's anti-Catholicism and anti-immigration ideas. Lawrence Bennion Davis, "The Baptist Response to Immigration in the United States, 1880–1925," (Ph.D. dissertation, University of Rochester, 1968), pp. 109–10. This work is published under the title *Immigrants, Baptists and the Protestant Mind in America* (Urbana: 1973). Paula K. Benkart, "Changing Attitudes of Presbyterians Toward Southern and Eastern European Immigrants, 1880–1914," *Journal of Presbyterian History*, 49 (Fall, 1971), 66–77.

40. See Henry Beardsell Leonard, "The Open Gates: The Protest Against the Movement to Restrict European Immigration, 1896–1924" (Ph.D. dissertation, Northwestern University, 1967).

41. For emphasis on Bowers as a more compulsive paranoiac personality, see John Higham, "The Mind of a Nativist: Henry F. Bowers and the A.P.A.," *American Quarterly*, IV (1952), 16–24. See also Kinzer, *An Episode in Anti-Catholicism*, pp. 38–40.

42. Kinzer, *An Episode in Anti-Catholicism*, p. 41.

43. Ibid., p. 44.

44. Ibid., p. 57.

45. Ibid., p. 59.

46. Herman L. Wayland, "About the A.P.A.," *Watchman*, LXXV (August 9, 1894), 1.

47. William J. H. Traynor, "Aims and Methods of the A.P.A.," *North American Review*, CLIX (1894), 69–70.

48. Kinzer, *An Episode in Anti-Catholicism*, pp. 74–79, 108–10; Fritz, *Movement for Indian Assimilation*, pp. 106, 220.

49. William J. H. Traynor, "The Menace of Romanism," *North American Review*, CLXI (1895), 129–40. Actually the Catholic hierarchy took a negative view of organized labor unions until the 1902 anthracite-coal strike. William E. Akin, "The Catholic Church and Unionism, 1886–1902: A Study of Institutional Adjustment," *Studies in History and Society*, III (1970), 14–24.

50. For Powderly's difficulties with the Catholic Church, see Henry J. Browne, *The Catholic Church and the Knights of Labor* (Washington, D.C., 1949). Powderly was not a radical; he opposed giving any support to the Haymarket Rioters. He felt there might be guilt by association. Niala McGann Drescher, " 'To Play the Hypocrite' : Terence V. Powderly on the Anarchists," *Labor History*, 13 (Winter, 1972), 60–62.

51. Kleppner, *The Cross of Culture*, pp. 173–74, 251–53; Kinzer, *An Episode in Anti-Catholicism*, p. 78.

52. Baldwin himself organized the American Patriotic League

(1889). Its program was similar to the APA's. Davies, *Patriotism on Parade*, p. 297.

53. Ibid., p. 298.

54. William J. H. Traynor to Henry Baldwin, March 3, 1891, in Baldwin Papers, New York Public Library.

55. For a list of the 58 organizations which attended, see Allen W. Burns, "The A.P.A. and the Anti-Catholic Crusade, 1885–1898," (Master's thesis, Columbia University, 1947), p. 21.

56. For the movement to restrict immigration which we will take up subsequently, see John Higham, "Origins of Immigration Restriction, 1882–1897: A Social Analysis," *Mississippi Valley Historical Review*, XXXIX (1952), 77–88.

57. A.P.A. Magazine, I (1895), 168; Fritiof Ander, "The Swedish American Press and the American Protective Association," *Church History*, VI (1937), 173.

58. Kleppner, *Cross of Culture*, pp. 251–56.

59. Lipset and Raab, *The Politics of Unreason*, p. 88.

60. Ibid., p. 89. See also Hadley Cantril, *The Psychology of Social Movements* (New York, 1941), pp. 63–66; Bruno Bettleheim and Morris Janowitz, *Social Change and Prejudice* (New York; 1964), pp. 48 and passim; Gordon Allport, *The Nature of Prejudice* (Cambridge, Mass., 1954), pp. 221–40.

61. William J. H. Traynor, "Aims and Methods of the A.P.A.," 74; George Parsons Lathrop, "Hostility to Roman Catholics," *North American Review*, CLVIII (1894), 565.

62. Charles Robinson, "The Threatened Revival of Know-Nothingism," *American Journal of Politics*, V (1894), 508.

63. A.P.A. Magazine, I (1895), 160. For Watson's xenophobic efforts, see C. Vann Woodward, *Tom Watson, Agrarian Rebel* (New York, 1963). For Southern efforts to recruit European immigrants, see Rowland T. Berthoff, "Southern Attitudes Toward Immigration, 1865–1914," *Journal of Southern History*, XVII (August, 1951), 330–31; Robert L. Brandfon, "The End of Immigration to the Cotton Fields," *Mississippi Valley Historical Review*, L (March, 1964), 591.

64. New York *Times*, October 15 and November 5, 1894, cited in Kinzer, *An Episode in Anti-Catholicism*, p. 100.

65. A.P.A. Magazine, I (1895), 161–62.

66. Kinzer, *An Episode in Anti-Catholicism*, p. 177; Higham, *Strangers in the Land*, p. 81.

67. Kinzer, *An Episode in Anti-Catholicism*, p. 138; Humphrey J. Desmond, *The A.P.A. Movement* (Washington, D.C. 1912), pp. 94–95.

68. For Linton, see *Biographical Directory of the American Congress, 1774–1961*, p. 1223; For the failure of other Congressmen

who received APA support to abide by the principles of the order, see William J. H. Traynor, "Policy and Power of the A.P.A.," *North American Review*, CLXII (1896), 663–64; Gustavus Myers, *History of Bigotry in the United States*, ed. and rev. Henry M. Christmas (New York, 1960), p. 187.

69. Kinzer, *An Episode in Anti-Catholicism*, p. 185.

70. Ibid., pp. 182, 214–17.

71. Ibid., pp. 185–86.

72. Ibid.

73. Explanations of riots are provided in Ted Gurr, *Why Men Rebel*, pp. 52, 193; Hans Toch, *Violent Men: An Inquiry into the Psychology of Violence* (Chicago, 1969), pp. 5, 154; Barrington Moore, Jr., "Thoughts on Violence and Democracy," *Urban Riots*, XXXIX (April, 1969), 5; Allen Grimshaw, ed., *Racial Violence in the United States* (Chicago, 1969), p. 372 and passim. See also Franz Fanon, *The Wretched of the Earth* (New York, 1963), p. 18.

74. Higham, *Strangers in the Land*, p. 84; Kinser, *An Episode in Anti-Catholicism*, pp. 186–88.

75. *New York Times*, July 6, 1895, cited in Kinzer, *An Episode in Anti-Catholicism*, p. 187.

76. Charles Robinson, "The Threatened Revival of Know Nothingism," *American Journal of Politics*, V (1894), 510–13.

77. *Public Opinion*, August 10, 1895, p. 201, cited in Kinzer, *An Episode in Anti-Catholicism*, pp. 193–94.

78. The order never had a national organ. The *A.P.A. Magazine* in effect violated a bylaw of the order when it took the initials of the order as its title. Traynor, "Aims and Methods," p. 74.

79. Kinzer, *An Episode in Anti-Catholicism*, p. 219.

80. As early as 1894, the politically ambitious Theodore Roosevelt condemned the APA as "un-American." Theodore Roosevelt, "What Americanism Means," *Forum*, VII (1894), 196. Then, too, some prominent Irish newspaper editors had become vocal supporters of the Republican party in the election of 1896. James P. Rodechko, "An Irish-American Journalist and Catholicism: Patrick Ford of the *Irish World*," *Church History*, XXXIX (1970), 525–40.

81. Kinzer, *An Episode in Anti-Catholicism*, pp. 236–39.

82. *New York Times*, June 19, 1894, p. 1.

83. Sydney G. Fisher, "Alien Degradation of American Character," *Forum*, XIV (1892), 615.

CHAPTER VIII

1. E. H. Johnson, Baptist Congress Proceedings (1888), 83–84, cited in Davis, "Baptist Response to Immigration," p. 116.

2. Act of March 3, 1891, 26 Stat. 1084, Sec. 1, U.S.C.

3. Steamship companies were also forbidden to encourage or solicit immigrants to the United States, and, in fact, the act forced these companies to bear the burden of returning illegal entrants to their country of origin.

4. For the administrative nature of the Act of 1893, see Bennett, *American Immigration Policies*, p. 23.

5. For the emergence of this racial concept, Gosset, *Race*, chapter 12: "Anti-Immigration Agitation, 1865–1915," esp. 293–94; Barbara Miller Solomon, *Ancestors and Immigrants: A Changing New England Tradition* (Cambridge, Mass., 1956), pp. 60–81. For the idea of excluding Catholics, see Anders, "Swedish American Press," p. 173; and Davis, "Baptist Response to Immigration," p. 120.

6. Solomon; *Ancestors and Immigrants*, p. 37. For Jewish efforts to offset this prejudice and discrimination, see Jacob M. Sable, "Some American Jewish Organizational Efforts to Combat Anti-Semitism," (Ph.D dissertation, Yeshiva University, 1964), passim.

7. Kenton J. Clymer, "Anti-Semitism in the Late Nineteenth Century: The Case of John Hay," *American Jewish Historical Quarterly*, LX (June, 1971), 341–54. For Hay's anti-Irish and anti-Italian feelings, see Frederick Cople Jaher, "Industrialism and the American Aristocrat: A Social Study of John Hay and His Novel," *Journal of the Illinois State Historical Society*, LXV (Spring, 1972), 69–93.

8. John Higham, "Anti-Semitism in the Gilded Age: A Reinterpretation," *Mississippi Valley Historical Review*, XLIII (March, 1957), 559–78; One author, however, insists that anti-Semitism did not become operative until the first decade of the twentieth century. Carey McWilliams, *The Mask of Privilege* (Boston, 1948), pp. 27–29.

9. De Conde, *Half Bitter, Half Sweet*, p. 117.

10. For opposition to Jewish workers, see Melech Epstein, *Jewish Labor in the United States of America: An Industrial, Political and Cultural History of the Jewish Labor Movement, 1882–1914* (New York, 1953), III, 186–88; Sheldon Neuringer, "American Jewry and United States Immigration Policy, 1881–1953" (Ph.D dissertation, University of Wisconsin, 1969), pp. 32–34.

11. Herbert G. Gutman, "The Knights of Labor and Patrician Anti-Semitism: 1891," *Labor History*, XIII (Winter, 1972), 63–67.

12. For the Greenbackers, see Irwin Unger, *The Greenback Era: A Social and Political History of American Finance* (Princeton, N. J., 1964), pp. 209–12. For the Populist as anti-Semite, see Richard Hofstadter, *The Age of Reform* (New York, 1960), p. 78. For a contrary view, see Norman Pollack, "The Myth of Populist Anti-Semitism," *American Historical Review*, LXVIII (October, 1962), 80; Walter T. K.

Nugent, *The Tolerant Populists: Kansas Populism and Nativism* (Chicago, 1963), 231–43.

13. William Jennings Bryan, *The First Battle: A Story of the Campaign of 1896, Together with a Collection of His Speeches and a Biographical Sketch by His Wife.* (Chicago, 1896).

14. S. E. W. Emery, *Seven Financial Conspiracies Which Have Enslaved the American People* (Lansing, 1892), p. 23.

15. Gordon Clark, *Shylock as Banker, Bondholder, Corruptionist, and Conspirator* (Washington, D.C., 1894), p. 55.

16. Mary E. Hobart, *The Secret of the Rothschilds* (Chicago, 1898), p. 40.

17. Ebenezer Wakely, *The Gentle Ass and the Judean Monetary Establishment* (Chicago, 1895), pp. 9–10.

18. Ibid., p. 152. Wakeley, nonetheless, was considered an anti-Semite by the American Jewish community. See *Reform Advocate,* September 26, 1896, p. 84, col. 1.

19. *Minneapolis Representative,* September 12, 1894, cited in Martin Ridge, *Ignatius Donnelly: The Portrait of a Politician* (Chicago, 1962), p. 337.

20. Ignatius Donnelly, *Caesar's Column* (reprint ed., Cambridge, 1960), p. 32. See also Ridge, *Donnelly,* 262–67.

21. William Hope Harvey, *Coin's Financial School* (Chicago, 1894), pp. 106–07.

22. William Hope Harvey, *Tale of Two Nations* (Chicago, 1894), passim. Harvey became disillusioned with the Democrats after 1896. Harvey wrote other books and even provided an analysis of the crash of 1929. In 1932, he received over 50,000 votes as the Liberal Party presidential candidate. He died in obscurity in 1936. Oren Stephens, " 'Coin' Harvey: The Free Silver Movement's Frustrated Promoter," *American West,* VIII (1971), 4–9.

23. *New York Times,* September 15, 1896, p. 9, col. 1.

24. Ibid., August 11, 1896, p. 3, col. 1.

25. Oscar Handlin, "American Views of the Jew at the Opening of the Twentieth Century," *American Jewish Historical Society,* XL (1951), 323–44. The Federal Civil Rights Law and the New York State Anti-Discrimination Law (1881) did nothing to hinder the harassment of Jews. *New York Times,* May 31, 1881, p. 4.

26. *Reform Advocate,* Oct. 3, 1896, p. 99, col. 2.

27. Samuel Joseph, *A History of the Baron de Hirsch Fund,* (New York, 1935).

28. Sewrey, "American Jewry," pp. 18–21; 25 and 27. Even the American Jews had an ambivalent attitude towards their Russian coreligionists. They feared that they would become a burden on Jew-

ish charitable organizations, and they also felt that they would increase
hostility to all Jews because of their strange language (Yiddish) and
customs. Ibid., p. 32; Zosa Szajkowski, "The Attitude of American
Jews to East European Immigration (1881–1893)," *Publications of
the American Jewish Historical Society*, XL (March, 1951), 240. Divi-
sions between the established Jews and the newcomers from Eastern
Europe persisted into the twentieth century. Moses Rischin, *The
Promised City: New York's Jews, 1870–1914* (Cambridge, Mass.,
1962), pp. 104–11.

29. *Journal and Messenger*, LXI (January 7, 1892), i; cited in
Davis, "Baptist Response to Immigration," pp. 123–24.

30. *American Organ*, December 6, 1855, p. 2, col. 3. See also
ibid., November 29, 1854, p. 2, col. 4.

31. Anonymous, "Confessions of a Roman Catholic," *Forum*, I
(1886), 523. For the difficulties of the Polish peasants' adjustments,
see William I. Thomas and Florian Znaniecki, *The Polish Peasant
in Europe and America: Monograph of an Immigrant Group* (New
York, 1927), II, 513, and Joseph A. Wytrwal, *America's Polish
Heritage: A Social History of the Poles in America* (Detroit, 1961),
passim. This latter work is marred by some factual errors.

32. Joseph S. Roucek, "The Image of the Slav in U.S. History
and in Immigration Policy," *American Journal of Economics and
Sociology*, XXVIII (January, 1969), 29–48. For the Greeks, see Theodore Saloutos, *The Greeks in the United States* (Cambridge, Mass.,
1964).

33. T. T. Munger, "Immigration by Passport," *Century Magazine*,
XXXV (March, 1888), 791–99.

34. Roucek, "Image of the Slav," p. 29. For the perpetuation of
this racist stereotype, see ibid., "The Roots of Racism of American
Social Scientists," *Indian Sociological Bulletin*, VI (April, 1969),
165–77.

35. See, for example, Morgan Appleton, "What Shall We do with
the 'Dago'?" *Popular Science Monthly*, XXXVII (1890), 172–79. For
early rejection of the Italians in America, see Luciano J. Iorizzo and
Salvatore Mondello, *The Italian-Americans* (New York, 1971), pp.
24–25.

36. For more details, see John E. Coxe, "The New Orleans Mafia
Incident," *Louisiana Historical Quarterly*, XX (October, 1937),
1067–1110; and John S. Kendall, "Who Killa de Chief," ibid., XXII
(April, 1939), 492–530. For Italian reaction, see De Conde, *Half Bitter,
Half Sweet*, pp. 121–25.

37. Henry Cabot Lodge, "Lynch Law and Unrestricted Immigration," *North American Review*, CLII (1891), 602–12. For a similar

point of view, see *Journal and Messenger*, LX (January, 1891), cited in Davis, "Baptist Response to Immigration," p. 119.

38. Prescott F. Hall, "New Problems of Immigration," *Forum*, XXX (1901), 555–67.

39. George E. Cunningham, "The Italian, a Hindrance to White Solidarity in Louisiana, 1890–1898," *Journal of Negro History*, L (January, 1965), 22–36; and for twentieth-century lynching, see Charles H. Watson, "Need of Federal Legislation in Respect to Mob Violence in Cases of Lynching of Aliens," *Yale Law Journal*, XXV (1916), 561–84.

40. Henry Pelling, *American Labor* (Chicago, 1960), pp. 101–2. While in the short run, large numbers of immigrants undoubtedly reduced wages, there is little evidence to suggest that, in the long run, immigration led to a decline in wages. Peter Joseph Mooney, "The Impact of Immigration on the Growth and Development of the United States Economy, 1890–1920," (Ph.D dissertation, University of North Carolina, 1971), passim.

41. Reuben Gold Thwaites, *On the Storied Ohio* (Chicago, 1903), p. 69, cited in Andrew F. Rolle, *The Immigrant Upraised: Italian Adventurers and Colonists in Expanding America* (Norman, 1968), p. 98.

42. Edward Saveth, *American Historians and European Immigrants, 1875–1925* (New York, 1948), pp. 13–14, 36, 49, 172, 176, 232–33, and passim.

43. *Journal and Messenger*, LXIII (March, 1894), cited in Davis, "Baptist Response to Immigration," p. 125.

44. Franklin H. Giddings, *The Principles of Sociology* (New York, 1904), pp. 328–29. In 1901 Giddings became a Vice President of the Immigration Restriction League. He replaced his colleague, Richmond Mayo-Smith.

45. Franklin H. Giddings, *The Theory of Socialization* (New York, 1897), pp. 15–17. See also Konrad Lorenz, *On Aggression*, trans. Marjorie Keer Wilson; (New York, 1966), pp. 262–63 and passim; Robert Ardrey, *The Territorial Imperative*, passim, and Anthony Storr, *Human Aggression* (New York, 1968), pp. 21–29 and passim.

46. For Ross, see Julius Weinberg, "E. A. Ross: The Progressive as Nativist," *Wisconsin Magazine of History*, L (Spring, 1967), 242–53; and ibid., *Edward Alsworth Ross and the Sociology of Progressivism* (Madison, 1972).

47. Morrell Heald, "Business Attitude toward European Immigration, 1880–1900," *Journal of Economic History*, XIII (Summer, 1953), 291–304.

48. Robert F. Foerster, *The Italian Emigration of Our Times* (New

York, 1968), p. 402. Opposition among native workers to the Italians also existed in Europe. Ibid., pp. 141–43, 163, 180–82 and 199.

49. H. S. Fukerson, *The Negro: As He Was; As He Is; As He Will Be* (Vicksburg, Miss., 1887), p. 68; cf. George M. Frederickson, *The Black Image in the White Mind: The Debate on Afro-American Character and Destiny, 1817–1914* (New York, 1971), p. 265.

50. Wade Hampton, "The Race Problem," *Arena*, II (1890), 21; cf. Frederickson, *Black Image*, p. 265.

51. [Carlyle McKinley], *An Appeal to Pharoah: The Negro Problem and Its Radical Solution*, 3rd ed. (Westport, Conn., 1970), pp. 115–23.

52. For example, the *North American Review* presented Gaetano D'Amato, "The Black Hand Myth," *North American Review*, CLXXXVII (1908), 543–49. For an evaluation of the magazines, see Salvatore Mondello, "Italian Migration to the U.S. as Reported in American Magazines, 1880–1920," *Social Science*, XXXIX (June, 1964), 131–42.

53. For the Italians, see Rudolph Vecoli, "Prelates and Peasants: Italian Immigration and the Catholic Church," *Journal of Social History*, II (Spring, 1969), 217–68. For a defense of the church and its dealings with Polish immigrants, see Thomas I. Monzell, "The Catholic Church and the Americanization of the Polish Immigrant," *Polish American Studies*, XXVI (January–June, 1969), 1–15. For the only effective schism in the American Catholic Church, see Paul Fox, *The Polish National Catholic Church* (Scranton, n.d.); also Eugene Kusielewicz, *Reflections on the Cultural Condition of the Polish American Community* (New York, 1969), pp. 11–13.

54. Stow Persons, "The Americanization of the Immigrant," in David F. Bowers, ed., *Foreign Influences in American Life: Essays and Critical Bibliographies* (New York, 1952), pp. 39–56.

55. Davies, *Patriotism on Parade*, p. 298; Edward George Hartmann, *The Movement to Americanize the Immigrant* (New York, 1948), pp. 31–33.

56. American Institute of Civics, *Organized Patriotism* (1891), p. 3.

57. For the perpetuation of this idea, see Edward C. Banfield and James Q. Wilson, *City Politics* (Cambridge, Mass., 1963). See the evaluation of the concept in Roger Durand, "Ethnicity 'Public-Regardedness' and Referenda Voting," *Midwest Journal of Political Science*, XVI (May, 1972), 259–68.

58. *New York Times*, June 14, 1891, p. 11, col. 6.

59. See *The Club Men of New York* (New York, 1893), which has arranged alphabetically the names of the club men and their

affiliations. Almost all of the Patria Club members also belonged to one or more of the hereditary societies.

60. Roberts had been defeated for reelection in 1874. He was a newspaper editor in Utica. For Roberts, see *Biographical Directory of Congress, 1776–1961*, p. 1526.

61. *New York Times*, March 12, 1892, p. 2, col. 7. Roberts would become president of the Patria Club.

62. Rev. Robert S. MacArthur, Pastor of the Calvary Baptist Church, made the same points in his speech. *New York Times*, November 26, 1891, p. 5, col. 1. Frederic Taylor, club member, called for restriction to stop Europe's practice of using America as "a cesspool into which may be turned all the sewage of Europe," mainly the non-Anglo-Saxon immigrants from Italy, Russia, and Austria-Hungary. Ibid., November 26, 1892, p. 5, col. 1.

63. Charles R. Skinner, *Manual of Patriotism* (Albany, 1900).

64. Solomon, *Ancestors and Immigrants*, p. 81.

65. *General Walker on Immigration* (Pamphlet No. 33, Immigration Restriction League); Solomon, *Ancestors and Immigrants* p. 79.

66. Francis A. Walker, *Discussions in Economics and Statistics* (New York, 1899), II, 215–26; Higham, *Strangers in the Land*, pp. 142–43. For the use of arguments on the survival of the fittest, see George W. Stocking, Jr., *Race, Culture and Evolution* (New York, 1968), and Richard Hofstadter, *Social Darwinism in American Thought 1860–1915* (New York, 1959), pp. 132–45.

67. Henry Graff, "A Decade of Nativism as Seen from New York, 1887–1897," (Masters' thesis, Columbia University, 1942), pp. 10–12; Richmond Mayo-Smith, *Emigration and Immigration* (New York, 1892), p. 165; ibid., "Control of Immigration," *Political Science Quarterly*, III (1888), 46–77.

68. Mayo-Smith, *Emigration and Immigration*, pp. 86 and 165.

69. John Fiske, the popularizer of the Anglo-Saxon myth; Robert Treat Paine, noted Philanthropist; Professor N. H. Shaler, Harvard geologist; former United States senator George Franklin Edmunds of Vermont; Samuel R. Capen, Boston merchant; and Richmond Mayo-Smith of Columbia University provided financial and moral support for the League. Fiske served as honorary president, the others as vice presidents of the organization. Joseph H. Taylor, "The Immigration Restriction League (1894–1924)," *Midwest Journal*, I (Summer, 1949), 51. See also ibid., "The Restriction of European Immigration, 1890–1924" (Ph.D dissertation, University of California, 1936).

70. Prescott Hall, *Immigration* (New York, 1907), p. 37.

71. Ibid., pp. 46, 55–57.

72. For his beliefs about immigrants, see Robert De Courcy Ward,

"The Restriction of Immigration," *North American Review*, CLXXIX (1904), 226–37.

73. Taylor, "The Immigration Restriction League," p. 52.

74. Immigration Restriction League, *Report of the Executive Committe*, 1901–1902 (n.p.d.).

75. Immigration Restriction League, *Report of the Executive Committee*, 1895 (n.p.d.); Taylor, "Immigration Restriction League," p. 55.

76. Immigration Restriction League, *Report of the Executive Committee* 1901–1902 (n.p.d.).

77. Immigration Restriction League, *Report of the Executive Committee, 1898, 1899, and 1900* (n.p.d.), presents a list of the documents that were issued. By 1902, over 170,000 pieces of propaganda had been issued. Ibid., 1901–1902.

78. As early as 1892, Lodge, then a member of the House of Representatives, had introduced a similar bill to ban all immigrants who could not read or write. John A. Garraty, *Henry Cabot Lodge: A Biography* (New York, 1965), p. 141.

79. *Congressional Record*, 54th Cong., 1st sess., pp. 2817–20.

80. Henry Cabot Lodge to Robert De Courcy Ward, May 30, 1896, Lodge Papers, Massachusetts Historical Society Library.

81. *Congressional Record*, 54th Cong., 2nd sess., pp. 1220–22.

82. Richardson, ed., *Messages and Papers of the President*, IX, 758–59.

83. Allan Nevins, *Grover Cleveland: A Study in Courage* (New York, 1947), pp. 725–26.

84. For the Immigration Protective League, see Leonard, "The Open Gates", pp. 32–38. This also deals with the antiliteracy test movement.

85. Henry Cabot Lodge to Prescott Hall, December 21, 1896, Lodge Papers; Immigration Restriction League, *Report of the Executive Committee*, 1901–1902.

86. Neuringer, "American Jewry and United States Immigration Policy," pp. 49–50. Many prominent Jews, however, feared making immigration a "Jewish issue." Henry B. Leonard, "Louis Marshall and Immigration Restriction, 1906–1924," *American Jewish Archives*, XXIV (April, 1972), 11.

87. In the 55th Congress, the Senate passed the measure in 1898, but the House failed to consider it. *Congressional Record*, 55th Cong., 2nd sess., pp. 196–97.

88. Immigration Restriction League, *Report of the Executive Committee*, 1898–1900.

89. Ibid.; Taylor, "Immigration Restriction League," p. 55.

90. See United States Senate Committee on Immigration, *Regulation of Immigration* (Senate Document No. 62; 57th Cong., 2nd sess.) Despite the fact that the Industrial Commission demanded a general stiffening of the immigration statutes, it did not recommend a literacy test. Higham, *Strangers in the Land,* p. 111; Industrial Commission, "Final Report of the Industrial Commission," *Reports,* XIX, pp. 1011–13.

91. Henry F. Pringle, *Theodore Roosevelt: A Biography* (New York, 1956), p. 173; William Preston, Jr., *Aliens and Dissenters: Federal Suppression of Radicals, 1903–1933* (New York, 1963), p. 4.

92. *Congressional Record,* 57th Cong., 1st sess., p. 5819, and ibid., 2nd Session, pp. 2750.

93. For the opposition, see Immigration Restriction League Scrapbook of Newspaper Clippings, IRL Collection.

94. Preston, *Aliens and Dissenters,* p. 32.

95. William Williams to Theodore Roosevelt, November 25, 1902, Williams Papers, New York Public Library.

96. Prescott Hall to William Williams, December 24, 1902, Ibid.

97. Frank P. Sargent to William Williams, October 6, 1902, Williams Papers. For a fuller explanation of Sargent's views on immigration, see Frank P. Sargent, "The Need of Closer Inspection and Greater Restriction of Immigrants," *Century Magazine,* LXVII (1904), 470–73.

98. Immigration Restriction League, *Report of the Executive Committee,* 1905.

99. For Jane Addams, see Jane Addams, *Twenty Years at Hull House* (New York, 1910), passim; Daniel Levine, *Jane Addams and the Liberal Tradition* (Madison, 1971), pp. 156–59. For Grace Abbott, see Robert L. Buroker, "From Voluntary Association to Welfare State: The Illinois Immigrants' Protective League, 1908–1926," *Journal of American History,* LVIII (December, 1971), 643–60, but esp. 647.

100. *Congressional Record,* 59th Cong., 1st sess., pp. 7293–98.

101. Cannon at one time supported the literacy test, but by 1906 he had changed his mind. Blair Bolles, *Tyrant from Illinois: Uncle Joe Cannon's Experiment with Personal Power* (New York, 1951), pp. 71–74.

102. Lodge to Henry Lee Higginson, February 18, 1907, Lodge Papers.

103. Bolles, *Tyrant from Illinois,* pp. 76–77.

104. Prescott Hall to Maxwell P. Beals, February 14, 1910, in Miscellaneous Publications of the National Liberal Immigration League, Columbia University.

105. The President, House, and Senate each appointed three

members. Roosevelt appointed Charles P. Neill, the Commissioner of Labor and William Wheeler, a San Francisco businessman, both of whom had no public stand on restriction. Roosevelt's third choice, Jeremiah Jenks of Cornell University, was pro-restriction. The Senate appointees were William Dillingham and Henry Cabot—notorious restrictionists. The third member from the Senate was Anselm McLaurin, a Mississippi Democrat. The House members were Benjamin Howell, a New Jersey Republican; William Bennett, New York Democrat; and John Burnett of Alabama, an active supporter of restriction. Oscar Handlin, *Race and Nationality in American Life* (Garden City, N. Y, 1957), pp. 79–80.

106. United States Immigration Commission, *Reports*, 61st Cong., 2nd sess., I, 106–7.

107. Prescott F. Hall, *Immigration*, pp. 91–101; Robert De Courcy Ward, "National Eugenics," *North American Review*, CXCII (1910), 59–64. See also Taylor, "Immigration Restriction League," p. 57. The American Breeders Association became the American Genetic Association in 1914. For the argument that supports increasing the genetic pool via immigration, see the British biologist's argument in C. D. Darlington, *The Evolution of Man and Society* (New York, 1969), pp. 608–12.

108. United States Immigration Commission, *Reports*, I, 33–36.

109. Ibid., p. 42.

110. Arthur Mann, "Gompers and the Irony of Racism," *Antioch Review*, XII (June, 1953), 203–14. Mollie Ray Carroll, *Labor and Politics: The Attitude of the American Federation of Labor toward Legislation and Politics* (Boston, 1923), pp. 118–19.

111. Handlin, *Race and Nationality*, pp. 79–80. For a scholarly attack secretly financed by the American Jewish Committee, See Isaac A. Hourwich, *Immigration and Labor* (New York, 1912), pp. 3–7 and passim. For the secret financing, see Leonard, "Louis Marshall," p. 16. A summary of the commission's findings can be found in Jeremiah W. Jenks and W. Jett Lauck, *The Immigration Problem: A Study of American Immigration Conditions and Needs* (New York, 1911).

112. Richardson, ed., *Messages*, XVI, 7848.

113. *Congressional Record*, 62nd Cong., 3rd sess., pp. 3318, 3429–3430.

114. Saveth, *American Historians and European Immigration*, pp. 141–45; Louis L. Gerson, *The Hyphenate in Recent American Politics and Diplomacy* (Lawrence, Mass., 1964), pp. 62–63.

115. *Congressional Record*, 63rd Cong., 2nd sess., p. 2899; Immigration Restriction League, *Report of the Executive Committee*, 1915.

116. Richardson, ed., *Messages*, XVII, 8043; Arthur S. Link, *Wilson, the New Freedom* (Princeton, 1956), p. 274.

117. *Congressional Record*, 63rd Cong., 3rd sess., pp. 3077–78.

118. See Hartmann, *Americanization*, pp. 97 ff.; Gerd Korman, *Industrialization, Immigration and Americanizers: The View from Milwaukee, 1866–1921* (Madison, 1967), pp. 148–66; and Gerson, *Hyphenate in Recent American Politics*, p. 42, 60–61, and 64–65.

119. *Congressional Record*, 64th Cong., 2nd sess., pp. 2456–57, 2629.

120. In 1917, only 391 immigrants were excluded because they were unable to read. Over 21,000 were admitted. United States Department of Labor, *Annual Report*, 1917, p. 13.

CHAPTER IX

1. Robert F. Foerster to Prescott F. Hall, April 28, 1919, Immigration Restriction League Collection.

2. Gerson, *The Hyphenate in Recent American Politics*, pp. 9–10.

3. For the mixed feelings of the Progressives toward the immigrant, see Hofstadter, *Age of Reform*, pp. 179–86; Eric F. Goldman, *Rendezvous with Destiny: A History of Modern American Reform* rev. ed. (New York, 1956), pp. 60–61; John Joseph Carey, Jr., "Progressives and the Immigrant, 1885–1915" (Ph.D dissertation, University of Connecticut, 1967), and Keslie Wayne Koepplin, "A Relationship of Reform: Immigrants and Progressives in the Far West (Ph.D dissertation, University of California at Los Angeles, 1971).

4. See Bruce Clayton, *The Savage Ideal: Intolerance and Intellectual Leadership in the South, 1890–1917* (Baltimore, 1972), passim.

5. European immigrants fared better in California, since the "Yellow peril" continued to dominate the thinking of the Far West. See Spencer C. Olin, Jr., "European Immigrant and Oriental Alien: Acceptance and Rejection by the California Legislature of 1913," *Pacific Historical Review*, XXXV (August, 1966), 303–15.

6. James A. Hyland, *Rome and the White House* (New York, 1928), p. 136.

7. For the Miles-Roosevelt controversy, see Pringle, *Roosevelt*, pp. 314–16. For other details of Miles's lengthy life, see Ezra J. Warner, *Generals in Blue: Lives of Union Commanders* (Baton Rouge, 1964), pp. 322–24.

8. Higham, *Strangers in the Land*, pp. 182–84.

9. Winfred Ernest Garrison, *The March of Faith: The Story of Religion in America Since 1865* (Westport, Conn., 1971), p. 212.

10. Woodward, *Tom Watson*, p. 385.

11. Garrison, *March of Faith*, p. 213.

12. For full details on Watson's stumbling into the issue, see Leo Dinnerstein, *The Leo Frank Case* (New York, 1968), esp. pp. 97–99 and passim.

13. Woodward, *Tom Watson*, pp. 438–45. Frank had been almost killed a month earlier in an attack by a fellow prisoner. Dinnerstein, *Frank Case*, pp. 137–38. For praise of the lynching, see ibid., pp. 146–47.

14. For Ford's rural sympathies, see Reynold M. Wik, *Henry Ford and Grass-Roots America* (Ann Arbor, 1972), passim. The definitive study remains Allan Nevins and Frank Ernest Hill, *Ford: The Times, The Man, the Company, and The Automotive Industry, 1863–1915 (New York, 1954): ibid., Ford, Expansion and Challenge, 1915–1933* (New York 1957); and ibid., *Ford: Decline and Rebirth* (New York: 1963); Also useful, but with the emphasis on Ford as the industrial genius, is Roger Burlingames's *Henry Ford, A Great Life in Brief* (New York, 1955).

15. Nevins and Hill, *Ford: Expansion and Challenge*, pp. 312–13. Thomas A. Edison may have been an influence on Ford's anti-Semitism. Ibid.

16. For a history of the forgery, see Parkes, *Antisemitism*, pp. 45 ff.

17. Nevins and Hill, *Ford: Expansion and Challenge*, p. 315. Ford ceased publication of the *Dearborn Independent* in 1927.

18. Woodward, *Watson*, p. 443.

19. Thomas R. Cripps, "Negro Reaction to Birth of a Nation," *Historian*, XXV (May, 1963), 344–62; Everett Carter, "Significance of Birth of a Nation," *American Quarterly*, XII (Fall, 1960), 347–57.

20. Dixon, by the way, had been a student of Woodrow Wilson's at Johns Hopkins University.

21. David M. Chalmers, *Hooded Americanism: The History of the Ku Klux Klan* (Chicago, 1968), pp. 28–29.

22. Ibid., p. 31.

23. Preston, *Aliens and Dissenters*, pp. 182–83.

24. Higham, *Strangers in the Land*, pp. 272–73. These articles were subsequently issued in book form in 1922 under the title, *Why Europe Leaves Home*. Ibid.

25. For a critique of the tests, see Daniel J. Kevles, "Testing the Army's Intelligence: Psychologists and the Military in World War I," *Journal of American History*, LV (December, 1968), 565–81; Joel H. Spring," Psychologists and the War: The Meaning of Intelligence in the Alpha and Beta Tests," *History of Education Quarterly*, XII (Spring, 1972), 3–15.

26. Hiram Wesley Evans, "The Klan: Defender of Americanism," *Forum*, LXXIV (1925), 810.

27. William E. Leuchtenburg, *The Perils of Prosperity, 1914–32* (Chicago, 1958), pp. 213–17; Kenneth T. Jackson, *The Ku Klux Klan in the City, 1915–1930* (New York, 1967), p. 18.

28. For the riots of 1917, see Elliot M. Rudwick, *Race Riots at East St. Louis, July 2, 1917* (Carbondale, Ill., 1964), passim; and William M. Tuttle, Jr., "Labor Conflict and Racial Violence: The Black Worker in Chicago, 1894–1919," *Labor History*, X (Summer, 1969), 408–32.

29. Elliot Rudwick and August Meier, "Negro Retaliatory Violence in the Twentieth Century," *New Politics*, V (Winter, 1966), 41–51; William Cohen, "Riots, Racism, and Hysteria: The Response of Federal Investigative Officials to the Race Riots of 1919," *The Massachusetts Review*, XIII (Summer, 1972), 373–400, esp. 376.

30. Arthur I. Waskow, *From Race Riot to Sit-In, 1919 and the 1960's* (Garden City, N.Y., 1966); and William M. Tuttle, Jr., *Race Riot: Chicago in the Red Summer of 1919* (New York, 1970), passim.

31. Cohen, "Riots, Racism and Hysteria," pp. 380–82.

32. Robert K. Murray, *Red Scare: A Study in National Hysteria, 1919–1920* (New York, 1964), p. 32.

33. Ibid., p. 30.

34. Preston, *Aliens and Dissenters*, p. 91.

35. Paul L. Murphy, "Sources and Nature of Intolerance in the 1920's," *Journal of American History*, LI (June, 1964), 65.

36. Stanley Coben, "A Study in Nativism: The American Red Scare of 1919–20," *Political Science Quarterly*, LXXIX (March, 1964), 66–67.

37. Coben, "A Study in Nativism," p. 72.

38. Murphy, "Sources and Nature of Intolerance," p. 72; for the role of Palmer, see Stanley Coben, *A. Mitchell Palmer: Politician* (New York, 1972), 217–45; for Wood, see Hermann Hagedorn, *Leonard Wood: A Biography* (New York, 1969), II, 342–43.

39. Preston, *Aliens and Dissenters*, pp. 220–21.

40. Ibid., p. 228.

41. *Congressional Record*, 66th Cong., 3rd sess., p. 3300.

42. Ibid., p. 3936.

43. Ibid., 67th Cong., 1st sess., pp. 1428, 1442–43.

44. Ibid., 67th Cong., 2nd sess., pp. 6208–09; 6238.

45. Chalmers, *Hooded Americanism*, pp. 31–32.

46. Ibid., p. 33.

47. Ibid., pp. 35–36.

48. John Moffatt Mecklin, *The Ku Klux Klan: A Study of the American Mind* (New York, 1963), p. 134.

49. Ibid., p. 130.

50. Ibid., pp. 140–41.

51. Jackson, *The Ku Klux Klan in the City*, p. 236; Lipset and Raab, *Politics of Unreason*, pp. 128–29.

52. Jackson, *The Ku Klux Klan in the City*, pp. 18–19.

53. Paul M. Winter, *What Price Tolerance* (New York, 1928), p. 12.

54. Charles Finch, *First Century of the Ku Klux Klan* (Philadelphia, 1964), p. 50.

55. Evans, "The Klan: Defender of Americanism," p. 807.

56. Hiram Wesley Evans, "The Catholic Question as Viewed by the Ku Klux Klan," *Current History*, XXVI (1927), 563.

57. Evans, "The Klan: Defender of Americanism," p. 805.

58. Hiram Wesley Evans, "Imperial Wizard, the Klan's Fight for Americanism," *North American Review*, CCXXIII (1926), 49.

59. Ibid., p. 43; Evans, "The Klan: Defender of Americanism," p. 812; C. M. Rork, "A Defense of the Ku Klux Klan," *Literary Digest*, LXXVI (January, 1923), 19. This anti-Catholicism proved to be so popular that the former APA leader tried once again to become an anti-Catholic spokesman. See W. J. H. Traynor, *The Devil's Catechism* (New York, 1920), passim.

60. Evans, "The Klan: Defender of America," p. 812.

61. *New York Times*, December 8, 1922, p. 19, col. 2.

62. Evans, "The Klan's Fight for Americanism," p. 55.

63. Jackson, *Ku Klux Klan in the City*, p. 16.

64. Chalmers, *Hooded Americanism*, pp. 171–172.

65. Ibid., pp. 173–74.

66. "The Klan as a Victim of Mob Violence," *Literary Digest*, LXXVIII (September, 1923), 12–13.

67. Jackson, *The Ku Klux Klan in the City*, p. 242.

68. United States House of Representatives, *Report No. 350*, 68th Cong., 1st sess. (1924), II, 4–5.

69. Donald R. McCoy, *Calvin Coolidge: The Quiet President* (New York, 1967), pp. 228–32.

70. For the election of 1928 and the anti-Catholicism that it engendered, see Edmund A. Moore, *A Catholic Runs for President* (New York, 1956), passim.

CHAPTER X

1. For American immigration legislation and policies during this time span, see Robert A. Divine, *American Immigration Policy, 1924–1952* (New Haven, 1957), passim.

2. For the unsuccessful efforts of the AFL in the 1920s, see Harvey A. Levenstein, "The AF of L and Mexican Immigration in the 1920's: An Experiment in Labor Diplomacy," *Hispanic American Historical Review*, XLVIII (May, 1968), 206–19.

3. See, for example, their arguments in *Hearings Before the Senate Committee on Immigration and Naturalization,* 71st Cong., 3rd sess. (1930), pp. 15–18, 22–28, 116–119.

4. Roscoe Baker, *The American Legion and American Foreign Policy* (New York, 1954), pp. 27–28, 52–59; Raymond Moley, Jr., *The American Legion Story* (New York, 1966), pp. 68–69, 93–94, 116, and 197.

5. *Congressional Record,* 71st Cong., 3rd sess., pp. 6574–77, 6971.

6. For the question of emigration loss from the United States, see Bernard Axelrod, "Historical Studies of Emigration from the United States," *International Migration Review* 6 (Spring, 1972), 32–47, esp. p. 46.

7. Baker, *The American Legion* pp. 59–60; Henry L. Feingold, *The Politics of Rescue: The Roosevelt Administration and the Holocaust, 1938–1945* (New Brunswick, N. J., 1970), pp. 149–151.

8. For the anti-Semitism of the 1930s, see Donald Strong, *Organized Anti-Semitism in America: The Rise of Group Prejudice during the Decade, 1930–1940* (Washington, D.C., 1941), passim.

9. Morris Janowitz, "Black Legions on the March," in Daniel Aaron, ed., *America in Crisis: Fourteen Crucial Episodes in American History* (New York, 1952), pp. 306–7; Lipset and Raab, *Politics of Unreason,* pp. 157–58.

10. Ralph Roy, *Apostles of Discord* (Boston, 1953), p. 28.

11. Lipset and Raab, *Politics of Unreason,* p. 167.

12. Neuringer, "American Jewry," p. 236.

13. For the changed attitudes of Protestants toward Catholics, see Lerond Curry, *Protestant-Catholic Relations in America: World War I through Vatican II* (Lexington, Ky., 1972), passim.

14. Arthur Schlesinger, Jr., *The Age of Roosevelt, The Politics of Upheaval* Vol. III (Boston, 1960), pp. 16–17.

15. Ibid., pp. 26–27.

16. Ibid., p. 19.

17. For his relations with the New Deal and his belief that Roosevelt was controlled by the Jews, see James P. Shenton, "The Coughlin Movement and the New Deal," *Political Science Quarterly,* LXXIII (1958), 360–70.

18. Edward C. McCarthy, "The Christian Front Movement in New York City, 1938–1940," (Master's thesis, Columbia University, 1965), pp. 7–8.

19. Lipset and Raab, *Politics of Unreason,* pp. 175–77.

20. See Samuel Lubell, *The Future of American Politics* (New York; 1956), passim; and Richard Rovere, *Senator Joseph McCarthy* (New York, 1960), passim.

Bibliography

IT WOULD BE BOTH REPETITIOUS AND SPACE CONSUMING to append a complete bibliographical listing. The footnotes for each chapter provide all the relevant primary and secondary sources used in this work. Some comments, however, are in order.

One manuscript collection, the Kenneth Rayner Papers, at the University of North Carolina Library proved to be a disappointment. There were no significant letters in the collection which dealt with the Know-Nothing movement despite the fact that Rayner was the author of the Union Degree in the Know-Nothing ritual. The recently discovered Millard Fillmore Collection, presently housed in the State University of New York at Oswego, contains a fund of information on the Know-Nothing strategy for the presidential election of 1856.

The following monographs and articles have been especially helpful. They do not include all of the major studies of xenophobic or nativist reaction to immigrants in the United States. They are, however, works that I have found quite useful.

Seymour Martin Lipset and Earl Raab have tried to cover the major American xenophobic outbursts in a single volume called *The Politics of Unreason: Right-Wing Extremism in America, 1790–1970* (New York, 1970). The book emphasizes the irrational aspects of these nativist organizations. A corrective to this view can be found in John Higham's "Another Look at Nativism," *The Catholic Historical Review*, XLIV (July, 1958), 147–58. This article proposes a more reasonable basis for nativism, that is, a loss of status.

A good one-volume history of American immigration is Maldwyn Allen Jones's, *American Immigration* (Chicago, 1960). Marcus Hansen's *The Atlantic Migration, 1607–1860: A History of the Continuing Settlement of the United States* (reprint ed., New York, 1961) is still a valuable contribution which emphasizes the events in Europe that precipitated much of the immigration to America.

For the early efforts in Colonial America to regulate and restrict immigration, there is the old but still adequate study by Emerson Edward Proper, *Colonial Immigration Laws: A Study of the Regula-*

tion of Immigration by the English Colonies in America (New York, 1900). For the positive side of colonial policy, that is, the moves to encourage immigration, see Erna Risch, "Encouragement of Immigration as Revealed in Colonial Legislation," *Virginia Magazine of History and Biography*, XLV (January, 1937), 1–10.

For the Alien and Sedition Acts, the best analysis is James Norton Smith's *Freedom's Fetters: The Alien and Sedition Laws and American Civil Liberties* (New York, 1956). The Federalists' relationship with xenophobia can be found in James M. Banner, Jr., *To the Hartford Convention: The Federalists and the Origins of Party Politics in Massachusetts, 1789–1815* (New York, 1970).

The early nativist movements are best followed in Ray Allen Billington, *The Protestant Crusade: A Study of the Origins of American Nativism* (New York, 1938), which places the stress on anti-Catholicism. See also William Darrell Overdyke, *The Know Nothing Party in the South* (Baton Rouge, 1950). For an evaluation of the nativist propaganda, a valuable article is David Brion Davis, "Some Themes of Counter-Subversion: An Analysis of Anti-Masonic, Anti-Catholic and Anti-Mormon Literature," *Mississippi Valley Historical Review*, XLVII (September, 1960), 205–24. See also Davis's "Some Ideological Functions of Prejudice in Anti-Bellum America," American Quarterly, XV (Summer, 1963), 115–25. Also useful for this early period is Oscar Handlin's *Boston's Immigrants: A Study in Acculturation*, rev. ed. (New York, 1969).

The post–Civil War period's reaction to the immigrant is best studied in the brilliant big book by John Higham, *Strangers in the Land: Patterns of American Nativism, 1860–1925* (New Brunswick, N. J., 1955). Roger Daniels' *The Politics of Prejudice* (Berkeley, 1972) is an important monograph that deals with the anti-Oriental prejudice in California before the Quota law of 1924. Mary Roberts Coolidge's 1909 study *Chinese Immigration* is still valuable and was reprinted by the *New York Times's* Arno Press in 1969.

The idea of intolerance and prejudice can still be best understood through a reading of Gordon W. Allport's *The Nature of Prejudice* (New York, 1954). There is also the much criticized but still useful study of the prejudiced personality by Theodore W. Adorno et al., *The Authoritarian Personality* (New York, 1950).

For racism in America, two valuable studies may be used: first, Thomas F. Gossett, *Race: History of an Idea in America* (Dallas, 1955), especially chapter 12, and Joel Kovel, the psychiatrist-historian's pessimistic *White Racism: A Psychohistory* (New York, 1970).

Alexander De Conde's *Half Bitter, Half Sweet: An Excursion into Italian-American History* (New York, 1971) is an excellent study of the Italian immigrant's impact on the United States. Donald Kinzer's *An Episode in Anti-Catholicism: The American Protective Association* (Seattle, 1964) is the best study yet of the APA.

Carey McWilliams's *The Mask of Privilege: Anti-Semitism in America* (Boston, 1948) is one of the few full-length studies available on anti-Semitism in the United States. It should be supplemented by John Higham's article, "Anti-Semitism in the Gilded Age: A Reinterpretation," *Mississippi Valley Historical Review*, XLIII (March, 1957), 559–78.

For the Immigration Restriction League, see Barbara Miller Solomon, *Ancestors and Immigrants: A Changing New England Tradition* (Cambridge, Mass., 1956).

For the 1920s, covering the antiradicalism and antialienism of the period, two provocative studies are William Preston, Jr., *Aliens and Dissenters: Federal Suppression of Radicals, 1903–1933* (Cambridge, Mass., 1963), and Kenneth Jackson, *The Ku Klux Klan in the City* (New York, 1967).

Index